A Philosophers' Manifesto: Ideas and Arguments to Change the World

T0384637

ROYAL INSTITUTE OF PHILOSOPHY SUPPLEMENT: 91

EDITED BY

Julian Baggini

CAMBRIDGE
UNIVERSITY PRESS

PUBLISHED BY THE PRESS SYNDICATE OF THE UNIVERSITY OF CAMBRIDGE
The Pitt Building, Trumpington Street, Cambridge, CB2 1RP,
United Kingdom

CAMBRIDGE UNIVERSITY PRESS
UPH, Shaftesbury Road, Cambridge CB2 8BS, United Kingdom
32 Avenue of the Americas, New York, NY 10013–2473, USA
477 Williamstown Road, Port Melbourne, VIC 3207, Australia
C/Orense, 4, planta 13, 28020 Madrid, Spain
Lower Ground Floor, Nautica Building, The Water Club, Beach Road,
Granger Bay, 8005 Cape Town, South Africa

Printed in Great Britain by Bell & Bain Ltd, Glasgow.
Typeset by Techset Composition Ltd, Salisbury, UK

A catalogue record for this book is available from the British Library

ISBN 9781009272667
ISSN 1358-2461

Contents

Notes on the Contributors

Myisha Cherry is an assistant professor of philosophy at the University of California, Riverside. Her research interest lies at the intersection of moral psychology and social and political philosophy. Cherry's books include *The Moral Psychology of Anger* co-edited with Owen Flanagan (Rowman and Littlefield, 2018) and *Unmuted: Conversations on Prejudice, Oppression, and Social Justice* (Oxford University Press, 2019).

Rajeev Bhargava is Former Professor, Honorary Fellow and Director, Parekh Institute of Indian Thought, Centre for the study of Developing Societies. His publications include *Individualism in Social Science, Secularism and its critics* (Ed) and *The Promise of India's secular democracy*.

Diane Coyle is Bennett Professor of Public Policy at the University of Cambridge. Her latest book is *Cogs and Monsters: What Economics is and What it Should Be*, and other recent publications are *Markets, State and People*, and *GDP: A Brief but Affectionate History*.

Fergus Green is Lecturer in Political Theory and Public Policy in the Department of Political Science, University College London. He works on the ethics, politics and governance of low-carbon transitions. Recent publications include *Engaged Climate Ethics* (2021) and *Legal Transitions without Legitimate Expectations* (2020), both in the *Journal of Political Philosophy*.

Ingrid Robeyns is Professor of Ethics of Institutions at the Ethics Institute, Utrecht University. She is currently writing a public philosophy book, provisionally entitled *Limitarianism. The Case Against Extreme Wealth*, to be published by Allen Lane/Penguin books.

Catherine Rowett is Professor of Philosophy, School of Politics, Philosophy, Language and Communication Studies at the University of East Anglia. In May 2019 she was elected to the European Parliament as the Green Party MEP, serving until the UK left the EU in January 2020. She now divides her time between research in philosophy and freelance political work.

doi:10.1017/S1358246122000108   © The Royal Institute of Philosophy and the contributors 2022
Royal Institute of Philosophy Supplement **91** 2022   v

Notes on the Contributors

Simon Duffy is President of Citizen Network and is based in Sheffield. His recent publications include *The Unmaking of Man* (Centre for Welfare Reform, 2013) and *Challenges-Responsive Guidelines: European roadmap for user-centred funding for Long-Term Care and Support* (EASPD, 2021).

Jonathan Wolff is the Alfred Landecker Professor of Values and Public Policy and Governing Body Fellow at Wolfson College. He has had a long-standing interest in health and health promotion, including questions of justice in health care resource allocation, the social determinants of health, and incentives and health behaviour. He writes a regular column on higher education for *The Guardian*.

Thaddeus Metz is Professor of Philosophy at the University of Pretoria in South Africa. Many of Metz's more than 250 books, chapters, and articles address themes in African philosophy. Recently Prospect Magazine named Metz one of the World's Top 50 Thinkers for having brought African philosophical ideas to global audiences.

Brian Wong is a Rhodes Scholar (Hong Kong, '20) and DPhil in Politics (Theory) candidate at Balliol College, University of Oxford. Their research interests primarily constitute rectifying historical and tackling structural injustices under non-ideal circumstances. They co-founded the Oxford Political Review.

Joseph Chan is a Professor in the Department of Politics and Public Administration at the University of Hong Kong and Global Scholar and Visiting Professor in the University Center for Human Values at Princeton University. His recent book is *Confucian Perfectionism: A Political Philosophy for Modern Times* (Princeton, 2014).

Lea Ypi is Professor in Political Theory in the Government Department, London School of Economics, and Adjunct Associate Professor in Philosophy at the Research School of Social Sciences, Australian National University. Before joining the LSE, she was a Post-doctoral Prize Research Fellow at Nuffield College (Oxford) and a researcher at the European University Institute where she obtained her PhD.

Martin O'Neill is Professor of Political Philosophy at the University of York. He is the co-author (with Joe Guinan) of *The Case for Community Wealth Building* (Polity Press, 2019), and the co-editor of *Taxation: Philosophical Perspectives* (Oxford University Press, 2018) and *Property-Owning Democracy: Rawls and Beyond* (Wiley-Blackwell, 2012).

Will Kymlicka is Canada Research Chair in Political Philosophy at Queen's University in Kingston. His publications include *Zoopolis: A Political Theory of Animal Rights* (OUP, 2011), co-authored with Sue Donaldson, and *Animal Labour: A New Frontier of Interspecies Justice?* (OUP, 2019), co-edited with Charlotte Blattner and Kendra Coulter.

Heisook Kim is Professor Emerita at Ewha Womans University. Her recent publications include *A New Interpretation of Yinyang: Deconstructing the Cultural Logic of East Asia* (Ewha Womans University Press, 2014), '*Moving the Contexts of Philosophy*' in *Philosophy By Women* (Routledge, 2021). Philosophical Methods are her main interest.

Debra Satz is the Marta Sutton Weeks Professor of Philosophy and of Political Science (by courtesy) at Stanford University. Her recent publications include *Economic Analysis, Moral Philosophy and Public Policy* (with Michael McPherson and Dan Hausman) (Cambridge: Cambridge University Press, 2017) and Ed. (with Anabelle Lever*)* *Ideas That Matter: Democracy, Justice, Rights* (Oxford: Oxford University Press, 2019).

Jesse Norman MP is Financial Secretary to the Treasury, and the author of recent biographies of Edmund Burke and Adam Smith.

Introduction

JULIAN BAGGINI

Twenty years ago in an interview, the then up and coming philosopher Jonathan Wolff told me, 'Political philosophers shouldn't, I think, be trying to create policy. They don't know how to' (Baggini and Stangroom, 2002, p. 48). At the time, this was an unremarkable remark. Philosophy as a discipline had moved on from its peak years of proudly impractical uselessness in the mid twentieth century. But in the English-speaking world there was still a suspicion of the kind of continental style *philosophe engagé*, pontificating on politics from a position of theoretical naiveté.

Wolff's contribution to this philosophers' manifesto does not show he has recanted his younger commitment. He and his collaborator Simon Duffy 'resist the temptation to make a simple policy recommendation', setting out broad 'policy goals' instead. Many others have explicitly left the filling out of the details of their proposals to others with more expertise in framing laws and policies. But most have been bold enough to make fairly specific proposals.

Times have changed. Philosophers have been increasingly unwilling to stick to the safety of their academic seminar rooms, indifferent to whether or not their arguments carry any weight beyond them. The drivers of this have been internal and external. From without, there is increasing pressure from the funders of higher education on academics to demonstrate 'impact', which in the UK is now a formal element of the quality assessment exercise all university departments have to undertake. But the desire to engage with those outside the classroom is in good part an endogenous phenomenon and not just a reaction to outside pressure. For all the worries that measuring impact would instrumentalise academic study, particularly for economic ends, many philosophers have found that they actually want to have some impact. A Philosophers' Manifesto is still an unusual kind of document, but its time has come.

The title of this manifesto was very careful chosen. First it is *a* manifesto. The absence of the definite article is essential: the contributors do not speak for any other philosophers, let alone all of them. The positioning of the inverted comma is also critical: this is a manifesto of plural, diverse philosophers. However, despite this very deliberate distancing from any kind of suggestion that this

doi:10.1017/S1358246122000091

volume speaks for the philosophical profession, it is interesting to consider whether these essays collectively give us some kind of rough sketch about what a government – or at least a political party – of contemporary philosophers would stand for.

Some might object that the views of philosophers are too diverse to profitably imagine any kind of single party that could represent them. That would be premature. First, it begs the question, since it assumes an incoherence that has not yet been demonstrated. Second, political parties are always coalitions in which members have a lot of disagreements. The coherence of a political project depends on having enough of what matters in common, not everything. Third, many parties represent sectors of society even when large minorities within those groups dissent. Not all workers support the policies of workers' parties, Christians those of Christian Democrats, environmentalists Green Parties. An imagined Philosophers' Party requires neither universal membership of philosophers nor unanimous support for every policy from its ranks.

Looking at the contributions to this manifesto, there does appear to be some striking convergence. I can see six general themes which each recur in two or more proposals: extending the role of state-funded education, expanding state ownership, increasing equity, making society less punitive, extending membership rights and countering excessive individualism. What's more, these themes are not only compatible, they form a more or less natural set

Regarding the first theme. Rajeev Bhargava argues for state-funded inter-religious education. In his own country, India, this is more controversial than it is in many other parts of the world, especially Europe. India has a secular constitution, albeit one which is being sorely tested by the rise of *Hindutva*, Hindu nationalism. As in the United States, it is widely believed that the state has to stay out of religion altogether to protect religious freedom.

But Bhargava is not arguing for formal religious *instruction* nor the teaching of the dominant religion. Rather, he argues that 'states must assume responsibility for teaching the ethical traditions of all religions'. If it does not, religions education is 'left to the family where learning is largely unsystematic and informal' or 'confined to schools funded and run by religious communities themselves, and where biases might go unchecked'. He argues that 'unbiased inter-religious education alone enables citizens to learn about and responsibly criticise each other's ethical values. It also helps place one's own ethical tradition in critical perspective'. This is 'necessary for social harmony'.

Myisha Cherry makes the case for state-funded anti-racist training, not just (or even primarily) in schools, but in public bodies, their contractors and nonprofit organisations funded by the United States government. Cherry carefully takes down the most common arguments against such training, which are mostly based on misconceptions – or perhaps deliberate misrepresentations – of what such training involves. (Anyone confused about what 'critical race theory' really means should read her lucidly clarifying account.) Cherry cleverly argues that the very fact critics don't understand what they are attacking is evidence that such training is needed. 'When a president says that "critical race theory is a Marxist ideology," and says it with confidence as if it is true, then it shows our leaders can benefit from the training they are tempting to halt [...] they will learn that there is more to learn about race and that there is a lot they do not know'.

Like Bhargava, Cherry argues that non-partisan state-funded education is important for creating a polis capable of promoting the liberal values governments claim to be committed to. 'If Americans really wanted to live up to their egalitarian principles,' she writes, 'the promise of equality for all, it was critical race theory that would help them move in that direction.'

These two very different proposals for state-funded education share a belief in the necessity of an educationally active state, not in order to impose a substantive, restrictive ideology, but to make the conditions of a diverse and fair society possible. To put it simply, in any culture in which people have diverse beliefs and backgrounds, we need to understand one another if our differences are not to lead to divisions. Those of one faith need to understand those of others or none, and those who receive the rewards of privilege need to understand how and why others do not, so that historic injustices are not perpetuated. Only the state has the resources to do this.

Two other contributions grant the state an arguably even more powerful role. In the latter part of the twentieth century nationalised industries went somewhat out of fashion. In Europe, many states still owned coal mines, steel works, railways and utility companies. Until 1976, the Italian government even had a monopoly on salt and tobacco, and the distinctive black and white *sali e tabacchi* signs can still be seen outside many stores. A growing confidence in the efficiency of markets led to many of these state assets being privatised. Today, however, the wisdom of many of those sales is increasingly questioned. Market competition seems impossible for natural monopolies such as water and energy supply. The case for private ownership is also somewhat undermined when some of the companies running railways and airports in the UK, for example, are owned by other European states.

So it is perhaps not surprising that we're seeing a revival of arguments that some public goods are too important to be left to the vagaries of the market, and that state ownership is a more direct and efficient means of keeping the private sector on the straight and narrow than complex regulation. This is the basis of Diane Coyle's argument that we need to establish a publicly funded social media platform. (Coyle is an economist, but one guiding principle of this manifesto is that philosophy's borders are porous and we find people who can be considered philosophers in adjacent disciplines.)

Coyle acknowledges her proposal might sound like 'wishful thinking', although some may fear it sounds more like a nightmare. But the basis of her argument is powerful. Until recently, we did not know how powerful social media would be. There is increasing evidence that it directly impacts not only on 'political discourse and choices' but on our mental wellbeing. As Coyle writes, 'The ascendancy of a small number of digital companies in the online world where most of us now spend a growing amount of our time means that their platforms can no longer be considered a private domain'. The online world has become a shared civic space yet it is owned and run by a small number of multinational giants. Imagine for example, that our city centres were all owned run by profit-making organisations, lightly regulated, with no obligation to serve the communities that surround them. The online world is like this. 'The features of digital markets mean they tend toward monopoly, so great economic and political power lie in the hands of a small number of giant companies.'

Coyle's public option is modelled on the BBC, the UK's state-owned broadcaster. Over its hundred-year history the BBC has managed to maintain its editorial independence and despite bullying has only rarely allowed itself to become an unwitting tool of the government. Its public service remit means that citizens have access to a more reliable news source than private alternatives, not just in Britain but around the world, thanks to the World Service. Coyle believes a similar body for social media would free users from 'the hunt for people's attention' which 'drives algorithmic promotion of viral content to get ever-more clicks'. This matters because 'Ideas build societies' and 'nothing is more important than the information and beliefs people acquire in determining the kind of society we have'.

Fergus Green and Ingrid Robeyns also reject the idea that 'the market is better at maximising aggregate welfare than the government' and argue for another radical form of nationalisation: states taking over the Fossil Fuel Industry. They argue that the urgency of the climate emergency provides strong reasons for a policy which would allow governments to take 'ten actions that are in the public interest, which will enhance social justice, enable a fair division of burdens and benefits, and strengthen democracy'. These include the end of all exploration for and development of new fossil fuel deposits; accounting for all emissions from the fossil fuels it produces; using its market power to raise the price of fossil fuels; expending research, development and demonstration resources on developing emissions reduction technologies; and ceasing all governmental and public affairs operations aimed at promoting fossil fuels.

Green and Robeyns acknowledge that the benefits they expect require making certain assumptions about government intentions and capacities, namely that 'the government is suitably motivated, has effective control over the companies it acquires, and is able to sustain this motivation and control for long-enough to wind-down acquired companies in the public interest'. But they argue these are reasonable and reject concerns that 'public ownership is the first step on the Road to serfdom'.

The presence of these four proposals for a strong state role may lead some to suspect that the Philosophers' Party would basically be a socialist one. However, none of these proposals is argued for on the grounds that the workers should own the means of production, that private ownership is illegitimate, or that capitalism exploits the surplus value of labour. Rather, in each case there is a more pragmatic set of arguments that, given the importance of certain public goods and the need for a fair society, the state is the body best placed to take control of certain keys aspects of the economy and social infrastructure. These arguments do not require anyone to buy into a thick political ideology. To have the chance of being persuaded, all you need to accept are some rather thin ideas of justice and equity.

These ideals are somewhat thickened by the contributions that explicitly aim to increase equity. Catherine Rowett – a former Green Party MEP as well as a philosopher – argues for a universal basic income (UBI). A UBI is 'an unconditional allowance, sufficient to live on, paid in cash to every citizen regardless of income'. This idea, for a long time dismissed as utopian, has attracted serious interest in many parts of the world, with some large-scale trials in progress.

Again, Rowett does not base her argument on socialist principles about the wrongness of private wealth or commerce. Rather, she presents what she thinks are some widely-accepted desiderata of a good society and argues that a UBI is the best way to achieve them. For example, almost every society accepts that we need to provide economic support for those in need. Yet our means of doing this creates 'a vast army of bureaucrats', fraud, 'the misery of a shame-based system' and enormous costs. A UBI would do away with all of these. It also eliminates the so-called benefits trap by which people receiving state money are disincentivized to find work. With a UBI 'there would be no penalty or deduction for earning a little, or a lot, of extra money on top of it'. Those who aspired to be rich would not be thwarted by a policy which prevents anyone from being poor.

Rowett also argues that a UBI would free many from 'the daily grind of going to a hateful job, and returning with not enough to live on, only to be obliged to apply for in-work benefits just in order to keep the family going is the source of enormous misery and distress'.

She accepts that a UBI would not entirely fulfil the criteria of the two most widely endorsed concepts of fairness, by which people get what they deserve and not something for nothing, or that 'disadvantages are remedied and reparations are made, to make good the unfairness of life-chances'. But current systems are even less fair, and the UBI, argues Rowett, does uphold the 'kind of fairness that says that being human is the same for all, and no one is worth more or less than anyone else'.

Arguments over UBI tend to focus on whether it is really affordable, with many arguing that it is not. Rowett cites studies that suggest otherwise. But her contribution to the debate fills out the moral and philosophical case for UBI which is too often lacking or assumed.

As has been mentioned, Simon Duffy and Jonathan Wolff do not offer a policy as such but a clear policy goal that dovetails neatly with Rowett. At the heart of their argument is the need for equity, expressed in their chosen epigram from Confucius: 'I have heard that [true] leaders of states or clans [...] do not worry about poverty, but inequity. [...] For if there is equity, there will be no poverty'.

For the kind of equity Duffy and Wolff seek, 'It is critically important to be able to offer a life of dignity for all'. That is something most benefit systems cannot do. In fact, they are often assaults on dignity. This is especially true of the ways in which benefits systems come accompanied by systems of punishment for anyone who breaks the rules. Stated as such, this might seem reasonable. But in practice, sticking by the rules can be extremely burdensome. If you do an odd-job for £50 pounds, for example, you face a choice of going through all the hassle of declaring it and perhaps losing the same amount in benefits as a result, or keeping it quiet and becoming a 'benefits cheat'. For Duffy and Wolff this is unacceptable: 'Compounding vulnerability with threats is the opposite of humanity'.

Hence their policy goal is to devise a system in which the threat of being charged as a benefit cheat is removed. This is not only faster, it is more humane. It would bring about 'a reduction of stress for claimants' and 'possibly a reduction in stress-related illness'. They accept that 'part of the social contract is to expect people to act responsibly in return for humane treatment' but argue that the current system absurdly makes 'following a set of arbitrary hurdles a test of responsibility'.

Rowett, Duffy and Wolff challenge us to rethink the ways in which we protect the most vulnerable by asking us to think harder about what equity and respect really mean and require. To stress once again, these are not highly ideological arguments but ones which, like all good philosophical arguments, are designed to appeal to any reasonable person, irrespective of their prior convictions.

Duffy and Wolff in particular seek to make our society less punitive, which is the key goal of two more of our manifesto proposals. Thaddeus Metz advocates state punishment for offenders which has reconciliation as its primary goal, rather than protection of the public or retribution against the offender. His argument draws on political and social values more dominant in the Global South, and especially sub-Saharan Africa, than in the West. In these societies, there is typically a greater emphasis on the relational nature of human beings, in which much of the value of human life is found in 'our capacity to relate positively or cohesively'. From this point of view, the main impact of crime is to undermine that value and 'the aims of punishment should be both to express disapproval when that value is degraded and to mend broken relationships'. Interestingly, something similar is found in Jesus's teachings about forgiveness, in which the goal is the healing of divisions. (Baggini, 2020, pp. 114–119)

Metz's argument, however, does not require us to fully take on board the relational model of human society. He also argues that the reconciliatory approach to sentencing 'avoids widely recognized problems with the rival protection and retribution models'. For example, in order for punishments to deter, they can sometimes be disproportionately harsh or lenient, which seems unjust. Retribution approaches promote the brutal logic of 'an eye for an eye' and take no account of the offender's character.

Brian Wong and Joseph Chan advocate for a different kind of reduction in the punitiveness of punishment. Democratic societies have long accepted that peaceful civil disobedience is sometimes morally warranted. In Rawls' famous account, civil disobedience may be permissible when it is public, non-violent, principled, a political act and has the aim of bringing about a change in the law or policies of the government.

Wong and Chan argue that there are forms of 'conscientious disobedience' which are morally justified but which do not meet all these criteria. Such 'uncivil disobedience' may be public, principled, and politically grounded but may involve some violence with no realistic chance of transforming society. Hong Kong, where Chan lives and works, may have provided recent examples of this. Wong and Chan argue that such conscientious disobedience is importantly distinct from other criminal acts and that this distinction is 'worthy of acknowledgment by public apparatus and actors'.

Their proposal is that when 'uncivil disobedients are wielding force that is *roughly proportionate* as a response to the egregious structural violence that they endure' they ought to be treated more leniently than ordinary criminals. Their paper proposes a 'comprehensive legislative scheme for governments to deal with prosecution, sentencing, and imprisonment of the conscientious disobedients' which is discussed in some detail.

The connections with Metz's reconciliatory approach are obvious. In both cases, retribution is judged inappropriate because it does not address the needs of the justice system to maintain and foster good relations between members of society. Punitive approaches increase divisions and exaggerate conflict. The existence of crime and uncivil disobedience highlights the fact that society always has its fractures and conflicts. Surely the goal of politics is to lessen these, to bring us closer together, not to drive us further apart.

This ideal of cohesion is developed more radically by three proposals to extend society's membership rights. Lea Ypi tackles the question of how far states are morally required to grant such rights to people who have crossed their borders illegally. Her starting point is the historical fact that many states were founded by the unjust appropriation of land by conquerors. This is not generally regarded as a reason to deny the legitimacy of these states today, thanks to something called supersession theory, which maintains that 'with the passage of time [...] a change in circumstances progressively mitigates the initial injustice, if certain conditions about supersession hold. A claim that was established through wrongdoing in the past could then be considered justified going forward'. To take a common example, a state founded illegitimately could in time be considered legitimate if it became properly democratic.

Ypi identifies a similarity between the position of illegal immigrants who have settled in a new land and initially illegal states that have settled in to government. In both cases, it can be argued that if the immigrant or state behaves properly, their initial crime can be overlooked. Opponents of regularising illegal immigrants argue that the differences are more important than the similarities. Most obviously, the passage of time is typically much longer with states than with immigrants. However, Ypi argues that supersession *both* justifies the rights of irregular migrants to stay *and* the states' right to exclude them. The way out of this, she argues, is to 'apply to states, the same criteria for supersession of injustice that they apply to individual immigrants'. These are that they fully recognise their previous wrongdoing and that they show their current good character. States that fulfil these criteria, she argues, have a weak right to exclude but also a responsibility to grant amnesty to illegal immigrants who also pass the tests.

Martin O'Neill proposes extending membership rights in a very different way: by reducing the voting age to twelve. This may sound recklessly radical but not so long ago many thought it dangerous to give the vote to ordinary working people, women, or those under thirty. As O'Neill argues, 'The franchise has expanded continually over the history of democratic societies, and this is a clear and obvious next step in this process of broadening the basis of democratic politics.'

O'Neill believes that this latest extension is required because 'Britain – like many other economically developed democratic societies – is now a society that does not serve its young people at all well'. These 'age-based injustices' need to be addressed and giving young people the vote is one important way of doing this. He argues that the twelve and overs 'are participating citizens whose lives are lived as part of our shared social and institutional environment' whose 'fundamental interests' are affected by 'the social, political and economic institutions of our society' and that they 'do not in general lack any specific capacity that would allow them to exercise their democratic rights as voters or as citizens more generally'.

O'Neill's is a good example of a philosophical argument that generates counter-intuitive conclusions that are nonetheless hard to fault rationally. He tackles the main objections head on and finds them very much wanting. I am sure that many will read his paper and find themselves convinced that he must be wrong but unable to explain convincingly why. In such cases, we may just have to accept that he is right.

Will Kymlicka's extension of membership rights is the most radical of all. He argues that domestic animals – which include livestock and companion animals – should be legally recognised as members of society. If that sounds preposterous, then just consider that already 'the vast majority of North Americans with companion animals consider them as "one of the family", to be treated according to an ethic of membership, and they increasingly expect the legal system to respect and honour this membership relationship'.

With the seemingly relentless march of animal rights, it might be wondered why membership rights should be necessary. Kymlicka argues that the status quo, described by Robert Nozick as 'Kantianism for humans, utilitarianism for animals' is a moral failure. On this view, human beings are treated as ends in themselves and animals as means to ends. Under this system, many farm animals in particular are subjected to cruel treatment in the name of the good that produces. However, Kymlicka argues that it is a non-starter to try to adopt utilitarianism for both humans and animals. It would cause outrage if we proposed that, for example, we should experiment on a few human beings in order to produce benefits for the rest of us. Kantianism for both humans and animals is similarly unrealistic. With in average of around 3% of most Western populations vegan, there is simply no prospect of gaining widespread support to give the likes of chickens and pigs the legal status of personhood. Membership rights 'to flourish within a shared society' can be more limited and take account of species differences. Such rights are 'group-differentiated' or 'relational' since 'they vary with an animal's relationship to human society'.

An interesting detail of Kymlicka's proposal is his claim that 'philosophers have largely been 'caught napping' on this issue. Part of the explanation is that their focus has been too much on moral philosophy and not enough on the political. When it comes to 'the animal question' he argues 'we desperately need to get political philosophy on board.'

As in so many contributions, Kymlicka picks up on the importance of the relational aspect of society to ground his arguments, extending these relations to other animals. This connects neatly with the sixth and final theme: countering excessive individualism. The West has not lost any of its enthusiasm for individual liberty and freedom. Over recent decades, however, there has been increasing concern that this may have gone too far, resulting in an unhealthy atomisation of society in which the social bonds that tie have become loose and sometimes severed.

The global coronavirus pandemic has put aspects of this issue into sharp focus as societies debate the need to balance personal freedom and collective security. Korean philosopher Heisook Kim challenges dominant Western assumptions about individuality, but begins her attack from within. John Stuart Mill, so often wheeled out when a philosophical defence of liberty is needed, famously wrote that 'the only purpose for which power can be rightfully exercised over any member of a civilized community, against his will, is to prevent harm to others. His own good, either physical or moral, is not a sufficient warrant'.

Kim points out that mask wearing mandates, far from being contrary to this principle, actually follow from it. 'It is difficult to view the mask use mandate as a violation of individual freedom, because even those who are not confirmed to have been infected may pass on the virus through asymptomatic spread'. This is a stark reminder that for many freedom is not longer a matter of principle but a kind of fetish, in which any restrictions on the rights of individuals to do what they like is an affront, even when those actions harm others.

Kim also questions the centrality of the individual to Western conceptions of liberty from without. As she explains, 'In the Confucian tradition, an individual never exists as an absolute unit. Individuals always exist in the network of relations carrying out their roles'.

We are asked to rethink what it means to be free because it is simply a fantasy to believe that in the age of the all-pervasive world wide web, individual freedom has an 'absolute value'. Our preferences are being modified and manipulated by global corporations like Amazon, to whom we willingly give information so that they can reconfigure the 'choice architecture' of our environment. Naive beliefs in autonomy simply don't hold water in this new world. Kim argues that a Confucian ethic based on community values is more suited to modern times than a notion of individual freedom which in the contemporary West is becoming 'more obscure than ever'. She warns, 'If we take individual freedom as an absolute value, we have to face a gloomy future'.

Debra Satz also asks us to think more of our duties as citizens and less of our rights as sovereign individuals when she argues for a mandatory public service requirement. 'Democratic citizenship is an achievement,' she says, not a basic right that can be conferred at will. A flourishing society cannot exist if it is not in the first place a *society*: a community of people living together, not as discrete islands. Her argument for compulsory national service rests on us accepting that what we owe to one another is more than just non-interference. She argues that 'democracy itself requires certain shared experiences and conditions and a commitment to democracy entails a commitment to the conditions needed to sustain it over time'.

She accepts that her proposal will not appeal to those 'who see society simply as an instrument for the optimal pursuit of individual interests'. But, she concludes, 'for those who see society as a framework for individuals – considered as free and equal but differing in many interests and values – to come together and rule themselves, a year of compulsory national service will count as a small price of admission'.

The conservative member of parliament and philosopher Jesse Norman also sees the need for society to be united by something more than just trade and legal obligations. It also requires *philia*, or civic friendship. For Aristotle, he writes, '*philia* is what holds states together, and he says that lawgivers almost care more for it than for justice. It is the social amity that they aim at most of all, and it expels faction, which is their worst enemy'.

How does a society create *philoi*, civic friends? It cannot do so by fiat. Rather, it must create the conditions for *philia* to flourish, and that in turn requires cherishing 'freedom of thought and speech and association, and the institutions, practices and habits that sustain them'.

Norman argues that mentoring is an effective means of promoting this. Mentoring binds generations and, if done well, different social classes. 'It is the stuff of meetings and conversation and personal contact, of shared projects and new friendships'. Echoing Satz, he suggests that the existing National Citizen Service could be extended and put to use facilitating more mentoring, which rewards both mentor and mentored.

The fact that it has been possible to seamlessly move from discussions of each of these six themes to the next suggests that there is some kind of natural connection between them. So what is it that links extending the role of state-funded education, expanding state ownership, increasing equity, making society less punitive, extending membership rights and countering excessive individualism?

First, there is a common thread of seeing society as a network of relations rather than simply a collection of atomic individuals. Criminals and dissidents are not just members of society, they are formed by it. To disown them is to deny the dark side of your own culture. Better to bring them back into the fold. Also, people believe different things and it is better to find ways to allow them to coexist harmoniously than it is to push them into their own ghettos. A too-mighty state can of course crush liberty, reducing citizens to vassals. But a too-weak state leaves its citizens to the mercy of fate, accidents of birth and the whims of rich, powerful, unaccountable organisations. Perhaps it is time to move away from tired debates about the small versus the big state and focus less on its size and more on what it should and should not do.

Second, there is a common theme of equity. State-funded religious and racial education programmes are essential for all groups of society to be given equal respect and recognition. State ownership of fossil fuels and a major social media provider ensures intergenerational justice, that the burdens of the energy transition are shared fairly, and that users of social media are not reduced to tools of the big tech companies. Less punitive criminal justice is fairer to those for whom life circumstances have made them more likely to become criminals as well as those whose 'criminality' is a principled and necessary resistance to injustice. Extending membership rights makes society more inclusive and horizontal, while countering excessive individualism reduces the inequalities that atomised capitalism has encouraged.

What unites the Philosopher's Party is therefore a politics of *equity* and *relationality*. This neatly brings together the conservative value of the organic society and the more left-wing values of greater equality of opportunity and access to resources. The vision being offered here is not a trade-off between solidarity and individuality, but the realisation that individuals can only really be fully free in an enabling society that allows each to fulfil their own potential.

Could such a programme be enough to unite a political party in the real world? It already is. The old parties have fractured and declined across the democratic world. It is no longer easy to distinguish neatly between right and left. Politicians can respond to this with one of two strategies for victory. One is divide and rule. Appeal to an angry faction of society, demonise the rest, and gain a parliamentary majority to impose your vision of the good society on others. The other is to try to unite the increasingly fractured electorate around the basic values that most people still share. Of these, surely equity and relationality are key.

Ever since Plato advocated the philosopher kings, people have worried that this would empower an out of touch elite to impose its values on an unwilling population. Our Philosophers' Manifesto suggests that if that were ever a worry, it no longer is. The values at its heart chime with ordinary people across the world. Wolff may be right that political philosophers shouldn't be trying to create policy. But this manifesto shows they could be invaluable in guiding it.

References

Julian Baggini and Jeremy Stangroom, *New British Philosophy: The Interviews* (New York and London: Routledge, 2002).
Julian Baggini, *The Godless Gospel* (London: Granta, 2020).

In Defense of Anti-Racist Training

MYISHA CHERRY

Abstract
I will argue for anti-racist training in federal and state funded programs. In order to do so, I will begin by discussing recent events occurring in the United States that have challenged such training. I will analyze criticisms of anti-racist programs, focusing particularly on those that began with the Trump administration and continue today. I will then consider what is happening in response and as a result of these criticisms, as well as make some suggestions for what should happen going forward.

In September of 2020, President Trump issued Executive Order 13950 that expressed concern for concepts and histories that were being taught in anti-racist training. His office also issued a memo to federal agencies, echoing in non-legal language some of the spirit of the executive order. In addition, there was a commission held at the White House on U.S. History to protest and counter what were perceived as inaccuracies in historical accounts expressed in the training. However, it was the executive order that had the power to do things on the ground. Here are some excerpts from the order:

> From the battlefield of Gettysburg to the bus boycott in Montgomery, and the Selma-to-Montgomery marches, heroic Americans have valiantly risked their lives to ensure that their children would grow up in a nation living out its creed, expressed in the Declaration of Independence, 'We hold these truths to be self-evident, that all men are created equal…' It was the belief in this inherent equality of every individual that inspired the founding generation to risk their lives, their fortunes, and their sacred honor to establish a new nation, unique among the countries of the world. Thanks to the courage and sacrifice of our forebears. America has made significant progress toward realization of a national creed. Today, however, many people are pushing a different vision of America that is grounded in hierarchies, based on collective social and political identities, rather than in the inherent and equal dignity of every person as an individual. This ideology is rooted in the pernicious and false belief that America is an irredeemably racist and sexist country, that some people, simply on account of their race or sex are oppressors.

doi:10.1017/S1358246122000054

And that racial and sexual identities are more important than our common status as human beings and Americans. This destructive ideology is grounded in misrepresentations of our country's history and its role in the world. Unfortunately, this maligned ideology is now migrating from the fringes of American society and threatens to infect core institutions of our country. But training like that discussed above perpetuates racial stereotypes and division and can use subtle, coercive pressure to ensure conformity of viewpoint. Such ideas may be fashionable in the academy, but they have no place in programs and activities sponsored by federal taxpayer dollars. Therefore, it shall be the policy of the United States not to promote race or sex, stereotyping or scapegoating in the federal workforce or in uniform services, and not to allow grant funds to be used for these purposes. In addition, federal contractors will not be permitted to inculcate such views in their employees.

It also summarizes the applicable groups that the executive order applies to. It includes federal contractors, executive agencies, the military, and recipients of federal grants. For anyone leading such training, whether as a contracter or a nonprofit organization funded by the United States government, there will be restrictions to what content they are allowed to communicate in the training.

What was the impact of the order? Applicable groups were required to submit all training materials to the proper authorities so that they could review the content to ensure that there was no presence of wording promoting the worries echoed in the executive order. Until such reviews were complete, training was suspended. There was also a hotline created so that anyone could report incidents involving training that violated the order. One of the things that happened as a result was the spread of fear. Many organizations were afraid to lose funding from the federal government. This fear led them to halt all diversity and inclusion work.

1. Terms Targeted

The order targeted any training that promoted 'the idea that America or Americans of any race or sex is inherently racist or evil'. More specifically, it's clear in documents and further communications that there were certain terms they believed echoed this particular idea. One of the terms was 'white privilege'. As defined, it is the belief that due to socially constructed racial hierarchies, as well as a history of colonialism and slavery, certain individuals have more access to certain rights, liberties, and fair treatment than others, based on race (e.g.., whites are, all things considered, more privileged than Black Americans). Other targeted terms in the order were 'critical race theory' and the 1619 Project. While I will not provide a full explanation of these terms and projects, I will provide a brief explanation of them to show where the order's concerns were misguided and ill-informed.

According to statements made by Trump at the 2020 White House conference on U.S. History, it is clear that he believed that 'critical race theory, the 1619 Project, and the crusade against American History is toxic propaganda, ideological poison that if not removed, will dissolve the civic bonds that tie us together. It will destroy our country'. He also went on to note that it is 'toxic propaganda, it's ideological poison'. His statement also reveals a fear. There is a worry that if these concepts and themes continued to be taught, then it would 'dissolve our civic bonds and destroy our country'.

One way that we can respond is that if this is true, if what the executive order and Trump have suggested is correct (as far as it being poison and propaganda), then we do have reasons to be suspicious of the training. And we also have reasons, if we are the federal government, to not fund them. Let's call this Option A. But there's a second option on the table. If these claims are false, if it's not the case that these concepts are ideological poison, then we have reasons to lessen our suspicion of these kinds of claim. Let's call this Option B. Option B means we have reason to continue to fund these programs in accordance with our diversity and inclusion goals. Let's try to analyze if indeed these claims are true.

2. Critical Race Theory and its Critics

Critical race theory was a term that Trump targeted. For him and others, critical race theory is a 'Marxist doctrine holding that America is a wicked and racist nation, that even young children are complicit in oppression. It's being deployed to rip apart families, neighbors, and families'. Are Trump and those who agree with him correct?

To answer this question it is best to find out how scholars in critical race theory define their field. UCLA Law School, a school known for having many faculty who are critical race theorists, issued an online response to what they took to be a misinterpretation of their field of study by Trump and others. One of the things they accused Trump of is *misinterpretation*. This is how they define critical race theory: 'Critical race theory invites us to confront with unflinching honesty, how race has operated in U.S. History in our present, and to recognize the deep and ongoing operation of structural racism through which racial inequality is reproduced'. One of the central principles that they hold, which is the opposite of what Trump claims, is not that America or Americans are inherently racist. Rather, they claim that there is nothing inherent about race. Therefore, there seems to be a mismatch between what theorists say they are doing in the field and what non-academic critics believe the theorizing involves.

Critical race theorists also suggest that Trump was creating a caricature of critical race theory. In their view, critics were reducing 'a sophisticated field of knowledge to the simplistic absurdities that America is inherently racist'. In response to criticisms that critical race theory is anti-American propaganda, the scholars stated in simple terms that this was not the case. As opposed to being propaganda that the country does not need, defenders noted that critical race theory is necessary. If Americans really wanted to live up to their egalitarian principles, the promise of equality for all, it was critical race theory that would help them move in that direction. Defenders believed the Trump administration was misinterpreting what critical race theory was all about.

But there also was also a *misguided implication*. Recall President Trump believed that critical race theory has no place; both in Federal programs and America in general. On the other hand, defenders suggested that if you look at the impact that critical race theory has had on legislation, on court cases, on programming, and on policies, you will see that indeed it has a proper place – one that is aligned with the goals and principles of the country.

Here are some theoretical concepts that defenders of critical race theory point to in order to show that critical race theory has been helpful – not only with how we relate to each other in our day-to-day practices, but also how we go about achieving justice and treating people fairly. First, if employees learn about the theory of intersectionality (i.e., the idea that there are distinct and multifarious oppressions based on one's intersecting identities), it can help motivate federal programs to address the disparities that individuals face.

As opposed to the theory being divisive, defenders suggest that when federal employees learn about the dangers of implicit bias, (i.e., the unconscious bias that informs the way in which we treat others) and are aware of the dangers, then this can spur improvement in how we process information about others and it can allow individuals to engage in fairer decision-making when they extend job opportunities to individuals, or to those receiving federal contracts. This is not divisive. This is in the service of promoting equality, which America professes it is committed to. If all of this is correct, then claims to the contrary reveal a misguided implication of these concepts.

3. The 1619 Project and its Critics

Another project that the Trump administration sought to rebuke is the 1619 Project. For Trump, 'by viewing every issue through the lens of race, they, individuals part of the project and the New York Times that sponsors it, they want to impose a new segregation, and we must not allow that'.

The 1619 project is a public history project sponsored by *The New York Times*, and created by Pulitzer Prize winner Nicole Hannah-Jones. According to its website, the project 'aims to reframe the country's history by placing the consequences of slavery, and the contributions of black Americans at the very center'. As opposed to this history being marginalized, as opposed to it being forgotten, as opposed to citizens acting like it never happened, the project wants to place the consequences of slavery, as well as the contributions of Black Americans at the heart of the U.S. National narrative. That's the explicit focus of the project. A look at the project's table of contents reveals its focus. In it, scholars provide a full history of slavery; explain the racial wealth gap; discuss the influence of Black music on freedom. Political theorists discuss the undemocratic assumptions of the U.S. Others provide a history and analyses of how Blacks have fought for freedom in the U.S. There are also essays that explore how race impacts the prison system.

For Trump and other critics, the 1619 project is viewing every issue through race. However, this too is a misinterpretation. The project is instead attempting to bring to the forefront that the history of America is a history of race. You can't talk about black music, for example, without talking about race. You can't also talk about the prison system without talking about race.

In response to the project, Trump and other critics, set up the 1776 Commission as way to rebuke the 1619 project and promote patriotic education. For critics, given the content of the 1619 Project, it is unpatriotic. And if it's unpatriotic, it is something that we do not need in America. But this is also a misguided implication. The 1619 project is reminding Americans that although our past and our present may be haunting, it is still true. And it's necessary for us to teach it. Just because it is haunting, doesn't mean that it's unpatriotic. There is no evidence that the 1619 project 'imposes segregation'. Instead, it exposes why America is segregated (e.g., by explaining how redlining occurred as well as its effects). Through public history, it exposes the history of segregation rather than imposes it. There is a valuable lesson to be learned. Just because we may be uncomfortable with the facts, doesn't mean that this discomfort equals or equates to 'division in the country.'

Claims made by critics in regards to these theoretical concepts and initiatives are untrue and unfounded. Therefore, the worries that stem from them are also unwarranted. This means that there is no justification for halting or defunding federal anti-racist training.

4. What Explains the Pushback?

I am going to provide an account of what I think is happening via these criticisms and defunding initiatives. I think reducing critics' reactions to being racist or sexist is too simplistic. More needs to be said.

One of the things on display in the critics' objection and worries is denial. There are several ways that we can deny our past and what's happening in the present. There's an explicit or literal denial in which we can claim that, 'Structural racism does not exist today.' But there's also a type of denial in which we acknowledge that wrongdoing has happened, but we overstate the progress we have made since. We may say, 'things are not as bad as they once were. Yes, wrongdoing may be happening, but it's not to the level that it once was'. This is downplaying of the wrongdoing. There are several ways in which individuals are experiencing these types of denials in relationship to racism.

But another thing on display in the critics' objections is a submersion of history. This occurs by not wanting to acknowledge the history of America. And there's no other scholar that has been able to articulate why and what happens when you try to submerge history better than W.E.B. Du Bois.

In *Black Reconstruction*, Du Bois attempts to provide a historical account of what Reconstruction in the United States was like for African-Americans. What were the impacts of it? And how did it help? In the last chapter – 'The Propaganda of History' – Du Bois discusses the seduction to submerge history. He says,

How the facts of American history have in the last half-century have been falsified because the nation was ashamed. What are American children taught today? We have too often a deliberate attempt so to change the facts of history, that the story will make pleasant reading for Americans. If we are going to use history for our pleasure and amusement, for inflating our national ego, and giving us a false but pleasurable sense of accomplishment, then we must give up the idea of history as in science. This may be fine romance, but it is not science. It may be inspiring, but it is certainly not the truth. And beyond this, it is dangerous. (1998, pp. 711–14).

By denying the reality that critical race theory is trying to illuminate; by denying our racial past which I think the 1619 project is trying to illuminate; and by getting in the way of how anti-racist trainers are trying to bring that knowledge into training to inform individuals, we repeat what Du Bois was concerned about. This denial and submerging are attempts to feed into a romance that we have of our nation. We pay a high price for depicting America or Britain or South Africa as equal in every way, as not racist, sexist, etc. One of the things that Du Bois reminds us is that this is not true, and purporting that it is can be dangerous.

So how is it dangerous? It can interfere with justice. How can you administer racial justice in your capacity as a federal employee when you are in denial that there are certain structures of racism that exists? This denial is going to interfere with your efforts. Also, submerging history affects our day-to-day lives. Think about what motivated Dylann Roof to go into a church in Charleston, South Carolina and kill eight African Americans after they invited him into their church. Roof had a different version of history and he wanted that romance of white supremacy to resurrect itself in reality. This is how denial and submerging negatively affects our day-to-day lives.

5. Going Forward

I am concerned about the precedent that this denial and submerging (via the executive order as well as current local initiatives) is going to have for future anti-racist training as well as school and university education.

If we accept that the claims and worries expressed through the executive order are false and therefore unwarranted, then we have reasons to lessen our suspicion of anti-racist training. And we can continue to fund them in accordance with our diversity and inclusion goals. That was Option B that I proposed earlier. However, given the misinterpretation and misguided implications I've described, they motivate me to make a revision.

Here's my revision: If the critic's claims are false then we have *more reason* to lessen our suspicion. And we have more reason to continue to fund these programs in accordance with our diversity and inclusion goals. Why? Because this shows that Americans are still misinformed about race, even our leaders. It shows that there's still a spread of misinformation from our leaders all the way down. It shows that Americans are still in denial about our racial past and also our racial present. It shows that the dangers that stem from them are occurring. And this all shows why anti-racist training and education needs to continue. The fact that there's so much misinformation, so much denial and so much mythmaking, makes a case for anti-racist training and education.

Frederick Douglass recalls in one of his biographies, *My Bondage, My Freedom*, the time when his mistress was teaching him how to read and his slave owner discovered her actions. His description of the experience illuminates the power of knowledge, but more particularly for our purposes, the power of racial knowledge. He says, 'Mr. Auld forbade continuance of her instruction telling her it was unlawful, it was unsafe and teaching …. a slave child how to read, could only lead to mischief… Learn him how to read, and he'll want to know how to write. And he'll be running away with himself'. Douglass continues, 'The effect of his words on me stirred up, not only my feelings into a sort of rebellion, but it awakened within me a slumbering train of vital thought. It was a special revelation'. This is what Douglass realized: 'Knowledge unfits a child to be a slave… And the very determination of his slave master to keep him ignorant,' he says, 'Only rendered me the more resolute in seeking intelligence' (Douglass, 2014, pp. 117–18).

I believe that certain kinds of racial knowledge, no matter how uncomfortable it is, not only makes a contemporary child unfit to be a slave to racism, but racial knowledge – the kind that is being taught in anti-racist training programs – also makes individuals unfit to be a master. The very determination for the administration to keep individuals ignorant of this racial knowledge, should render us all the more resolute in seeking this racial intelligence through anti-racist training.

I also believe this misinformation makes a case for state funded programs too. So of course, the executive order's jurisdiction is federally-funded programs. The federal government can only have a say about those programs that the federal government is funding. But given that it's not just federal programs that administer justice, there's a case to be made to take very seriously the continuation of anti-racist training for state-funded programs. If denial and submersion of history interferes with racial justice, but there are state-funded programs whose sole purpose is to administer justice, then they also need to be trained in these matters. If critical race theory, for example, shapes legislation, court cases, programs, and policies, this doesn't just take place on the federal level. It also takes place locally.

Going forward, anti-racist curricula should be peer reviewed and not politician reviewed. In academia, if there's a paper that I want to get published, that paper is sent to other experts in the field to evaluate the tenability of my claims, to ensure that the work is up to certain standards. Similarity, anti-racist programs should not be reviewed based on politically charged buzzwords. The training curricula need to be evaluated, not by politicians, but by historians, theorists, and other experienced trainers. They are more in a position to let us know if indeed the training violates the principles of the United States and historical facts, and if they are promoting not only propaganda, but false ideology.

Lastly, those with funding power, (e.g., political leaders and donors) should also participate in anti-racist training. If they are in positions of power and administering funds, there are certain facts and virtues they need to learn and cultivate. It's pretty clear that they need to learn to cultivate intellectual humility. When a president says that 'critical race theory is a Marxist ideology,' and says it with confidence as if it is true, then it shows our leaders can benefit from the training they are attempting to halt. In this training, they will learn that there is more to learn about race and that there is a lot they do not know. And it will help them learn certain facts and continue to learn them. This training can also help them cultivate racial, emotional intelligence. There are many critics who are responding to anti-racist training with fear, discomfort, and shame. But racial, emotional intelligence will teach them how to analyze their emotions (their racial emotions) and to manage them. It can help them make sure that just because they are uncomfortable with certain histories, that this shouldn't be reason to stop the dissemination of knowledge; a knowledge that can make us all free.

UC Riverside
myisha.cherry@ucr.edu

References

Derrick Clifton, 'How the Trump administration's '1776 Report' warps the history of racism and slavery', *NBC News,* (January 20, 2021) https://www.nbcnews.com/news/nbcblk/how-trump-administration-s-1776-report-warps-history-racism-slavery-n1254926.

Frederick Douglass, *My Bondage, My Freedom* (New Haven: Yale University Press, 2014).

W.E.B. Du Bois, *Black Reconstruction in America America, 1860–1880* (New York: Free Press, 1999).

Executive Order 13950 https://www.federalregister.gov/documents/2020/09/28/2020-21534/combating-race-and-sex-stereotyping

UCLA Law School, 'UCLA Law Professors Set the Record Straight', (July 15, 2021), https://law.ucla.edu/news/critical-race-theory-news-ucla-law-professors-set-record-straight-0

For State-Funded Inter-Religious Education

RAJEEV BHARGAVA

Abstract
In this paper I address the vexed question of the relationship between secular states and religious education.

In this paper I address the vexed question of the relationship between secular states and religious education. In theocracies and in states with an established religion, all publicly funded schools are required to impart religious instruction. The issue of whether or not this should be done never arises in such states. But in secular states, this question is important and urgent. This is why I raise it here, and my answer is that states already committed to the rule of law, that guarantee a bundle of meaningful individual rights, criminalize hate speech and have an established system of 'secular' education, should shed their inhibition about religion and adopt a policy of inter-religious education.[1]

This is neither an argument for formal religious instruction in schools, something that states might legitimately discourage, nor, given deep religious diversity in all modern societies, the advocacy to teach the dominant religion.[2] In fact, this is not even an argument for teaching the dominant religion but giving the option to children from non-dominant religions not to take part in such education. Instead, my claim is that states must assume responsibility for teaching the ethical traditions of all religions.

Religious education should not be left to the family where learning is largely unsystematic and informal, nor be confined to schools

[1] This has been a criticism levelled against Western European states where religious education has been dominated by Christianity. Critics have legitimately argued for a more 'capacious' understanding of humanism and world-religions, as has been articulated in the introduction to Smyth et al (2013).

[2] This argument has some validity in places where good education is unavailable in school run by non-dominant religions. In such schools, children should be provided education without discrimination on grounds of religion and also be exempt from specific instruction in the dominant religion.

doi:10.1017/S1358246121000424   © The Royal Institute of Philosophy and the contributors 2022
Royal Institute of Philosophy Supplement **91** 2022

funded and run by religious communities themselves, and where biases might go unchecked. Unbiased inter-religious education alone enables citizens to learn about and responsibly criticize each other's ethical values. It also helps place one's own ethical tradition in critical perspective. This is necessary for social harmony, a value irreducible to individualistically-construed moral values. I illustrate my argument by discussing the case of India.

Before exploring this issue, I must specify what I mean by 'religious education'. 'Religious education' means a deeper, more thorough understanding of the cumulative tradition of a particular religion. I borrow the term 'cumulative tradition' from Wilfred Cantwell Smith which he takes to be, the historic deposit of the past religious life of the community in question: temples, scriptures, theological and philosophical systems, dance patterns, legal and social institutions, moral codes, myths, and so on, anything that can be transmitted from one person or generation to another and that even a scholar (an outsider) can grasp more or less objectively (Smith, 1991, pp. 156-57). So, while aspects of particular religious experiences can only be grasped from the inside, traditions are knowable even by outsiders.

To repeat, education *in* the cumulative tradition of a particular religion is different from education *about* it. Education in religion is a part of the larger process of religious instruction, the whole purpose of which is to initiate the child into a faith or to strengthen it if she already has it. Education about the cumulative tradition, as I have mentioned may be possessed even by the outsider. Hence, the phrase 'religious education' is ambiguous between education in religion (religious instruction) and education of the cumulative tradition of a religion. I wish to sharply distinguish the two.

For those who hold the view that all religious education is religious instruction, and in addition, religion is an outdated form of living and knowledge, a storehouse of superstition and obscurantism that systematically inculcates blind acceptance of authority, and undermines any capacity for independent thought, the answer to the question is obvious. The true function of education is to impart a sense of individual autonomy (critical thinking, independence of thought) and make children into good citizens (openness, capacity to deliberate and to listen to others, reasonableness, respect for difference, solidarity, a sense of justice, inclusiveness, and accommodation), features believed to be central to a liberal-democratic, secular vision. Religious education, it is claimed, undermines both. Thus, religious education must not be part of the curriculum of any school, public or private. Rather, there must be one common school which provides only secular education to believers and non-believers alike.

How plausible is this view? When a particular religion takes a dogmatic form, systematically undermines individual curiosity and critical thinking and valorizes religious identity above citizenship, then quite clearly it should not be taught in high schools run by secular states. Perhaps, such religions should be even actively discouraged by these states. But there is no cumulative religious tradition which wholly fits the above description, so aspects of every known religion can always be part of the school curricula.

Indeed, it is hard to deny that humans invariably relate to something beyond themselves, that for many this means relating to god, gods and goddesses or some other higher entity, that they do so in different ways, and that this manifests itself as individual belief and feeling as well as social practice in the public domain, embodied, under modern conditions, in different religious and secular spiritual traditions. As the scientist Merlin Donald has argued, humans as we know them always need all three systems of cognition: mimetic, mythic and the theoretic (Donald, 2012). If this is so, religion which emphasizes the mimetic (ritual) and mythic (cosmic narratives), will never entirely disappear. If so, a democratic secularist must find a way to reconcile the importance of citizenship and individual autonomy on the one hand, and strong religious convictions and commitments on the other. She must understand that while they wish to make their children into citizens, parents may also wish to give them the opportunity to learn about their religious traditions, have their identities shaped by them.

This raises an important issue which is rarely addressed in India but has been a topic of extensive discussion among liberal educationists in Europe. European liberals have rightly argued that children must not be treated as entirely passive, their agency must also be taken into account. This recognition of children's agency can be seen 'as occurring along a continuum that ranges from listening to children, supporting them in expressing their views, taking their views into account, involving them in decision-making processes to children sharing power' (Shier, 2001, p. 112).

I am partly sympathetic to this critique. At the same time, it cannot be ignored that until children reach a certain age, say 14-16, they remain dependent for most significant aspects of their lives on their parents. The most radical advocate of individual autonomy must concede the point that choosing with care and judgement with an understanding of the context and anticipation of potential consequence presuppose a wide-ranging, informal, and formal education. This is as true of religion as of other life choices. Indeed, one can well argue that for one's eventual choice of religion, a grasp of a wide variety of religious experiences and knowledge of the cumulative traditions of all major religions is crucial. Inter-religious education is necessary not only to satisfy one's curiosity about other religions, to learn from one another, to enable mutual enrichment but also to eventually decide which religion to have, whether or not exclusive allegiance to one religion is sufficient. And indeed, whether one must attach oneself to any religion at all.

But a liberal secularist can respond by asking: why cannot this take place at home? One reason why religious education at home may not be adequate is that parents may wish the transmission of this identity-shaping religious deposit to be stable, something not feasible without formal and systematic training. Moreover, they may not themselves have the time and quality required for such training.[3] Second, even when they have the time and inclination, they may additionally require the help of formal teaching and curriculum to supplement instruction at home. Thus, they may wish religious education to take place in schools. Third, the tradition may be so rich that it can be taught only by institutions much larger than the family.

The liberal-democratic secularist might accept this argument but then ask why can't this be done by separate private schools run by each community? Why get schools funded and run by public money involved in such education? This and other related issues were debated in the Constituent Assembly of India.[4] In the assembly, the case against religious education in state schools was made on four grounds. First, the financial cost of providing such education is borne by citizens who do not benefit from it. In an egalitarian and democratic society, public funds raised by taxes must not be utilized for the benefit of any particular religious community. Consider a school established by a local government that gives religious instruction in Hinduism on the ground that a majority of students in the area are Hindus. This violates the given principle because it requires that children of Muslims and other religious communities would nonetheless pay for this instruction. But why should they carry this unfair burden? The cost of religious instruction must be borne by the religious community itself. As one member of the Constituent Assembly put it, all funds for the provision of religious education must be supplied by the community that desires it, not by everyone. Since state schools are publicly funded, religious education must remain a wholly private affair.[5]

---

[3] For these arguments, see Spinner-Halev (2000).
[4] *Constituent Assembly Debates*, Vol. VII, 8 December 1948, Lok Sabha Secretariat, New Delhi (1999, pp. 877–78).
[5] Ibid. (pp. 832-33).

This argument is sound if state schools teach the cumulative tradition of one, dominant religion but loses force if multi-religious education is imparted in schools. Moreover, this argument is valid only for separate schools that impart only religious education. But multi- religious education in my view remains only a fraction of the overall secular curricula. So no religious or secular parent shares any unfair burden for funding the education of his or her child. This takes care of the problem of the unfair burden.

But several other arguments were put forward in the Assembly against the proposal of multi-religious education. First, some liberal members claimed that religious education/instruction usually teaches students obedience but not the art of questioning. A second objection was that such education frequently inculcates insulation from the rest of the political community. The boundaries of religious and politically communities do not always coincide. Loyalty to one, it was argued, may conflict with loyalty to another.[6] These limitations obstruct the growth of students into good citizens of a free, democratic society. A state may just about tolerate the presence in society of schools that undermine the value of citizenship, but surely it cannot permit this to occur in state-owned educational institutions. Third, a point was made by the great Dalit leader Ambedkar: given that many religions claim that their teachings are the only right path for salvation, social peace and harmony are bound to be disturbed when doctrinal controversies are brought into the public domain.[7] Social peace is possible only if all religions publicly declare that they do not have monopoly over the ultimate truth or are publicly silent on this matter. Since religions that believe that they have monopoly over ultimate truth cannot publicly deny it, the most that can be expected from them is that they do not publicly assert this belief, but remain silent instead. This means that the doctrines of such religions must not be brought into the public domain. It follows that instruction in this religion should not be permitted in publicly funded institutions. Further, a commitment to egalitarianism, and therefore to state-neutrality, implies that no religious community should be given the right to religious instruction in educational institutions funded by the state.

A fourth related objection came from those who feared that religious instruction exacerbates communalism and communal conflict. One member wanted the article concerning religious education to be framed keeping in mind not sects and denominations as they might

6   Ibid. (pp. 881-82).
7   Ibid. (pp. 883-84).

exist in some ideal world but as they really are. Real existing sects and denominations frequently forget the basic truth of all religion, he argued, and 'exalt their own particular brand as any advertiser in the market lauds his own wares.'[8]

Another member, argued that religion 'had been exploited and marketed in the country and has led to the worst horrors that could be perpetrated in the name of religion.'[9] Yet another Parsi member, R.K. Sidhwa, argued that 'the religious books of the various communities are translated by various authors in a manner that has really brought disgrace to religion. The authors have translated the beautiful original phrases to suit their own political ends with the result that today on religious grounds, the country has broken into various pieces.' Therefore, 'under existing circumstances, there should be no religious education provided in any educational institution which receive state aid.'[10] The constitution cannot give people 'the freedom to teach religion in any manner they like. Finally, fifth, there was an argument propelled simply by anti-majoritarian impulse. For instance, most Sikh members supported a total ban on religious instruction in educational institutions maintained wholly out of state funds because they feared that this inevitably favours the religion of the majority community.[11]

I concede straightaway that in contexts where religious passions are inflamed recurrently, hate speech against one another is common, the system of rule of law has virtually collapsed and conservative communitarianism trumps individual rights, in short where liberal-democracy has ceased to function, secular states should refrain from religious education in schools they fund. Indeed, there should be stringent laws against negative stereotyping, hate speech and incitement to violence. This is why my suggestion that secular states should shed their inhibition about religious education is limited to functioning liberal democracies.

The argument that religion teaches obedience rather than critical questioning takes a narrow, one-sided view of religion. For starters, debates and arguments were a part and parcel of ancient Hindu and Buddhist cultures, as indeed they were even in 'medieval Islamic cultures' shaped by Indian ethos. Second, theological debates were common in Islam and Christianity too. But even if the doctrinaire versions of religions were also given space in the curricula, they

---

[8]   Ibid. (p. 902).
[9]   Ibid.
[10] Ibid., (p. 906).
[11] Ibid.

would be only be taught in schools that give a strong emphasis on critical scrutiny and questioning. What pupils must learn in religiously diverse societies is critical respect for all religions. They must learn to respect genuine difference in ethical viewpoints, and as the ancient Indian emperor Asoka put it, learn to criticize each other when they have good reason to, on appropriate occasions and always moderately in a manner that does not humiliate others. Equally they must learn to be self-critical and not glorify their religion. No praise is justified where there are no good reasons to do so, articulated on inappropriate occasions and immoderately. One must learn not to brag about one's religion. When interaction takes place in the right way, there is a good chance that people would shed dogma and become less doctrinaire (Bhargava, 2014). How else have religiously diverse societies existed for so long? The motto of schools that impart multi-religious education should be critical respect, not excessive uncritical indulgence for one's own and disdain for other religions.[12] This also takes care of Ambedkar's worry of religious conflict.

Second, schools that inculcate critical reasoning and virtues of citizenship equip their pupils to think contextually and sensitively about all ethical conflicts. This would help them resolve problems of potential divided loyalties too. Finally, the argument that majoritarianism may be fueled by funding religious education is invalidated if schools run or funded by the state give equal weight to the teaching of all religions, regardless of their numbers or social dominance. On the contrary, imagine a school run by the majority community that admits students from the minority community. Here, the ethos of the school is likely to be permeated by the culture or religion of the majority, resulting in the estrangement of minorities who may have strong feelings of being misfits. To avoid having this feeling of alienation, they may even wish to assimilate. On the other hand, in publicly funded schools with multi-religious education, maintaining community identity will be easier, if not always without problems. If so, state funding is likely to benefit the minority community.

Third, communalism is exacerbated because people misunderstand each other's religion.

Though some religious conflicts could arise if people began to better understand each other's religion, most are intensified instead by false propaganda, stereotyping, and caricature.

---

[12] On critical respect as an integral feature of Indian secularism, see Bhargava (2010, p. 91).

Proper teaching of different religions assists in dispelling these and also diffuses tension between religious groups. It should do so as much by minimizing prejudice as by helping us see the futility of trite answers such as all religions are essentially the same.

Fourth, multi or inter-religious education is crucial because just and peaceful societies cannot be built either without persons of faith or when people of different faiths clash with one another. Nor can they be built any longer by foolishly persevering with the belief that all religions other than one's own are wrong, by the desire to dominate people of other faiths. They can be built only when diverse groups of believers and non-believers can come to effective mutual understanding, accommodation, and acceptance.

A final objection can come from those who acknowledge asymmetries in a community's capability to undertake multi or inter-religious education, perhaps even non-religious education. In such cases, parents who wish to provide good education to their children have no option but to send them to schools run by one particular religious community. The relevant liberal argument here would be those children from religions other than the one taught in the school must have a right to be exempted from any religious instruction. Such precedents have been available in India since the time of Akbar who was the first 'to establish an exclusive department of education wherein Hindus and Muslims were taught in the same madrasa but were given the option of separate syllabi. The Hindu elite was not averse to sending its children to madrasas to receive Islamic education' (Ara, 2004, p. 36). Indeed, this provision is available even in the Indian Constitution (Art. 28). However, in my view this is a stopgap arrangement. There is no substitute for schools that provide multi or inter-religious education to all children.

What is needed today is not just that Muslims, Hindus, Christians or atheists be good Muslims, Hindus, Christians, atheists only in their respective religious communities but rather that they be good Muslims, Hindus, Christians or atheists in a world where other intelligent and sensitive people are not Hindus, or Muslims, Christians or atheists. This is possible only with sensible multi-religious education. Indeed, historical precedents of this already exist in India. It also requires a proper setting where children from different religious backgrounds have the opportunity to meet one another, as they normally do in common state-run schools, and learn that ways of thinking and being exist in forms other than the one taught by their parents. They may even learn to respect other ways of life and thought.

This is crucial for civic friendship, for realizing the values of citizenship. We need schools to encourage students to listen to one another, to learn from and accept each other. We need multi-religious education to become good citizens, for after all existing individuals are not abstract citizens but members of various sub-cultures and communities. We do not interact with them only in religion-free public domains but also in political domains mediated by religions. To learn how to negotiate these is a skill that must be learnt not just at home but in schools. Nor can schools run privately by religious communities carry the burden of teaching children how to be good citizens, sensitive to the religious sensibility of others. The prime function of community-run, private schools is education in one religion or religious instruction. In short, only schools with a predominantly secular or common curricula, that neither discriminate on grounds of religion in their policy of admission nor compels children to be instructed in one religion, which teach the strengths and weaknesses of every religion but refuse to foster negative stereotypes of others, in short state-funded public schools alone can perform this task.

A final argument for religious education in India – and to some extent in all societies with sufficient number of Hindus – is grounded in a peculiar feature of religious perspectives such as Hinduism. The very distinction between religion, philosophy, and culture makes no sense in Hinduism. Therefore, taking religion out of public education would mean excluding a large chunk of Indian culture and civilization. In this context, Ambedkar draws upon the distinction between religious instruction and religious education and argued in favour of religious education. When asked if institutions where the Vedas, the Smritis, the Gita, the Upanishads are taught and which are maintained wholly out of state funds will be shut down once the constitution comes into force, Dr Ambedkar replied that there is a distinction between religious instruction and religious study. Religious instruction means the teaching of dogma. Religious study or religious education is different (religious study must imply that we also question dogma because all education implies possible critique, that is, critical questioning of anything under scrutiny). The implication was clear. The critical study of religious texts is not only permissible but must be positively encouraged.

My argument has been that we must wriggle out of the dichotomy of state schools without religious education and separate, community-run private schools, on the other hand, that provide religious instruction. Even if these schools teach their own religion in the right way, for example, without deriding other religions, they would not teach other religions. If so, we are in a situation where no school imparts proper inter-religious education, necessary for inter-religious understanding and eventually, civic friendship. This is unhealthy in liberal-democratic, secular polities.

Now it might finally be objected by some that states that teach religions are violating a basic principle of secularism, namely that state and religion should not mix, that they should maintain something akin to a wall of separation between one another. But this confuses a specific strategy of a particular phase in a single's country's self-understanding with a general principle. It is commonplace that political secularism means the separation of state and religion. But, the metaphor of separation needs to be unpacked. Moreover, to get a handle of what is at stake here, separation must be viewed as disconnection at three levels. A state may be disconnected from religion at the level of ends (first level), at the level of institutions (second level), and the level of law and public policy (third level). A secular state is distinguished from theocracies and states with established religions by a primary, first-level disconnection. A secular state has free standing ends, substantially, if not always completely, disconnected from the ends of religion. A secular state also endorses an institutional disconnection. Both the Church and the priestly class has virtually no role in running the affairs of the state. To some extent, this features secular states share with states that establish religion.

States with established religions have something in common with secular states – at least a partial institutional disconnection. But unlike them secular states tend to break completely away from the church and the priestly class. But secular states go further in the direction of disconnection; they break away completely. They withdraw privileges that established churches take for granted. Finally, a state may be disconnected from religion even at the level of law and public policy. When it disconnects at even this third level, it excludes religion altogether from every form of state activity. Such a state maintains a policy of strict or absolute separation.

In this incarnation, secularism becomes a doctrine of political taboo; it prohibits the state to come into contact with religious activities. It proposes that religious and political institutions live as strangers to each other, at best with benign respectful indifference. When a state is disconnected from religion at all three levels in this particular way, then we may say that a 'wall of separation' has been erected between the two. A state can be secular also if it excludes religion from its activities, but continuously interferes in religious affairs and therefore does not exclude itself from religion. It maintains a one-sided connection in order to control religion or suppress it altogether. Finally, instead of mutual or one-sided disconnection the state may keep a principled distance from all religions.

Now, this conception of a secular state in which the state is disconnected from the religion at all three levels is not the only available conception of secular state. A state can be secular if it disconnects itself from religion at the first two levels but is connected at the third level. In short, when, instead of excluding religion at the third level, it keeps a principled distance from it. The policy of principled distance entails a flexible approach on the question of inclusion/exclusion, engagement/disengagement, and intervention/abstention, dependent on the context, nature, or current state of relevant religions. It accepts a disconnection between state and religion at the level of ends and institutions but does not make a fetish of it at the third level of policy and law.

Principled distance is premised, therefore, on the idea that a state that has secular ends and that is institutionally separated from the church or some church-like entity may engage with religion at the level of law and social policy. This engagement must be governed by principles that flow from a commitment to the values of a secular state. For example, citizens may support a coercive law of the state grounded purely in a religious rationale if this law is compatible with, or promotes freedom and equality. A state may grant aid to religious institutions or may itself provide multi-religious education if this promotes equality or fraternity. Since a third level disconnection is not constitutive of all secular states, a state does not lose its secular character if it aids religiously-affiliated schools or provides multi-religious education. I have argued that under some circumstances, a secular state may directly provide multi-religious education.

I am not here claiming, of course, that this is the only function of schools run by states. In short, multi- or inter-religious education can and in some circumstances, must be an integral part of the larger project of publicly funded education. I have also argued that secularism is a critical perspective against all forms of inter- and intra-religious domination. To reduce domination, the state may engage with religion or disengage from it – it may engage with it positively (say provide multi-religious education) or negatively (by intervening in those religious practices that are demeaning and oppressive towards its own vulnerable members and which its leaders continue to neglect.) Providing multi-religious education for the sake of reducing the alienation of some citizens and for enhancing social and political fraternity is perfectly in keeping with the core principles of secularism.

I have argued that under some circumstances, a secular state may directly provide multi-religious education as an integral part of the larger project of secular education by the state. This is necessary because only such schools can teach young boys and girls a language to engage each other respectfully across different religious traditions as well be critical of one another in the right way. In societies with a vibrant religious past or with citizens with a lively involvement in their respective religions, religious education is crucial for strengthening mutual respect, and in turn for enhancing fraternity. Only then will they less likely to be prejudiced against the religions of others and be more self-critical.

I end this essay with the hope that one day we will discard the idea of religion presupposed by the idea of multi-religious education that I endorse in this paper. In the present form, multi-religious education means learning about a religion that is one's own and then, secondarily, learning about religions that are not one's own, which belong to others. However, this idea of separate religious systems to which each of us owe distinct allegiance is not a natural idea, as Wilfred Cantwell Smith, the great historian of comparative religions, so brilliantly showed. Asian faiths, the great faiths of the East, are not and can become religions only with cataclysmic distortion.

It is well known that until the late 19th century, and in many parts of rural India perhaps even today, a person could easily be both a Hindu and a Muslim. Much the same is true of contemporary China – a single Chinese person may be and usually is a 'Confucian, a Buddhist, and a Taoist'. This may baffle many for it is difficult for some of us to imagine how a single person can belong to three different religions. But as Smith reminds us, this perplexity arises from an inappropriate imposition of the concept of a religious system on what really are three rich and complex traditions of thought. These schools of thought have been cherished for centuries in China. Their teachings are available and everyone partakes of them but what each person does with them is entirely up to him. An analogy with Political Thought and Theory may help us appreciate this point. As a student of political thought, I cherish the thought of Plato, Aristotle, Locke, Burke, Rousseau, Marx, Gandhi, and Ambedkar but I do not necessarily become an ideologically committed Lockean or Burkean or even Gandhian as I do when I embrace a religion or an atheistic ideology. I embrace a part of their thought, without swallowing the whole. Nor do I feel the need to build a closed community around each tradition of thinking. Religions too should be understood as such traditions of thought and practice. Why then is it not possible for each one of us to partake of the rich traditions of the Jains, the Buddhists, the several communities that fall under the umbrella of Hindus, the Muslims, the Jews, the

Christians, as well of the many indigenous peoples without the compulsive need to publicly display that we belong first and foremost to only one of these?

Centre for the study of Developing Societies
rbhargav4@gmail.com

References

Arjumand Ara, 'Madrasas and Making of Muslim Identity in India', *Economic and Political Weekly*, (2004).

Rajeev Bhargava, *The Promise of India's Secular Democracy*, (OUP, 2010)

Rajeev Bhargava, 'Beyond Toleration: Civility and Principled co-existence in Asokan Edicts' in Alfred Stepan and Charles Taylor eds. *The Boundaries of Toleration*, (Columbia University Press, 2014).

Merlin Donald, 'An Evolutionary Approach to Culture' In Bellah, Robert N., and Hans Joas eds. *The axial age and its consequences*, (Harvard University Press, 2012).

W. Cantwell Smith, *The Meaning and End of Religion,* (Minneapolis: Fortress Press, 1991).

Harry Shier, 'Pathways to participation: Openings, opportunities and obligations', *Children & society* 15 (2001).

Emer Smyth, Maureen Lyons, and Merike Darmody's *Religious education in a multicultural Europe: Children, parents and schools*, (Springer, 2013).

Jeff Spinner-Halev, *Surviving Diversity*, Baltimore: The John Hopkins University Press, 2000

Constituent Assembly Debates, Vol. VII, 8 December 1948, Lok Sabha Secretariat, New Delhi (1999, pp. 877–78).

The Public Option

DIANE COYLE

Abstract

People value highly the digital technologies that are so pervasive in everyday life and work, certainly as measured by economists. Yet there are also evident harms associated with them, including the likelihood that they are affecting political discourse and choices. The features of digital markets mean they tend toward monopoly, so great economic and political power lies in the hands of a small number of giant companies. While tougher regulation may be one way to tackle the harms they create, it does not get at the structural problem, which is their advertising-driven business model. The hunt for people's attention drives algorithmic promotion of viral content to get ever-more clicks. An alternative policy intervention to reclaim public space would be to create a public service competitor that could drive competition along other dimensions. Online space must be reclaimed as a public space from the privately-owned US and Chinese digital giants.

1. Weighing up the digital age

Digital technology has become pervasive. It is reshaping the way we lead our lives. The average adult in Britain spent 28 hours a week online in 2020 (Ofcom, 2021), more than a whole day a week, sleep included. This was less than the average German or American; in one survey nearly one in three American respondents said they were online 'almost constantly' (Perrin and Kumar, 2021). This digital dependence has been cemented by the pandemic lockdowns; entertainment, studying, shopping and social life could only happen online, as could work for many people. People in lower income countries are still less tethered than this to the Internet and World Wide Web but catching up rapidly. Less visible in everyday experience, but just as pervasive, is the way much business activity happens digitally, from control systems in factories to logistics chains to urban sensors, and much government activity too. This is without doubt the digital age.

This has happened within just two or three decades. Digital technologies have been the most rapidly adopted in history. It took a century after the introduction of the flush toilet in the 1850s for nine in ten US households to get one, but less than 20 years for

doi:10.1017/S1358246121000394

Internet access to reach the same milestone (Comin & Hobeijn, 2010, data appendix). As well as spreading very rapidly, digital has had far-reaching effects. Economists describe this cluster of related information and communications innovations as a 'general purpose technology': they have a wide range of uses across different areas, and profoundly change the way people, and businesses, carry out their activities. Yet despite the presence and profound impact of these technologies on our lives, neither formal regulation nor informal social norms of behaviour have adjusted to them. The costs as well as the benefits have become all too clear, from disinformation and conspiracy theories online to security breaches and loss of privacy.

Even so, many people derive great value from digital services, especially as the most familiar ones – such as online search, social media, travel planners or email – do not need to be paid for directly. High usage rates speak for themselves (for instance two thirds of UK adults use social media, four in five use online search); and when people are asked what they would need to be paid to go without Google or Facebook for a year, the typical (median) figures are high: £1,500 for online search, or £150 for Facebook (compared with £750 for access to a public park and £3,500 for a TV set) according to one study (Coyle & Nguyen, 2020). Some respondents state much higher figures than these, but in any case all are above the zero price they need to pay.

For economists, estimates like these are a measure of the utility people derive from digital services, providing a metric of value. For economics remains fundamentally utilitarian in its view of the good life – or social welfare, to use the term of art. The benefits gained from the consumption and use of different economic goods depend on the extent to which they satisfy their users' preferences (subject to the constraint of having enough money to buy them). Economic analysis assesses policies or business practices in terms of whether or not they increase social welfare in this specific sense. What's more, despite the evident ethical framework embedded in this approach, economists also generally insist (in the jargon) that their task is 'positive' and not 'normative'. In other words, they are concerned with what is, not what ought to be, with value judgments to be made by politicians or others once they are in possession of the objective economic evidence (Friedman 1953, Duflo 2017).[1] The behavioural economics revolution has introduced human psychology,

---

[1] This separation of normative from positive is discussed in Coyle (2019), and the welfare framework for economic analysis in for example Coyle (2020) and Hausman et al. (2016).

but this is generally taken to mean that individuals' preferences are 'biased': the economic analyst (or social planner) still then has the task of maximising aggregate utility by incentivising people to behave according to their 'true' preferences. In short, the high stated monetary values for digital services, and the 'revealed preference' of their widespread use, are taken as a valid measure of society's economic gain.

Economic analysis is certainly not blind to concerns such as loss of privacy, misinformation, bias, or manipulation of voting. These disbenefits of the digital world are clearly relevant to any evaluation of the impact of the technologies on social welfare. But they are harder to accommodate within the standard framework of value in terms of the metric of money. There have been numerous critiques of the one-dimensionality of the utilitarian calculus, such as Elizabeth Anderson's (1995) argument for an irreducibly multi-dimensional ethical framework, Michael Sandel's (2012) emphasis on 'republican virtues' or Amartya Sen's (1993) capabilities approach. In the end, though, when it comes to making policy decisions concerning the role of digital technologies and companies in our lives, these incommensurable outcomes need to be weighed in the same scale: how should Facebook and Google be regulated? It depends on how we think the value of their services compares to the cost of their adverse effects. Evaluation of the social impact of the digital revolution involves their many different consequences. We all love being able to plan journeys, do our banking online to avoid queues in the branch, or shop conveniently. Against this we might want to consider the explosion of child pornography, or the role of social media in inciting violence or vaccine conspiracy theories, or the scope for algorithms to shift voting behaviour by altering search results and timelines.

2. The winner-takes-all phenomenon

The evaluation needs to be informed by the fact that digital service use is concentrated among a very few giant companies, almost all based in the US or China. Most people choose the services provided by a handful of companies (Alphabet/Google, Amazon, Apple, Facebook, Microsoft, or Alibaba, Baidu, ByteDance and Tencent) and this is itself an aspect of the economic calculus. Might the negative consequences of digital be mitigated if so much power were not held by a small number of companies and their immensely rich executives?

This tendency toward monopoly, known as a 'winner takes all' market, is related to the essence of digital as a suite of information and communications technologies. Many industries from aircraft manufacture to banking now have a few large, dominant firms because there are large economies of scale: it is costly to get into activities such as manufacturing vaccines or creating sophisticated software. Once in, the average costs per user decline faster the larger the business, so big firms can generally supply the market at better prices and often also better quality (thanks to accumulated experience) than their smaller or newer competitors. But in the case of the digital sector, this normal scale phenomenon is reinforced by other distinctive characteristics.

One is what are known as network effects. This refers to the benefits users of a communications network gain from their being other users. A telephone call with nobody at the other end is of no value. The more people you can call the better. In the case of digital platforms including social media, these network effects can also be 'indirect' as the platform will be mediating between users and suppliers of a service: think of diners and restaurants, or advertisers and consumers. More diners makes it worthwhile for restaurants, while more restaurants mean more choice for diners. Any business facing such network effects will have a tricky task, when it is new, to keep both 'sides' in appropriate balance. This is known in the literature as the chicken-and-egg problem for obvious reasons (Evans, 2002). When they reach a critical mass of users on each side, though, digital platforms grow extremely quickly and one generally dominates the market.

A second digital characteristic is the importance of data for delivering services to users. Every key stroke or tap on our devices provides data to the big companies. This helps them improve their services over time, the more they know about what we want. It also enables their business model. Platforms will generally charge different prices to each 'side', often zero on the consumer side with all the commission charged to suppliers (Rochet & Tirole, 2006). This reflects the usually greater sensitivity of consumers to pricing; we do not have to go out to dine but restaurants need customers to survive. When the consumer price is zero, all the revenues need to come from suppliers. For many of the heavily-used digital service, the second 'side' consists of advertisers. The more the platform can tell advertisers about their potential customers, the more they can charge them. Data drives advertising revenues and further growth in user numbers, as the companies know so much about us as to be able to provide a compelling service. The data feedback loop reinforces market dominance and creates another barrier to potentially competing services.

For these reasons, the most successful digital companies have become astonishingly large and powerful. Google took over from Yahoo as market leader by having a better search algorithm, and Facebook from MySpace thanks to its improved features. But it is hard to see how the next generation of innovators could replace them now. The winner-takes-all dynamics have produced the winners. To underline their scale, the five most valuable (according to the stockmarket) American companies are the digital big five. Their combined valuation of $10 trillion is about one fifth of the total for the entire US stockmarket. Apple is worth about $2.4 trillion compared to, say, Exxon Mobil's $2.4 billion: it is an order of magnitude bigger than the giants of old.

With such economic power comes political power. Overt lobbying is a crude measure of political influence, but US advocacy group Public Citizen reports that Amazon and Facebook are the two biggest lobbyists in the US (Chung, 2021), and they and other tech firms are also among the biggest spenders on lobbying in the EU as well.[2] More influential although harder by far to measure will be the political and social consequences of the way they run their businesses. These might include the influence of search results or viral social media memes on people's beliefs and behaviours, the spread of material inciting terrorism or of child pornography, or any of the other online harms poisoning society.

Digital concentration has also hollowed out traditional news media in many countries, undermining both subscription and advertising revenues. Newspapers and broadcasters feel compelled to make content available for free via the digital platforms, as it is increasingly the only way to reach audiences. Relatively few can sustain paywalls. As for advertising, Google and Facebook between them earn the lion's share of online advertising revenues. Many newspapers have closed, particularly local ones, diminishing the scrutiny by the media so essential to the healthy functioning of a democracy. The amounts available to support investigative reporting have shrunk steadily. A few countries, such as Australia and France, have forced the digital giants to make payments to other news organisations. Information markets are not like markets for apples; when there are just a few dominant providers the consequences will be far reaching.

The conditions of everyday life in ways both trivial and profound are therefore to a startling degree shaped by a handful of large

---

[2]   https://lobbyfacts.eu/reports/lobby-costs/companies

corporations. If governments and citizens want to tackle the negative consequences of the digital age, they can do so only by getting companies like Google and Facebook to change their practices.

3. Tackling digital power

The public intervention intended to ensure the market economy continues to deliver for society is competition policy, intended to promote energetic rivalry between firms for customers ensuring positive rather than negative outcomes. Yet it has been hard to get a grip on how competition policy should tackle digital markets. After all, if the giants deliver services people love, for free, and with continuing innovation, what is there to complain about? Competition authorities have traditionally not been concerned about corporate growth when consumers are evidently so satisfied. Eventually, though, the wider societal concerns led to a number of high profile reports in recent years (e.g. Cremer et al., 2019; Furman et al., 2019) recommending a change in policy, a tougher approach to policing digital markets. Joseph Schumpeter (1942) saw markets as a field of creative destruction with a succession of winners putting weaker competitors out of business over time. The market might be concentrated at a moment in time but a serious threat of new entry can perhaps discipline the behaviour of the incumbents. The problem with digital dominance is that it has become impossible for new entrants to break in as the winner-take-all features make the threat of new entry rather weak. So many jurisdictions are updating their competition policy frameworks now with new powers intended to enable the digital incumbents to be challenged.

Some of the new proposals concern questions such as the prominence the big platforms give to services provided by rivals, or the commission fees they charge. The intention is to regulate to make competition more effective. A particular focus, though, is the data loop, as this gives the tech giants a self-reinforcing and almost-insurmountable defence against new competition. Privacy campaigners object to the data harvesting on intrinsic grounds, quite correctly arguing that there is no meaningful consent given to handing over personal data when people click 'accept' on long and impenetrable terms and conditions notices.

Others have objected to the unfair division of the gains from the data transaction. Although users get the service for free, the companies make large profits from us. One line of argument therefore advocates for considering 'data as labour', and the payment of small sums of money to users for their attention and data (Arrieta-Ibarra et al., 2018). However, this notion of an individual transaction does not capture the fact that the valuable information content – what advertisers pay for – comes from the combination of individuals' data. An advertiser does not want to know only my tastes but those of all people like me in relevant ways. The legalistic framing of data as property to be owned (the default is that the digital companies that collect it have economic ownership of it, having won our consent by a click) is based on a misconception (Coyle et al., 2019; Viljoen, forthcoming). Data is more like air than a normal economic good; it should not be considered as something over which property rights can be held.[3]

Data can furthermore be combined with other data to be turned into useful information that can help people more effectively do what they want – save time, invent new things, make their business more profitable. It is potentially a rich social resource, but one locked in the data centres of a small number of big corporations. The concern for privacy, understandable as it is, has strengthened the grip of the digital giants over the data hoards. So an alternative approach to lowering the data barrier to entry is to consider ways to make it interoperable and transferable – not simple, given the need to protect privacy and ensure security and data quality, but technically possible.

While making data more accessible to others, and breaking into the data loop, might help strengthen potential competitors to the digital giants, it will not avert all the digital harm that concern us. To see why, consider that Google and Facebook are not the pioneers in the use of personal data for corporate profit. Other kinds of company such as credit rating agencies and marketing companies have collected and sold data and the market analytics based on it. Yet they have not generated the same kind of troubling societal harms.

The feature that makes the role of some of the big tech companies today problematic is their business model: the collection of data to sell advertising space on digital real estate. In order to make money this way, they have to be able to demonstrate that they have users' attention through clicks. They need to corral more and more of our time, more minutes in every day and more of those minutes on their platform rather than others. Given that leisure time is limited by the need to earn money through work and to sleep and eat, the battle

---

[3]   In technical terms, it is non-rival: it can be used simultaneously by many people. If access is restricted by technical or legal means it would be designated a club good; otherwise a public good.

for clicks is an arms race. This race is being conducted between a few advertising-funded companies: Google including You Tube, Facebook including Instagram, TikTok, Twitter. The Alphabet and Facebook families account for more than two thirds of online advertising revenue in the UK. The fundamental need to get people clicking, to earn advertising revenues, is at the heart of the societal costs imposed on us by big tech. Conspiracy theories, misinformation, hatred of minorities (such as the Rohingya in Myanmar) – along with celebrity news, sourdough recipes and cute pet videos – are among the viral memes that get people clicking.

Advertising is to some degree a means of providing useful information to consumers. For example, nobody would buy innovative products if they had not been brought to their attention by advertising; think of the iconic Apple '1984' advert. Advertising is also, though, a form of rivalry between companies in markets where there are similar but differentiated products, such as different varieties of toothpaste or home printers. Nicholas Kaldor (1950) pointed out this had adverse effects: 'Advertising is mainly a device for strengthening monopoly power and weakening competition, and is, therefore, anti-social in its effects'. Even this understates the anti-social element. From quack remedies advertised in 19th century newspapers onwards, it has always conveyed pure misinformation to consumers, which regulators struggle to control. This context might make us wary of advertising-funded businesses to start with. Layered on top of this in today's (mis)information environment is the character of the content driving clicks and advertising. Neither the digital platforms nor their advertisers create this content; but they need it. Without viral, click-worthy content, they would have no profits because they give away their services for free.

The scale of their operations, the sheer number of their users, makes it challenging for the tech giants to monitor and police the content on their own platforms. Many governments are beginning to demand that the platforms tackle harmful online information, which has prompted them to introduce enhanced monitoring, or deploy AI algorithms to take down some kinds of content automatically (with some odd results given the gap between artificial and human judgement). When there are specific outrages or crises, obnoxious material (such as terrorist videos) is now removed relatively quickly. Yet it is only minimally rhetorical to say the drive for clicks causes much harm, including many deaths, whether from the incitement of hatred or the spread of anti-vax beliefs.

4. The public option

This reactive approach is inadequate; the quantity of hate or misinformation will always be unmanageable, and anyway it needs to be prevented in the first place. A much bolder intervention is needed to tackle the pernicious effects of the click-bait and advertising based economic model. It needs to be an intervention that does not depend on unwinding the digital age. We will continue to spend many hours each day online. Specifically, an intervention is needed to ensure that competition for people's attention does not require maximising the number of clicks. The only way to achieve this will be to introduce into the market for attention an alternative business model, one not driven by profit maximisation: a public option whose platform is shaped not by whatever will generate most clicks but by public service aims.

In case this sounds like wishful thinking, there is already a highly successful example of content markets delivering public service aims through competitors with a mixture of advertising, subscription and tax-based revenues: broadcasting. The example I have in mind is of course the BBC. It was established in 1922 as an offshoot of the Post Office with explicitly economic aims, an industrial policy intended to make sure the UK had a foothold in the exciting new tech frontier of radio (Coyle, 2015). Originally the only broadcaster, in due course commercial rivals came along, supported by advertising and regulated with public service requirements. This competition explicitly further encouraged by Mrs Thatcher's Government by establishing Channel 4 as an advertising funded, publicly-owned broadcaster with a public service remit. Even more recently, subscription-based and profit-motivated services entered the market too, delivered by cable and satellite as well as broadcast platforms. Thus, by happenstance, Britain has had a broadcast market supported by a diversity of business models, ownership structures, and corporate purposes.

The BBC has been under sustained political attack from successive Conservative governments, and its finances seriously squeezed. The current Conservative Government intends to privatise Channel 4, albeit promising it will be sold with public service purposes intact. The ideological lenses through which Conservatives have seen the market have blinded them to the economic and social benefits of the mixed broadcasting ecology in the UK. These include the kind of benefits a successful industrial policy can deliver: training for the sector as a whole, blue skies research, derisking innovation for smaller suppliers (such as musicians or special effects studios) by

47

providing a large market for their wares, encouraging consumer adoption of new technologies (such as on-demand viewing through the launch of the iPlayer, in 2007). However, the key point for present purposes is that while the BBC has competed vigorously with its commercial rivals for audiences, the nature of that competition has ensured high average quality and no race to the bottom in terms of types of content. Although it is regulation that ensures all UK broadcasters have to provide reasonably impartial news bulletins, it is the varied nature of the competition among business models and governance structures that ensures none of the widely-viewed UK TV channels or radio stations only shows soap operas or American movies, by far the most popular genres. Variety and quality are dimensions of the competition for attention.

Given the toxin spreading through society because of the widespread imperative to get users clicking online, and given the unmanageable scale of the problem with the billions of users and billions of hours spent on the giant tech platforms, incremental tightening of regulations on YouTube or Facebook seem unlikely to have a big impact. And yet these platforms now entirely shape the arena for public debate in our societies. People's information and beliefs, shaping how they vote, whether they get vaccinated, where they shop, whom they hate and how they think it is acceptable to act on that – all are acquired from online spaces. This includes 'traditional' media such as newspapers and indeed broadcasters, who also now depend on the tech giants to get access to their readers and viewers.

Nothing will change unless there is a significant intervention by the state, in the face of the platforms' extraordinary private concentration of power. This is a fundamental challenge to the body politic.

Regulation could work. The Chinese solution demonstrates this. Not content with exercising tight oversight of what people see and say online, with a large digital police force, the Chinese government has recently launched an all-out political attack on the privately-owned platforms. While not nationalised, they have been effectively brought under the strict supervision of the state, with a suite of new regulations regarding their practices, closer party supervision, and a massive extension of the state's control over the data held by the tech companies. Prominent commentators have denounced 'big capitalists'.[4] This suggests that sufficiently determined regulation and punishment could reclaim the digital arena. Unfortunately only the US (if it wanted to) and China have the ability to take this

[4]   Financial Times, 6 & 7 September 2021 https://www.ft.com/content/bacf9b6a-326b-4aa9-a8f6-2456921e61ec

route. Other countries' governments can demand compliance with rules about moderating access to certain kinds of content, or enforcing age limits, or could even try to insist on data sharing, but their enforcement powers are weak. If it came to a game of chicken, which government would risk Facebook shutting up shop inside their borders?

So establishing a public service social media platform, at sufficient scale to attract users, perhaps through easy linkage with other online public services, or indeed by brilliant viral content that does not rely on misinformation or hatred, seems an attractive alternative. It would need to be paid for, and there is plenty of alternative need for public spending now, so perhaps this seems an unrealistic proposal. Yet we have such a degraded information environment and poisoned public debate that, when everything people believe and do is shaped by the information they acquire, it might be worth it. We could consider it a National Health Service for the body politic.

5. Claiming public space

Ideas build societies. Ideas triggered the Enlightenment and Industrial Revolution, shaping the modern world (Mokyr, 2002). Economic growth is a matter of new ideas about how to produce things or about new services and products. Ideas and beliefs cause political debate or compromise – or conflict. People die – or kill – for them. As both authoritarians and democrats have long realised (Ben-Ghiat, 2020), nothing is more important than the information and beliefs people acquire in determining the kind of society we have.

The ascendancy of a small number of digital companies in the online world where most of now spend a growing amount of our time means that their platforms can no longer be considered a private domain. Just as the presumption that they hold private ownership rights over data must be challenged, so must the presumption that the world online is a private economic space, a market. Introducing information into the picture immediately implies that market solutions are not the best ones for society (Stiglitz and Greenwald, 2014).

States have always played a strongly interventionist role in the means of communication, from post to telegraph to phone networks to broadcasting (with the US something of an anomaly, albeit regulating these markets). Communications companies have often been publicly-owned. They have also often been publicly financed. The American state through its funding and Cold War requirements

Diane Coyle

laid the foundations for the Internet, and European governments did the same for the World Wide Web, developed by Tim Berners-Lee at the CERN research facility and made freely available. Initially the Web was considered public space. The rise of the private platforms has occurred mainly in the past 15 years (Wu, 2016) because the growth of most of these services we all use has occurred in the United States, with its distinctive economistic, pro-market and anti-government instincts.

The instinct to let the market decide unconstrained by government limits, the utilitarian calculus making it easier to count economic gain than social or political loss, and the nature of digital technologies themselves have brought us to the point where it is widely accepted that something must be done. We have become reliant on huge and powerful privately-owned companies based in the US or China. They decisively shape our information environment. Online space must be reclaimed as public space, and one way to do so will be to build public spaces online. Digital platforms do not all need to be publicly-owned but they do need to serve the public good.

University of Cambridge
dc700@cam.ac.uk

References

E. Anderson, *Value in ethics and economics*, (Cambridge MA: Harvard University Press, 1995).

I. Arrieta-Ibarra, L. Goff, D. Jiménez-Hernández, J. Lanier and E.G. Weyl, 'Should we treat data as labor? Moving beyond 'free''. *AEA Papers and Proceedings* 108 (2018), 38-42.

R. Ben-Ghiat, *Strongmen: How they rise, Why they succeed, How they fall* (London: Profile Books, 2020).

J. Chung, *Big tech, BIG Cash: Washington's new power players*. (Public Citizen, 2021). Available at: https://mkus3lurbh3lbztg254fzode-wpengine.netdna-ssl.com/wp-content/uploads/Big-Tech-Big-Cash-Washingtons-New-Power-Players.pdf

D. Comin and B. Hobijn, 'An exploration of technology diffusion', *American economic review*, 100 (2010), 2031–59.

D. Coyle, 'The Scale of the BBC', in J. Mair, R. Tait and R. Keeble (eds) *The BBC Today: Future Uncertain*, (London: Abramis, 2015).

D. Coyle, 'Homo Economicus, AIs, humans and rats: decision-making and economic welfare', *Journal of Economic Methodology*, 26 (2019), 2–12.

D. Coyle, *Markets, State, and People: Economics for Public Policy*, (Princeton University Press, 2020).

D. Coyle, S. Diepeveen, J. Wdowin, J. Tennison and L. Kay, *The Value of Data: Policy Implications*, Bennett Institute for Public Policy (2019). Available at: https://www.bennettinstitute.cam.ac.uk/publications/value-data-policy-implications/

D. Coyle and D. Nguyen, 'Free Goods and Economic Welfare', *Economic Statistics Centre of Excellence, Discussion paper 2020–18*, (2020).

J. Cremer, Y. -A de Montjoye, H. Schweitzer, *Competition policy for the digital era*. Report prepared for the European Commission, *Directorate-General for Competition*, (2019).

E. Duflo, 'The economist as plumber', *American Economic Review*, 107 (2017), 1–26.

D. Evans, 'The Antitrust Economics of Two-Sided Markets', (2002). Available at SSRN: https://ssrn.com/abstract=332022 or http://dx.doi.org/10.2139/ssrn.332022

M. Friedman, *Essays in positive economics*, (Chicago: University of Chicago Press, 1953).

J. Furman, D. Coyle, A. Fletcher, D. McAuley and P. Marsden, 'Unlocking digital competition: Report of the digital competition expert panel'. *UK government publication, HM Treasury* (2019).

D. Hausman, M. McPherson and D. Satz, *Economic analysis, moral philosophy, and public policy*, (Cambridge: Cambridge University Press, 2016).

N. Kaldor, 'The economic aspects of advertising', *The review of economic studies*, 18 (1950),1–27.

J. Mokyr, *The Gifts of Athena: Historical Origins of the Knowledge Economy*, (Princeton and Oxford: Princeton University Press, 2002).

Ofcom, Online nation. (2021). Available at: https://www.ofcom.org.uk/__data/assets/pdf_file/0013/220414/online-nation-2021-report.pdf

A. Perrin and M. Kumar, 'About three-in-ten US adults say they are 'almost constantly' online' *Pew Research Center*, 25 (2021). Available at: https://www.pewresearch.org/fact-tank/2021/03/26/about-three-in-ten-u-s-adults-say-they-are-almost-constantly-online/

Jean-Charles Rochet and Jean Tirole, 'Two-Sided Markets: A Progress Report', *The RAND Journal of Economics*, 37, (2006), 645–67.

M. Sandel, *What Money Can't Buy: The Moral Limits of Markets*, (New York: Farrar, Strauss & Giroux, 2012).

J. Schumpeter, *Capitalism, Socialism, and Democracy*, (New York: Harper & Bros, 1942).

A. Sen, 'Capability and Well-being', in Nussbaum and Sen (eds.), *The Quality of Life*, (Oxford: Clarendon Press, 1993), 30–53.

J. Stiglitz and B. Greenwald, *Creating A Learning Society: A New Approach to Growth, Development and Social Progress*, (New York: Columbia University Press, 2014).

S. Viljoen, 'Democratic Data: A Relational Theory For Data Governance', *Yale Law Journal* Vol 131 (forthcoming). Available at SSRN: http://dx.doi.org/10.2139/ssrn.3727562

T. Wu, *The Attention Merchants: The Epic Scramble to Get Inside Our Heads*, (New York: Knopf Publishing, 2016).

On the Merits and Limits of Nationalising the Fossil Fuel Industry

FERGUS GREEN AND INGRID ROBEYNS

Abstract

We explore the desirability of an idea that has not received the attention it deserves by political philosophers: that governments should bring privately-owned fossil fuel companies into public ownership with a view to managing their wind-down in the public interest – often simply referred to as 'nationalising the fossil fuel industry'. We aim to make a conditional case for public ownership of fossil fuel companies. We will assume certain conditions about government motivations and capacities that are similar to assumptions made generally in the philosophical and economic analysis of climate policies: that the government is suitably motivated, has effective control over the companies it acquires, and is able to sustain this motivation and control for long-enough to wind-down acquired companies in the public interest. We argue that bringing fossil fuel companies into public ownership, under these conditions, allows the government to take ten actions that are in the public interest, which will enhance social justice, enable a fair division of burdens and benefits, and strengthen democracy. We consider four plausible objections. While some of these point to the need for further research, they do not undermine our claim that nationalising the fossil fuel industry is a policy option that merits serious consideration.

1. Introduction

Climate change, or global heating, is one of the most profound crises facing humanity. It threatens the ecological and social preconditions for wellbeing and social justice. To safeguard those preconditions as best we can, the rise in global average temperatures must urgently be restrained. It is now widely agreed that average temperature increases should be kept within 1.5°C above pre-industrial levels (they have already risen 1.2°C). To do so, the greenhouse gas (GHG) emissions that cause climate change must be rapidly reduced and carbon dioxide (CO_2) needs to be removed from the atmosphere (the balance between GHG additions and CO_2 removal is known as *net* GHG emissions). The policies and measures aimed at reducing GHG emissions and removing CO_2 are collectively known as

doi:10.1017/S1358246122000030   © The Royal Institute of Philosophy and the contributors 2022

Royal Institute of Philosophy Supplement **91** 2022

climate change mitigation.[1] A great many mitigation policies and measures have been discussed, proposed and implemented, to varying degrees on all continents and across all levels of society. But emissions keep rising, year on year. The United Nations Environment Program (UNEP) estimates that if governments' current, unconditional 2030 emissions reduction pledges were implemented (but no more), average temperatures would rise by 2.7°C by the end of the century (UNEP 2021). Worse still, many countries have a long history of failing to achieve their previously pledged (inadequate) emissions reduction targets. Yet, to restrain global heating to within 1.5°C above pre-industrial levels, it is estimated that net emissions must fall by 55% between now and 2030 (UNEP 2021). For every year that mitigation efforts fail, and net GHG emissions continue to rise, the rate at which they must subsequently fall in order to meet the goal becomes steeper.

The mainstream social-scientific paradigm in which the climate problem, *qua social* problem, has been studied takes its cues from this description of the proximate causes of climate change, i.e. excessive net emissions. On this 'pollution paradigm', the social problem of climate change is understood in reductionist terms, as an issue of cumulative anthropogenic GHG emissions, and agents – be they persons or collectives – are typically assumed to have extensive control over their emissions-relevant choices (F. Green, 2021). Climate ethicists have almost universally accepted the pollution paradigm as the social-scientific frame within which to undertake their ethical theorising. Consequently, the seminal debates in the field have focused on the correct principles for distributing the 'burden' of reducing emissions, and the correct subjects to whom those principles should apply (see Caney, 2020, secs. 5–6). Insofar as philosophers have debated desirable mitigation policies and measures, the debate has, again, largely paralleled the pollution paradigm, with the bulk of attention focused on GHG emissions trading schemes (Caney and Hepburn, 2011; Hyams, 2009; Page, 2013).

Social scientists working on climate change have begun to question the pollution paradigm, arguing for a more holistic, systems-level frame of analysis, and placing greater emphasis on the structural determinants of emissions-intensive activities (Bernstein and

---

[1]   The other key category of policies and measures to respond to climate change is known as *climate change adaptation.* Adaptation is about preparing for and responding to the effects of climate change, now and in the future – for example, by giving farmers access to affordable seeds that are resistant to more extreme weather.

Hoffmann, 2019; Farmer et al., 2019; Otto et al., 2020). Bernstein and Hoffman redescribe the social problem of climate change as one of 'global carbon lock-in':

> multiple, interdependent systems at local, regional and national levels, as well as the economic activity within and among them, are locked into the use of fossil energy. In other words, carbon lock-in is a multilevel and multisectoral challenge of similar, overlapping and interdependent political, economic, techno-logical and cultural forces that reinforce dependence on fossil fuels in many places simultaneously. (Bernstein and Hoffmann 2019, p. 919)

Understanding the problem in this way, they argue, suggests a need to 'reorient research and action from a dominant focus on the collect-ive action problem of distributing emissions reductions to preserve the global commons, to analysing and deploying strategies that disrupt carbon lock-in at multiple levels and scales' (ibid, p. 919). In a similar vein, Jessica Green and others have called for radically different thinking about the kinds of policy options for mitigating global climate change (e.g., J. F. Green, 2021).

In this spirit, we explore in this paper the desirability of an idea that has, at least on the face of it, the potential to 'disrupt carbon-lock in': that governments should bring privately-owned fossil fuel companies into public ownership with a view to managing their wind-down in the public interest.[2] There has been growing interest in the US and elsewhere in such a strategy – often simply referred to as 'nationalis-ing the fossil fuel industry' (Alperovitz, Guinan, and Hanna, 2017; Aronoff 2020a; 2020b; 2021; Bozuwa and Táíwò, 2021; Paul, Skandier, and Renzy, 2020; Sweeney, 2020). But to our knowledge the issue has not received the attention it deserves by political philo-sophers. We aim to contribute to this debate by making a case for public ownership of fossil fuel companies, under certain assumed conditions.

The three conditions we will assume for the sake of our argument are as follows. First, we assume that each public acquisition of a fossil fuel company is undertaken by a *suitably motivated government*, by which we mean a government that is genuinely committed to achiev-ing deep and rapid decarbonisation, and doing so via a portfolio of policies and measures that includes winding down fossil fuel

---

[2] We will provide a *normative* analysis (rather than, for example, a descriptive or explanatory analysis), thus we develop an answer to the ques-tion what we *should do*, and what *reasons* we have for doing something.

companies in the public interest. Second, we assume that each (suitably motivated) government acquisition results in the government enjoying *effective control* over the company. By effective control, we mean control that is sufficient to carry out the Public Interest Actions described in section 2.1. We assume this is obtained by the government acquiring a majority stake in each relevant company that is large enough to enable the government to (i) amend the company charter or constitution to specify that the company shall be governed for public purposes / in the public interest, and (ii) appoint a majority of the company's board of directors, effectively giving the government control over company strategy and policies, and over the hiring and firing of senior management. Third, we assume that the motivation specified in the first assumption and the effective control specified in the second assumption are *sustained* (i.e. continue to obtain) throughout the period of time necessary for achieving the wind-down of the company's assets in the public interest. Given these assumed conditions, our argument should be understood as pertaining to *suitably motivated and effective public ownership of fossil fuel companies*.

We acknowledge that these are 'big' assumptions. However, they are no bigger than the assumptions that are standardly made by normative theorists, and in the mixed normative/social-scientific field of 'public policy analysis', when discussing other climate change policies. For instance, the merits and 'effectiveness' of global systems of carbon pricing (taxation or emissions trading) have been debated at length in the mainstream climate policy community (e.g., High-Level Commission on Carbon Prices, 2017). Most such analyses assume that governments are motivated to deeply cut emissions, have the capacity to successfully implement carbon pricing, and will sustain that motivation and capacity for as long as necessary to achieve the policy's goals. That said, we think that issues of motivation and feasibility, including the successful enactment of policies and laws, and their sustained implementation, merit much more consideration by philosophers and social scientists – and this plea applies equally to our own proposal. While we cannot explore these issues in-depth in this paper, we set out some of the key issues meriting further attention (section 3.4).

Our focus on the conditional desirability of public ownership of fossil fuel companies means we must bracket certain practical issues, many of which raise additional philosophical questions. First, while we focus on the case for governments acquiring majority stakes in those fossil fuel companies that are currently majority privately owned, we do not specify which governments should acquire which companies, nor do we discuss the principles by which such acquisitions should be distributed between governments. Rather, we implicitly assume the perspective of a hypothetical suitably motivated, high-capacity government acquiring a hypothetical privately-owned fossil fuel company. Second, we do not discuss the means by which a controlling majority stake should be acquired. We assume the acquisition will occur via an acquisition of shares (rather than an acquisition of business assets) since this is a necessary incident of our assumption that governments will obtain effective control via a 'controlling majority stake'. However, we do not consider whether the shares should be purchased on the open market or compulsorily acquired. Nor do we consider, in the latter case, how much compensation (if any) should be paid to current shareholders. Third, we do not directly consider what should be done about those fossil fuel companies that are currently majority state-owned (or those that do not even have a separate legal existence from the state). Finally, while we focus on the case for public ownership of fossil fuel *production/supply* companies, we will not here defend this supply-side orientation. The case for supply-side (upstream) climate policy − as part of a portfolio of climate policies that includes strong measures to decarbonise downstream industries and greatly reduce energy demand − has been made by one of us elsewhere (F. Green and Denniss 2018). We discuss the benefits of including ownership of fossil fuel (production) companies as part of a portfolio of policies and measures in section 3.1. We acknowledge that the case for public ownership may apply similarly to other links in the fossil fuel supply chain (e.g. coal-fired power stations) and other sources of emissions, and we are open to extensions of our argument to such other targets of public ownership.

Given the contentiousness of our three assumptions and the numerous issues that we bracket, what our argument amounts to is the proposition that *the idea of public ownership of fossil fuel companies, as one component in a portfolio of climate mitigation policies and measures, has conditional merit and deserves to be seriously considered and debated.* In this sense, our contribution is to use the techniques of political philosophy to advance the exploration of an important idea. In doing so, we contribute not only to the literature on climate ethics and climate policy, but also to an orthogonal debate concerning the appropriate role of the state in the economy and whether (some of) the means of production should be state-owned (see Gilabert and O'Neill, 2019).

Our argument is structured as follows. In Part 2, we outline our positive case for suitably motivated and effective public ownership of fossil fuel companies. Section 2.1 specifies the key actions that such ownership would allow such governments to take. In section 2.2, we evaluate these actions, explaining how they would enhance *social justice*, which we stipulate to be the primary evaluation criterion. For this purpose, we simply adopt a widely held principle of justice, namely that all persons, current and future, should enjoy genuine opportunities to pursue the most central human functionings (Robeyns, 2017). In section 2.3, we evaluate these actions by reference to two additional (secondary) criteria: *fairness* in the sharing of burdens and benefits and *democracy*. In Part 3, we consider and respond to four potential objections to our proposal: that public ownership of fossil fuel companies would be redundant because similar outcomes could be achieved (at lower cost) with other policies and measures (3.1); that it would not be welfare-maximising because perfectly competitive markets are better at maximising welfare, and markets for fossil fuels could be rendered approximately perfectly competitive through other policies (3.2); that state acquisitions of fossil fuel companies are a step on the road to serfdom (3.3); and that our three assumed conditions do not hold (3.4). Part 4 concludes.

2. The desirability of suitably motivated and effective public ownership of fossil fuel companies

2.1. *The Public Interest Actions that public ownership enables governments to take*

The desirability of suitably motivated and effective public ownership of fossil fuel companies rests on the effective control the relevant government would gain over fossil fuel companies and their associated assets and operations, enabling it to manage these in the public interest. Specifically, such control would enable the government unilaterally to take the following actions, which we shall subsequently refer to as the Public Interest Actions:

1. cease all exploration for and development of new fossil fuel deposits;
2. account for and disclose the emissions embodied in the fossil fuels it produces, and phase out existing production in a timeframe consistent with the achievement of the relevant emission reduction targets and other relevant goals (e.g. ensuring a sufficient supply of energy to satisfy requirements of social justice);

3. use its market power to raise the price of those fossil fuels it continues to sell (i.e. those sales that are compatible with the phase-out timeframe).[3]
4. disclose and minimise the company's Scope 1 and Scope 2 greenhouse gas emissions, and comply with the letter and spirit of all (other) government laws and regulations relating to climate change and energy efficiency;[4]
5. expend research, development and demonstration (RD&D) resources on developing emissions reduction technologies that are likely to be necessary to the global decarbonisation effort and that leverage the company's existing assets (e.g. geological expertise);
6. cease all governmental and public affairs operations aimed at promoting fossil fuels, obstructing climate policies and re-pressing local opposition to operations (e.g. lobbying, political donations, advertising, public relations, litigation, surveillance of anti-fossil fuel protestors etc.);
7. cease all forms of tax avoidance and evasion, and comply with the letter and spirit of applicable tax laws;
8. undertake ongoing operations in accordance with high standards for occupational health and safety, labour relations, community relations and environmental/pollution management.
9. fully decommission former production sites and restore them to high standards of safety, amenity and ecological functioning, and carry out associated maintenance and monitoring of decommissioned sites to a high standard;
10. justly manage the transition of the workforce and of local communities dependent on company operations.

---

[3] The oil market is highly globalised and so governments would have limited market power to set prices *directly*, but reductions in supply increase prices, all else equal. Other fossil fuel supply markets are typically based on longer-term supply contracts and only some markets are open to cross-border trade (e.g. the markets for liquefied natural gas and certain types of coal), meaning governments acting unilaterally would have some power to set prices directly.

[4] Scope 1 emissions are emissions from point sources under the operational control of the company, such as CO_2 from gas flaring, CO_2 from on-site electricity production and combustion, company vehicle usage, and fugitive methane emissions from oil and gas production. Scope 2 emissions are emissions from electricity and heat production supplied to the company by third parties for use in the company's operations. Relevant scope 3 emissions are primarily addressed through action 2, above.

2.2. Primary desirability criterion: social justice

All of the above-mentioned 10 actions advance social justice. The first six do so by more effectively achieving decarbonisation at a scale and speed consistent with maintaining the ecological and social preconditions for social justice.

The combined effect of actions 1–3 would be to increase the price of fossil fuels that remain on the market, effectively constraining the (very large amount of) 'scope 3' emissions that are released when fossil fuels are burned by downstream customers, such as by drivers of petrol-based cars and trucks. Basic economic theory tells us that an increase in price results in a contraction in demand and hence, all else equal, a reduction in greenhouse gas emissions. Of course, all else is not equal. In particular, the higher price of remaining fossil fuels will incentivise other suppliers (in other countries) to expand their supply – a phenomenon known as cross-border *production leakage*. The new equilibrium price will depend on the relative price elasticities of demand and supply – an empirical question that depends on numerous factors. Existing studies of relative elasticities in various fossil fuel markets show mixed results, but the balance of literature suggests that unilateral reductions in fossil fuel supply tend to be replaced elsewhere at a ratio of less than 1:1, meaning unilateral fossil fuel supply restrictions tend to lead to genuine net global emissions reductions. For example, here is the conclusion of Fæhn and colleagues from their empirical study of cost-effective climate mitigation in Norway:

> The global combustion of fossil fuels extracted in Norway leads to CO_2 emissions that are about ten times higher than total emissions of CO_2 within Norway. Even though leakages are likely to be larger with supply side measures than demand side measures, we conclude that it is cost-effective for Norway to let most of the contribution to global emission reductions be achieved through supply side measures. In our benchmark scenario, only one third of a given global reduction should be realised through demand side measures; the remaining two thirds should come through supply side measures, that is, by reducing oil extraction. (Fæhn et al., 2017)

The more countries that pursue a supply reduction strategy, the more they will foster a new global moral norm against fossil fuel production, which will raise the *social costs* of non-cooperation, incentivising supply reductions (Collier and Venables, 2015; F. Green, 2018). First-movers have a crucial role to play in modelling such 'anti-fossil fuel norms' and persuading other countries to cooperate

(F. Green, 2018). We assume that such a foreign policy strategy would be part of the policy mix of a suitably motivated government seeking to adopt ambitious climate mitigation strategies. Ultimately, such actions could lead to international cooperation among like-minded governments to phase-out fossil fuel production (Asheim et al., 2019; Collier and Venables, 2015; F. Green, 2018; F. Green and Denniss, 2018; Newell and Simms, 2020; Piggot et al., 2018).

The effect of action 4 would be to directly reduce the emissions produced in the course of the company's operations. These operational emissions can be significant: for example, the International Energy Agency (IEA) estimates that emissions from the upstream production, processing, transportation and refining of oil and gas account for 10-30% of the lifecycle emissions of oil and 15-40% for gas (IEA, 2018).

Action 5 would contribute to global climate mitigation through the innovation of new technologies and processes that ultimately accelerate global emissions reductions. Stockmarket listed firms tend to be myopic, pursuing short-term strategies to boost stock prices and dividends at the expense of investments in technological innovation that are profitable in the longer term and that benefit the firm's wider stakeholders (Lazonick and Shin, 2019; Mazzucato, 2013; Stout, 2012). Fossil fuel companies are no exception to this myopia (Kenner and Heede, 2021). Under suitably motivated and effective public ownership, this trend could be reversed: the assets of the acquired companies could be utilised for the RD&D of emissions reduction technologies.

Action 6 would remove powerful sources of pro-fossil fuel influence over politics, policy, civil society, and consumer beliefs, attitudes and preferences. Instead, fossil fuel companies under the effective control of suitably motivated governments would become advocates of decarbonisation. The effect of this political shift in the strategic orientation of fossil fuel companies could be great (see section 3.1).

Actions 7–10 enhance social justice in the transition process.[5] There is considerable evidence that the fossil fuel industry as a whole (albeit with regional variability on some measures) performs poorly – at best, patchily – with regard to transparency, payment of taxes, occupational health and safety, site decommissioning and restoration, local environmental management, labour

---

[5] Since social justice informs the decarbonisation objective (which we consider a *precondition* for social justice) consistency demands that the transitional effects of alternative climate policies also be evaluated by reference to social justice.

Fergus Green and Ingrid Robeyns

relations, and community relations (Olson and Lenzmann, 2016). Consequently, considerable injustice is done to workers in these firms and to (other) persons who are killed or harmed by these firms' operations (Wenar, 2015). Meanwhile, the low levels of tax paid by the industry constrains governments' ability to provide public goods and services that advance social justice (J. F., Green 2021). A suitably motivated government would run such firms according to high standards across these areas (see actions 7–10), enabling large social justice gains relative to current ownership patterns.

Consider, for example, the issue of workforce transition. Privately-owned fossil fuel companies tend to treat their workers as mere factors of production. They are often swiftly made redundant when labour-saving technologies and processes are implemented to reduce costs and in adverse circumstances (e.g. when fossil fuel prices fall), with little thought given to their career development, their skills or their general wellbeing and that of their families and communities. Many fossil fuel firms have used bankruptcy as a means to escape their liabilities to fund their workers' pensions and other entitlements (Aronoff, 2021). In the context of debates about a 'just transition' of the carbon-dependent workforce, it is often assumed that only governments have obligations to support workers, or that, if firms do have obligations, they are unlikely to fulfil them. However, if such firms were in the employ of a suitably motivated government, the government would be able to secure a just transition for fossil fuel workers (F. Green and Gambhir, 2020; International Labour Organization, 2015). A publicly owned fossil fuel company could, for example, engage its workers in a workplace-democratic process concerning transition arrangements; ensure pension liabilities are paid out to eligible beneficiaries; facilitate voluntary early retirement for older workers; redeploy workers to site decommissioning, restoration, maintenance and monitoring operations, RD&D operations or other (sustainable) parts of the business; and facilitate the training and reskilling of non-retiring workers for employment in good quality jobs in growing, zero-carbon industries (as part of the wider policy mix, we assume the government would be facilitating and investing in such industries).

2.3. Secondary criteria: fairness and democracy

A public controlling majority stake performs well not only on the primary desirability criterion of increased social justice, but also on the following two secondary desirability criteria.

Fairness

Consider first the issue of fairness. The public ownership and management of fossil fuel companies, post-acquisition, will entail costs and benefits the distribution of which needs to be judged from the standpoint of fairness. A key issue is the distribution of financial costs or benefits from fossil fuel operations. Whether the operations of a fossil fuel company, once government-owned (and thus on a rapid phase-out trajectory), result in net costs or benefits depends on whether revenue exceeds operating costs over a relevant time-frame. We shall assume for the sake of argument that the companies will be operated at a loss. Public ownership effectively socialises these (assumed) losses, so the relevant question becomes: what fiscal and monetary arrangements most fairly distribute these losses across the population?

The answer to this question depends on one's preferred principle of fairness. Much has been written elsewhere on what fairness requires by way of distribution of burdens and benefits, including in the climate context (see Caney, 2020) and, more specifically, with regard to phasing out fossil fuel production (Kartha et al., 2018; Lenferna, 2018; Muttitt and Kartha, 2020). Contributing, let alone resolving, this more abstract debate is beyond the scope of this paper. We simply claim that *whatever one's preferred principle of fairness*, an advantage of the socialisation of fossil fuel companies' operational losses through public ownership is that, in principle, it is possible for governments to arrange their fiscal and monetary institutions and policies such that the burdens are borne ultimately as directed by the relevant principle. To illustrate, consider the plausible principle that burdens should be borne by those with the greatest ability to pay (i.e. progressively according to income or wealth). The government could manage its fiscal and monetary policies so as to recoup losses from its fossil fuel companies' operations by increasing the progressivity of taxes on income and/or wealth.

We can also say something about fairness in the sharing of burdens and benefits internationally. We do not here propose any particular fair global distribution of rights to extract. However, as we discuss later (section 3.4), the conditions of effective control and/or suitable motivation may effectively limit the case for public ownership of fossil fuel companies to rich democracies. If this results in rich countries phasing out fossil fuels faster than poorer ones, then the policy is likely to be consistent with principles of historical responsibility and capacity to pay that have been advocated in the ethical literature on fossil fuel extraction (Kartha et al., 2018; Muttitt and Kartha, 2020).

63

Democracy

A public controlling majority stake in fossil fuel companies is likely to improve democracy in two respects. First, when democratic countries bring fossil fuel companies into public control, citizens gain collective authority over a larger sphere of economic decision-making than they otherwise would, which itself arguably counts as a democratic improvement (Arnold n.d., sec. 4). To the extent that economic decisions affect the public, the underlying idea behind the expansion into the economic sphere of the scope of democratic decision-making is the principle that 'those affected by a decision should enjoy a say over that decision, proportional to the degree to which they are affected' (ibid, sec. 4(a)). The decisions of fossil fuel companies about the extraction of fossil fuels have profound, potentially existential impacts on the public. As such, there is a particularly strong case for bringing them under democratic control.

Second, majority public control over fossil fuel companies would indirectly increase the influence of ordinary citizens over the democratic process. Democracy is strengthened when (all else equal[6]) citizens have more equal influence over, or more equal opportunity to influence, democratic decisions (Christiano, 2012). In capitalist societies, those who own the means of production use their structural, instrumental and cultural power to disproportionately influence democratic decision-making. Public control over the means of production reduces this distortive influence over democratic decision-making, making it more egalitarian (Arnold n.d., sec. 4(b); Bowles and Gintis, 1986; Meiksins Wood, 1995; Wright, 2010). This argument applies particularly forcefully in the case of fossil fuel companies: perhaps no other industry in modern history has more profoundly corrupted government decision-making and distorted the informational basis for democratic accountability (Carroll, 2021).

3. Objections

3.1. Public ownership is redundant: other policies could achieve similar outcomes (at lower cost)

The first objection we consider is that public ownership of fossil fuel companies would be redundant because similar outcomes could be

---

[6]   This caveat is necessary to accommodate the principle, discussed in the previous paragraph, that those more affected should enjoy greater decision-making authority.

achieved (at lower cost) with other regulations. For example, the government could remove fossil fuel subsidies, ban new fossil fuel exploration and development, reduce existing production (by instituting a system of declining production quotas – which could be tradeable – or by taxing fossil fuel production), price carbon, mandate higher standards for energy efficiency, and so forth. The same could be said for the regulation of fossil fuel companies' decommissioning and site restoration, technological innovation, local environmental protection, labour relations and community relations obligations.

We certainly think that many such regulations could be valuable elements of the climate policy mix. However, we think these other regulations are more likely to be effective if combined with suitably motivated and effective public ownership of fossil fuel companies. There are two reasons for this, both of which have to do with *post-enactment dynamics*. For the purpose of responding to this objection, we shall therefore assume that the government enacts some set of the aforementioned regulations such that, *if fully implemented*, this set of regulations would achieve similar results to what would be achieved with public ownership alone. Our claim is that those policies would have feedback effects that mean they would be less effective than they would be if fossil fuel companies were publicly owned, under the conditions outlined in Part 1, because of different – and superior – feedback effects of such ownership.

First, all regulation of private corporate activity faces *implementation and enforcement challenges*. These challenges arise from the strategic (e.g. profit-maximising) orientation of the privately-owned firms that the regulation seeks to control, combined with the information asymmetry between what firms know about their own activities compared with what the government can know. The fewer resources a government has available for monitoring and verifying (i.e. auditing) firms' behaviour, the greater these information asymmetries will be. Moreover, the larger and more powerful the regulated firms are, the more likely they will 'capture' regulatory agencies, thus influencing executive rule-making as well as auditing and enforcement policies and practices. Larger firms are also more likely to be able to avoid enforcement actions or penalties for non-compliance, and to engage in forms of 'creative compliance' / 'gaming' (Baldwin, Cave, and Lodge, 2011; McBarnet and Whelan, 1991). The fossil fuel industry has proven itself highly adept at capturing and gaming regulatory and tax systems (Bergin and Bousso, 2020; J. F. Green, 2021; Stokes, 2020). By contrast, a fossil fuel company controlled by suitably-motivated government owners would by definition be motivated by the public interest objectives that govern its mandate, thus eliminating the motivation for strategic evasion of regulations (see action 4 on our list in section 2.1).

The second set of relevant post-enactment dynamics concerns the incentives and capacities of regulated firms to mobilise politically in order to repeal or dilute the enacted legislation itself (Patashnik, 2008). If a government were to enact mainstream climate policies, the affected fossil fuel firms would have every incentive to redouble their political efforts to repeal or weaken the legislation. To be sure, the enacted policies themselves would inevitably weaken these firms' capabilities. Still, the incentive for fossil fuel companies to use their remaining capabilities to mobilise politically would continue. This incentive would be eliminated if a suitably motivated government controlled the relevant firms – hence action 6 on our list.

3.2. The market is better at maximising aggregate welfare than the government

A second objection is that public ownership of fossil fuel companies would not be welfare-maximising because perfectly competitive markets are better at maximising welfare.[7] Before we respond to the core of the objection, note that it only gets off the ground if markets for fossil fuels are perfectly competitive, or could be made so with additional regulation. In reality, markets for fossil fuels are about as far from perfectly competitive as a market can get. Fossil fuel companies are propped up by massive direct and indirect government subsidies that support production (e.g., production tax credits), or downstream consumption of their products (e.g., consumer fuel rebates) (Coady et al., 2015). Most discussions of subsidies don't even count government investments in military operations to protect fossil fuel production sites, infrastructure, and transport routes, or government diplomatic efforts to secure favourable contracts and other arrangements (Olson and Lenzmann, 2016). Aside from subsidies, the industry pays nowhere near (plausible estimates of) the social cost of its externalities, which include not only its greenhouse gas emissions but also air pollution and other environmental impacts (Coady et al., 2015), not to mention human rights abuses and democratic distortions across the world (Olson and Lenzmann,

---

[7] We do not accept that maximising welfare *qua* preference-satisfaction should be the ultimate normative objective, but we will assume it is for the sake of responding to this objection.

2016; Wenar, 2015). Finally, the supply of fossil fuels is oligopolistic, as there are high barriers to entry to the industry and it requires natural monopoly infrastructure such as pipelines, railways and ports. If the industry received no subsidies (other than for any positive externalities it provides), and paid the full social costs of its externalities (e.g. through carbon and pollution taxes), much – perhaps all – of it would be unprofitable, and perfect competition would bid down any remaining rents.

However unlikely it is that a perfectly competitive fossil fuel market comes about, let us assume for the sake of argument that it does and consider the original objection on its merits.[8] The objection is that, under perfectly competitive market conditions, the (*ex hypothesi* highly-regulated) market would achieve higher aggregate welfare than if fossil fuels were produced and distributed according to government priorities. This, so the argument goes, is because markets enable fossil fuels to go to those who have the greatest willingness to pay for them.

The objector's argument rests on an implicit assumption that efficient outcomes (which we are assuming for the sake of argument) are welfare-maximising, where welfare is understood to mean the aggregate satisfaction of consumption preferences. But efficiency and welfare are not the same. Rather, given the diminishing marginal propensity of money to satisfy preferences, aggregate preference satisfaction is a function of how economic resources are *distributed*. Efficiency is, therefore, at best an indication of society's *potential* to satisfy preferences (assuming costless redistribution); realising that potential requires actual redistribution (which is not costless) (Hausman, McPherson, and Satz, 2016, pp. 159–61). The more unequally economic resources are distributed, the greater the distance between efficiency and aggregate preference satisfaction (i.e. the less efficiency is a proxy for welfare) because a wealthy person is able and willing to pay more for a good they value than a poorer person who values the good just as much. It follows that the more unequal a society is, the more effective government rationing (as compared with market allocation) will be as a means of maximising welfare (Weitzman, 1977). Income and wealth inequalities are

---

[8] It is not even theoretically clear what this would mean in the case of internalising the social costs of GHG emissions. Calculating social costs assumes that the disvalue of GHGs can be determined by what current consumers are willing to pay to avoid the effects of climate change. But this poses insuperable empirical difficulties and requires questionable normative assumptions (Stern, 2013).

currently extremely high (Chancel et al., 2021). Consequently, some individuals can fly around the world in private jets, while others can barely heat their homes in winter, and others still don't have access to housing at all. Under these conditions, our objector cannot rely on neoclassical welfare theory alone to argue that the allocation of fossil fuels via the market mechanism is more welfare-maximising than is its allocation according to the priorities determined by the government.

3.3. Public ownership is the first step on the Road to serfdom

A second objection comes from those who are worried that the government taking over economic production entails the undermining of economic freedoms. Following Hayek's famous arguments in *The Road to Serfdom* (1944), economic and political liberties go hand in hand, hence the increase of government ownership over the means of production will eventually lead to tyranny: the government will start by curtailing economic freedoms of entrepreneurs in the fossil fuel industry, and once they have taken this step, we are on a slippery slope to further restrictions of economic freedoms and eventually a totalitarian state.

Given the prevailing ideological background in many countries, the idea of public ownership of a large sector may come across as radical. But that position may reveal more about the biases in those prevailing ideologies, since contemporary governments – even prosperous, democratic ones – already own many assets. Indeed, all rich democracies have mixed economies that combine private, public and common ownership, yet there is no evidence that this public and common ownership has set those countries on a path towards totalitarianism.

The relevant question, then, is: which sector, or the production of which goods and services, should be organised in what way? The answer will likely vary from case to case, and depend on a wide range of factors, including values and social-scientific knowledge (Bayliss and Fine, 2020). Focusing on the normative issues at stake, we have made a specific set of arguments as to why governments should take fossil fuel companies into public hands, assuming they are suitably-motivated and capable of exercising effective control. We do not argue in this paper for public ownership in a broad range of sectors, let alone in the entire economy. At most, the arguments we have made could be extended to encompass other links in the supply chain of fossil fuels (e.g. large coal-fired and gas-fired power generators), and other large sources of emissions. The onus therefore lies with the objector to explain the causal dynamics by which suitably motivated and effective public ownership of fossil fuel companies – or other public ownership of other targets to which our arguments may extend – would lead to serfdom.

3.4. Motivation and feasibility issues

In this final section, rather than considering a specific objection, we explore a set of issues concerning motivation and feasibility.[9] These issues are linked in that they question one or more of our main assumptions in ways that have significant implications for our arguments – especially concerning the effectiveness of public ownership as a means of decarbonisation. We do not propose to treat these issues comprehensively, let alone to resolve them. Rather, we merely aim to lay out the relevant issues and invite further multi-disciplinary discussion.

Our first two assumptions are that in each case of a public acquisition of a fossil fuel company it is undertaken by a suitably motivated government that acquires sufficient control over the company to carry out the Public Interest Actions. Following the philosophical literature on feasibility, these can be thought of as assumptions about *accessibility*, i.e. the attainability of an outcome, by way of a set of possible transformations (social, political, economic etc.) from the status quo (cf. Gilabert, 2017; Gilabert and Lawford-Smith, 2012). Our third assumption is about *stability*, i.e. the maintenance of the requisite motivation and control over a relevant time period (Cohen, 2009), and this assumption can be decomposed into an assumption about the stability of the requisite motivation and an assumption about the stability of the requisite control. Objections can be envisaged targeting each of these assumptions.

Accessibility of the requisite motivation: An objector may argue that governments are unlikely to be motivated to incur the economic and political costs of acquiring fossil fuel companies only to wind down production in the global public interest. The objector may point to the fact that, historically, where governments have been motivated to acquire fossil fuel assets their motivation has been to gain control over a higher share of short- to medium-term revenue from the sale

---

[9] We are grateful to participants in the 2021 Princeton Climate Futures Workshop, especially Paasha Mahdavi and Alexandra Gillies, for raising and discussing many of the below issues with us.

of oil and to use this to retain power, consistent with an overall objective of *maximising net benefits to the ruler* (Mahdavi, 2014; 2020).

However, just because some rulers in some countries in the past nationalised oil companies to enrich themselves and entrench their
power does not preclude other governments in other countries in
the future acquiring fossil fuel companies in the interests of decarbonisation. Numerous governments have pursued policies to
manage the phase-out of fossil fuel production or power generation
assets on climate mitigation grounds, especially in the coal sector
(Rentier, Lelieveldt, and Kramer 2019). Moreover, we do not
assume that public ownership would necessarily involve expropriation / compulsory acquisition, as did the oil nationalisations of the
1970s: as we note in Part 1, we are open to the possibility that
shares could be acquired on the open market or some amount of compensation could be paid for a compulsory acquisition (though we acknowledge that would be controversial, so we remain neutral on this
issue here).

As for whether the requisite motivation might extend to *using
public ownership* to engineer such a phase-out, we note that free-
market ideology is increasingly being called into question among
the public and among segments of the intellectual elite in many
parts of the world, and there is substantial interest in expanding
public ownership of essential assets (Guinan and O'Neill, 2018;
Hanna, 2018; Kishimoto, Steinfort, and Petitjean, 2020; Lawrence
and Hanna, 2020). The imperative to decarbonise is often a central
motivation for such proposals (Aronoff et al., 2019; Galvin and
Healy, 2020; Pettifor, 2019; Prakash and Girgenti, 2020). To
provide just two examples, proposals for a Green New Deal in the
US, advocated by the socialist-progressive wing of the Democratic
party, have proved extremely popular with the public (Bergquist,
Mildenberger, and Stokes, 2020; Gustafson et al., 2019) and have
clearly influenced the policies of the Biden administration
(Kurtzleben, 2021). In the UK, the nationalisation of a wide range
of strategic assets, and implementing a Green New Deal, were
central planks of the Labour Party manifesto for the 2019 national
election (Labour Party 2019). Clearly, this political-economic trajectory faces barriers in the US and UK, and we do not necessarily think
it is *likely* to eventuate. Our point is simply that the probability that a
future progressive government in the US, UK or elsewhere would be
motivated to acquire fossil fuel companies as part of their decarbonisation strategy seems sufficient to warrant further debate.

Still, this response has its limits. Even if all rich democracies (say)
underwent a progressive revolution in which suitably motivated

governments came to power, stubborn facts about the geographic dispersion of fossil fuel reserves and their current ownership are likely to limit the effectiveness of the decarbonisation actions we envisage (in section 2.1). This is a particularly thorny issue for oil, since the vast majority of reserves are controlled by national oil companies, most of which are currently owned by poorer and/or undemocratic states where, to put it mildly, the requisite motivational state seems less accessible for the foreseeable future (Heller and Mihalyi, 2019; Manley and Heller, 2021). It is somewhat less of an issue for coal – where large deposits exist in the US, Australia, Germany and other rich democracies, and where markets are more regionalised. Future research could usefully explore the feasibility of suitably motivated governments coming to power in different countries with significant fossil fuel reserves.[10]

Sustainability of the requisite motivation. A further issue concerns whether the requisite motivation, once attained, could be sustained for sufficiently long to carry out the Public Interest Actions. If it turns out that the probability of suitably motivated governments coming to power is only sufficiently high to warrant serious consideration in rich democracies, then we must also recognise that those governments could lose power at a subsequent election and be replaced by a government with contrary motivations. Indeed the replacement government might even be motivated to use its newfound control over the fossil fuel sector to *increase* production, or otherwise pursue the opposite actions that we have envisaged. Much depends on the political feedback effects of the initial acquisition: are these likely to entrench or weaken support for the incumbent and its decarbonisation strategy? Future research could usefully explore this question in relevant democracies.

Accessibility and sustainability of the requisite control: Finally, it may be objected that many states lack the fiscal or administrative capacity necessary to acquire and sustain ownership of private fossil fuel companies, or obtain and sustain sufficient control over the companies they own to implement the Public Interest Actions.

Whether a government has the capacity to *acquire ownership* of relevant companies depends much on the acquisition strategy pursued

---

[10]   We are assuming in this paragraph that governments will only be able to exercise control over operations *in their* jurisdiction. Legal and other factors may limit the ability of such governments to wind-down operations in overseas jurisdictions, and in any case they are unlikely to be able to prevent the overseas government from engaging another company to exploit the resources.

(see Part 1) and jurisdiction-specific features, and is therefore difficult to evaluate in the abstract. Further analysis of specific feasibility constraints, and the feasibility trade-offs associated with different acquisition strategies, in key jurisdictions would be valuable.

Whether a government that acquires a fossil fuel company can then obtain and sustain sufficient control over it to carry out the Public Interest Actions is likely to be contingent on the capacities of the relevant government and the motivations and behaviours of managers and employees in the relevant company. Historical and contemporary case studies suggest two kinds of generic risks. First is the principal-agent problem, which might be called the 'state within a state' problem: that the acquired fossil fuel company is so large, and so wedded to its (former) objectives of profit-maximisation through fossil fuel production, that it remains *de facto* autonomous – both motivated and able to ignore government mandates. This might manifest as successful resistance to either the initial bid for government control, or an ability to thwart the directives of the government-installed directors and their appointed senior managers, or to co-opt them over time. A related problem applicable to a company that exhibits this kind of autonomous resistance to the government's desired public interest strategy is what might be called the 'fox in the henhouse' problem: that the company, once brought into the government apparatus, is able to exert *more* corruptive influence over the government's energy and climate policy than it did when it was privately owned. Again, the conditions under which these kinds of dynamics are likely to be triggered vs avoided in specific contexts is a worthy object of further study.

4. Conclusion

Philosophers – in particular political philosophers – have often presented the philosophical case for new institutions they think will improve the world, from the implementation of an unconditional basic income, to the abolition of borders.[11] We are unlikely to think all such ideas were, upon closer analysis, *good* ideas; but they make us think about how the world could be different. We believe that climate change demands from us that we think out of the box, and consider seriously proposals that go against the ideological mainstream.

[11]   For a discussion of fifty of such proposals, see Gosseries and Vanderborght (2011).

It is in this spirit that we have explored the idea of nationalising privately-owned fossil fuel companies, on the assumed conditions that such national acquisitions are undertaken by a suitably motivated government that is able to obtain effective control over such companies, and that such motivation and control are able to be sustained for long enough to phase out the companies' production of fossil fuels in the public interest. We argued that, under such conditions, public ownership would advance the achievement of social justice – both climate justice (via increased / more effective climate mitigation) and the justice of the transition to a net-zero emissions economy. We also argued it would facilitate a fair sharing of burdens and benefits, and would enhance democracy. Finally, we responded to four types of objections to this argument. The strongest of these was a set of objections to the feasibility of our assumed conditions and the implications for our argument of applicable feasibility constraints: could the requisite motivation and control really be obtained and sustained? In what countries is there a sufficiently significant probability of this occurring to be worthy of serious consideration? Would nationalisations in *those* countries alone be sufficient to achieve significant advances in climate mitigation, given the global distribution of fossil fuels? These are important questions that we hope to continue to discuss with social scientists and other philosophers.

Without claiming to have resolved the debate, this paper has made two contributions to literatures at the intersection of political philosophy and political economy. First, the literature on climate ethics has predominantly adopted the mainstream 'pollution paradigm' within which to deliberate about how states ought to respond to climate change. Alongside the social-scientific turn towards a systems paradigm in the climate field, and calls for radically different thinking about climate policy options, political philosophers have begun to think about how the substance and methods of normative theorising need to evolve if they are to be relevant to the challenge of decarbonisation (e.g., F. Green, 2021; F. Green and Brandstedt, 2021). Both substantively and methodologically, our open-textured and non-definitive exploration of what is a normatively and social-scientifically complex idea contribute to a mode of climate ethics that we think well-suited for the precarious historical moment in which we find ourselves.

Second, we contribute to a longstanding debate about the role of the state in the economy, encompassing both the desirability and feasibility of government ownership of (some of) the means of production (Gilabert and O'Neill, 2019). In recent years, there has been a resurgent exploration of public ownership models for a wide range of essential goods and services (Guinan and O'Neill, 2018; Hanna, 2018; Kishimoto, Steinfort, and Petitjean, 2020; Lawrence and Hanna, 2020; Mazzucato, 2013). In these cases, the aim is to reclaim the production of a good or service from the market, in order to deliver it in a more democratic and equitable way, or to ensure a fairer balance of risks, costs and benefits, between private and public actors in systems of production and innovation. Examples of governments taking on enterprises to *phase them out* in the public interest are less commonly discussed. Although the public acquisition of loss-making assets is not historically anomalous – for example, in the banking sector (e.g., Schäfer and Zimmermann, 2009) – the unique aims of fossil fuel nationalisations raise novel issues of distributive justice that merit deeper debate among political philosophers, which we hope that this paper will encourage.[12]

University College London
fergus.green@ucl.ac.uk
Utrecht University
I.A.M.Robeyns@uu.nl

References

Gar Alperovitz, Joe Guinan, and Thomas M. Hanna, 'The Policy Weapon Climate Activists Need.' *The Nation* (2017) https://www.thenation.com/article/archive/the-policy-weapon-climate-activists-need/.

Samuel Arnold, 'Socialism.' In *Internet Encyclopedia of Philosophy*, https://iep.utm.edu/socialis/.

Kate Aronoff, 'A Moderate Proposal: Nationalize the Fossil Fuel Industry', *The New Republic*, (2020a) https://newrepublic.com/article/156941/moderate-proposal-nationalize-fossil-fuel-industry.

Kate Aronoff, 'The Death of the Fossil Fuel Industry Could Be Disastrous for Workers. Now's the Time to Nationalise It', *Novara Media* (2020b) https://novaramedia.com/2020/12/08/

[12] For comments on earlier drafts, we thank audiences at the Chair Hoover (Louvain-la-Neuve), the Princeton Climate Futures Workshop, and our former colleagues at the Fair Limits group. Both authors acknowledge research funding by the European Union's Horizon 2020 Research and Innovation Programme, ERC Consolidator Grant Number 726153.

the-death-of-the-fossil-fuel-industry-could-be-disastrous-nows-the-time-to-nationalise-it/.

Kate Aronoff, *Overheated: How Capitalism Broke the Planet – And How We Fight Back*, (PublicAffairs, 2021).

Kate Aronoff, Alyssa Battistoni, Daniel Aldana Cohen, and Thea Riofrancos, *A Planet to Win: Why We Need a Green New Deal*, (London: Verso, 2019).

G. B. Asheim, et al. 'The Case for a Supply-Side Climate Treaty', *Science* 365 (2019), 325–28.

Robert Baldwin, Martin Cave, and Martin Lodge, *Understanding Regulation: Theory, Strategy, and Practice,* (Oxford: Oxford University Press, 2011).

Kate Bayliss and Ben Fine, *A Guide to the Systems of Provision Approach: Who Gets What, How and Why*, (Palgrave Macmillan, 2020).

Tom Bergin and Ron Bousso, 'Special Report: How Oil Majors Shift Billions in Profits to Island Tax Havens', *Reuters* (2020) https://www.reuters.com/article/global-oil-tax-havens-idUSKBN28J1IK.

Parrish Bergquist, Matto Mildenberger, and Leah C. Stokes, 'Combining Climate, Economic, and Social Policy Builds Public Support for Climate Action in the US.' *Environmental Research Letters* 15(n.054019) (2020).

Steven Bernstein and Matthew Hoffmann, 'Climate Change, Metaphors and the Fractal Carbon Trap.' *Nature Climate Change* 9 (2019) 919–25. http://dx.doi.org/10.1038/s41558-019-0618-2.

Samuel Bowles and Herbert Gintis, *Democracy and Capitalism: Property, Community and the Contradictions of Modern Social Thought,* (New York: Routledge, 1986).

Johanna Bozuwa and Olúfẹ́mi O. Táíwò, 'It's Time to Nationalize Shell. Private Oil Companies Are No Longer Fit for Purpose' *The Guardian* (2021) https://www.theguardian.com/commentisfree/2021/jun/07/its-time-to-nationalize-shell-private-oil-companies-are-no-longer-fit-for-purpose.

Simon Caney, 'Climate Justice.' In *The Stanford Encyclopedia of Philosophy*, ed. Edward N. Zalta. Stanford: The Metaphysics Research Lab, Center for the Study of Language and Information (CSLI), Stanford University (2020) https://stanford.library.sydney.edu.au/entries/justice-climate/.

Simon Caney and Cameron Hepburn, 'Carbon Trading: Unethical, Unjust and Ineffective?' *Royal Institute of Philosophy Supplement* 69 (2011) 201–34.

William K. Carroll, ed. *Regime of Obstruction: How Corporate Power Blocks Energy Democracy*, (Edmonton: Athabasca University Press, 2021).

Lucas Chancel, Thomas Piketty, Emmanuel Saez, and Gabriel Zucman, *World Inequality Report 2022*, (2021) https:// wir2022.wid.world/.

Thomas Christiano, 'Money in Politics' In *The Oxford Handbook of Political Philosophy*, ed. David Estlund, (Oxford: Oxford University Press, 2012), 241–57.

David Coady, Ian Parry, Louis Sears, and Baoping Shang, *How Large Are Global Energy Subsidies?* (Washington, DC, 2015).

G.A. Cohen, *Why Not Socialism?* (Princeton, N.J.: Princeton University Press, 2009).

Paul Collier and Anthony J. Venables, 'Closing Coal: Economic and Moral Incentives.' *Oxford Review of Economic Policy* 30 (2015), 492–512.

Taran Fæhn et al., 'Climate Policies in a Fossil Fuel Producing Country: Demand versus Supply Side Policies' *Energy Journal* 38 (2017), 77–102.

J D Farmer et al., 'Sensitive Intervention Points in the Post-Carbon Transition' *Science* 364 (2019), 132–34.

Ray Galvin and Noel Healy, 'The Green New Deal in the United States: What It Is and How to Pay for It', *Energy Research and Social Science* 67 (n.101529) (2020).

Pablo Gilabert, 'Justice and Feasibility: A Dynamic Approach.' In *Political Utopias: Contemporary Debates*, eds. Kevin Vallier and Michael E. Weber, (Oxford: Oxford University Press, 2017) 95–126.

Pablo Gilabert and Holly Lawford-Smith, 'Political Feasibility: A Conceptual Exploration' *Political Studies* 60 (2012), 809–25.

Pablo Gilabert and Martin O'Neill, 'Socialism' In *The Stanford Encyclopedia of Philosophy*, ed. Edward N. Zalta. The Metaphysics Research Lab, Center for the Study of Language and Information (CSLI), Stanford University (2019). https:// stanford.library.sydney.edu.au/entries/socialism/.

Axel Gosseries and Yannick Vanderborght, eds. *Arguing about Justice: Essays for Philippe van Parijs*, (Louvain-la-Neuve: Presses universitaires de Louvain, 2011).

Fergus Green, 'Anti-Fossil Fuel Norms' *Climatic Change* 150 (2018) 103–16.

Fergus Green, 'Radically Rethinking Climate Ethics: Carbon Lock-in and the Ethics of Decarbonisation.' Working paper (on file with author) (2021).

Fergus Green and Eric Brandstedt, 'Engaged Climate Ethics', *Journal of Political Philosophy* 29 (2021), 539–63.

Fergus Green and Richard Denniss, 'Cutting with Both Arms of the Scissors: The Economic and Political Case for Restrictive Supply-Side Climate Policies' *Climatic Change* 150 (2018) 73–87.

Fergus Green and Ajay Gambhir, 'Transitional Assistance Policies for Just, Equitable and Smooth Low-Carbon Transitions: Who, What and How?' *Climate Policy* 20 (2020), 902–21.

Jessica F. Green, 'Beyond Carbon Pricing: Tax Reform Is Climate Policy' *Global Policy* (2021).

Joe Guinan and Martin O'Neill, 'The Institutional Turn: Labour's New Political Economy.' *Renewal* 26 (2018) 5–16. https://renewal.org.uk/archive/vol-26-2018/the-institutional-turn-labours-new-political-economy/.

Abel Gustafson et al., 'The Development of Partisan Polarization over the Green New Deal.' *Nature Climate Change* 9 (2019), 940–44. http://dx.doi.org/10.1038/s41558-019-0621-7.

Thomas M. Hanna, *Our Common Wealth: The Return of Public Ownership in the United States,* (Manchester: Manchester University Press, 2018).

Daniel M. Hausman, Michael S. McPherson, and Debra Satz, *Economic Analysis, Moral Philosophy and Public Policy*, 3rd ed, (Cambridge: Cambridge University Press, 2016).

Patrick R. P. Heller and David Mihalyi, *Massive and Misunderstood: Data-Driven Insights into National Oil Companies* (2019). https://resourcegovernance.org/sites/default/files/documents/massive_and_misunderstood_data_driven_insights_into_national_oil_companies.pdf.

High-Level Commission on Carbon Prices, *Report of the High-Level Commission on Carbon Prices*. (Washington, DC, 2017).

Keith Hyams, 'A Just Response to Climate Change: Personal Carbon Allowances and the Normal-Functioning Approach' *Journal of Social Philosophy* 40 (2009), 237–56.

IEA, *World Energy Outlook 2018*, (Paris, 2018). https://iea.blob.core.windows.net/assets/77ecf96c-5f4b-4d0d-9d93-d81b938217cb/World_Energy_Outlook_2018.pdf.

International Labour Organization, 'Guidelines for a Just Transition towards Environmentally Sustainable Economies and Societies for All' (2015) http://www.ilo.org/wcmsp5/groups/public/---ed_emp/---emp_ent/documents/publication/wcms_432859.pdf.

Sivan Kartha, Simon Caney, Navroz K. Dubash, and Greg Muttitt, 'Whose Carbon Is Burnable? Equity Considerations in the

Allocation of a "Right to Extract"', *Climatic Change* 150 (2018), 117–29.

Dario Kenner and Richard Heede, 'White Knights, or Horsemen of the Apocalypse? Prospects for Big Oil to Align Emissions with a 1.5°C Pathway', *Energy Research & Social Science*, (2021) https://doi.org/10.1016/j.erss.2021.102049.

Satoko Kishimoto, Lavinia Steinfort, and Olivier Petitjean, eds. *The Future Is Public: Towards Democratic Ownership of Public Services*, (Amsterdam: Transnational Institute, 2020).

Danielle Kurtzleben, 'Ocasio-Cortez Sees Green New Deal Progress In Biden Plan, But "It's Not Enough"' *NPR* (2021). https://www.npr.org/2021/04/02/983398361/green-new-deal-leaders-see-biden-climate-plans-as-a-victory-kind-of?t=1622721551495.

Labour Party, *Labour Party Manifesto 2019*, (2019). https://labour.org.uk/manifesto-2019/.

Mathew Lawrence and Thomas M. Hanna, *Ownership Futures: Towards Democratic Public Ownership in the 21st Century* (2020). https://www.common-wealth.co.uk/reports/ownership-futures-towards-democratic-public-ownership-in-the-twenty-first-century#chapter-1.

William Lazonick and Jang-Sup Shin, *Predatory Value Extraction,* (Oxford: Oxford University Press, 2019).

Georges Alexandre Lenferna, 'Can We Equitably Manage the End of the Fossil Fuel Era?' *Energy Research and Social Science* 35 (2018) 217–23. https://doi.org/10.1016/j.erss.2017.11.007.

Paasha Mahdavi,. 'Why Do Leaders Nationalize the Oil Industry? The Politics of Resource Expropriation' *Energy Policy* 75 (2014) 228–43.

Paasha Mahdavi, *Power Grab: Political Survival through Extractive Resource Nationalization,* (Cambridge: Cambridge University Press, 2020).

David Manley and Patrick R. P. Heller, *Risky Bet: National Oil Companies in the Energy Transition.* (2021). https://resourcegovernance.org/analysis-tools/publications/risky-bet-national-oil-companies-energy-transition.

Mariana Mazzucato, *The Entrepreneurial State: Debunking Private vs Public Sector Myths,* (London: Anthem, 2013).

Doreen McBarnet and Christopher Whelan, 'The Elusive Spirit of the Law: Formalism and the Struggle for Legal Control' *Modern Law Review*, 51 (1991) 848–73.

Ellen Meiksins Wood, *Democracy Against Capitalism: Renewing Historical Materialism,* (Cambridge: Cambridge University Press, 1995).

Greg Muttitt and Sivan Kartha, 'Equity, Climate Justice and Fossil Fuel Extraction: Principles for a Managed Phase Out' *Climate Policy* 20 (2020), 1024–1042.

Peter Newell and Andrew Simms, 'Towards a Fossil Fuel Non-Proliferation Treaty' *Climate Policy* 20 (2020), 1043–54.

Carol Olson and Frank Lenzmann, 'The Social and Economic Consequences of the Fossil Fuel Supply Chain' *MRS Energy & Sustainability*, 3 (2016) 1–32.

Ilona M. Otto et al., 'Social Tipping Dynamics for Stabilizing Earth's Climate by 2050', *Proceedings of the National Academy of Sciences* 117 (2020), 2354–65.

Edward A. Page, 'The Ethics of Emissions Trading' *WIRES Climate Change* 4 (2013) 233–43.

Eric M. Patashnik, *Reforms at Risk: What Happens After Major Policy Changes Are Enacted*, (Princeton: Princeton University Press, 2008).

Mark Paul, Carla Santos Skandier, and Rory Renzy, *Out of Time: The Case for Nationalizing the Fossil Fuel Industry* (2020). https://thenextsystem.org/sites/default/files/2020-06/OutofTime-Report_Final%282%29pages.pdf.

Ann Pettifor, *The Case for the Green New Deal*, (London: Verso, 2019).

Georgia Piggot, Peter Erickson, Harro van Asselt, and Michael Lazarus, 'Swimming Upstream: Addressing Fossil Fuel Supply under the UNFCCC' *Climate Policy* 18 (2018), 1189–1202.

Varshini Prakash and Guido Girgenti, eds., *Winning the Green New Deal: Why We Must, How We Can*, (London: Simon & Schuster, 2020).

Gerrit Rentier, Herman Lelieveldt and Gert Jan Kramer, 'Varieties of Coal-Fired Power Phase-out across Europe' *Energy Policy* 132 (2019), 620–32. https://doi.org/10.1016/j.enpol.2019.05.042.

Ingrid Robeyns, *Wellbeing, Freedom and Social Justice: The Capability Approach Re-Examined*, (Cambridge: Open Book Publishers, 2017).

Dorothea Schäfer and Klaus F. Zimmermann,. 'Bad Bank(s) and the Recapitalisation of the Banking Sector' *Intereconomics* 44 (2009) 215–25.

Nicholas Stern, 'The Structure of Economic Modeling of the Potential Impacts of Climate Change: Grafting Gross Underestimation of Risk onto Already Narrow Science Models', *Journal of Economic Literature* 51 (2013), 838–59.

Leah C. Stokes, *Short Circuiting Policy: Interest Groups and the Battle Over Clean Energy and Climate Policy in the American States,* (New York: Oxford University Press, 2020).

Lynn A. Stout, *The Shareholder Value Myth: How Putting Shareholders First Harms Investors, Corporations, and the Public,* (San Francisco: Berrett-Koehler, 2012).

Sean Sweeney, 'There May Be No Choice but to Nationalize Oil and Gas – and Renewables, Too.' *Jacobin* (2020). https://jacobinmag. com/2020/08/nationalize-fossil-fuels-green-new-deal-big-oil.

UNEP, *Emissions Gap Report 2021: The Heat Is On – A World of Climate Promises Not Yet Delivered*, (Nairobi, 2021).

Martin L. Weitzman, 'Is the Price System or Rationing More Effective in Getting a Commodity to Those Who Need It Most?' *The Bell Journal of Economics* 8 (1977), 517–24.

Leif Wenar, *Blood Oil: Tyrants, Violence, and the Rules That Run the World,* (Oxford: Oxford University Press, 2015).

Erik Olin Wright, *Envisioning Real Utopias,* (London: Verso, 2010).

Philosophical Reflections on the Idea of a Universal Basic Income

CATHERINE ROWETT

Abstract
A universal basic income is an unconditional allowance, sufficient to live on, paid in cash to every citizen regardless of income. It has been a Green Party policy for years. But the idea raises many interesting philosophical questions, about fairness, entitlement, desert, stigma and sanctions, the value of unpaid work, the proper ambitions of a good society, and our preconceptions about whether leisure (time for recreation and free creativity) or jobs (working to give the proceeds of our labour and the luxury of free time to someone else) are the thing we should prize above all for free citizens. Coming from the perspective of ancient philosophy, I consider the answers offered in the ancient world to some of these questions, and how we might learn from re-thinking our notions of how to create a good society in which people can be free and realise their creative and intellectual potential.

1. Introduction: if we had a Universal Basic Income, what would change?

My proposal is that we – the UK, or whatever country or federation of countries you belong to – should have a universal basic income. A 'universal basic income', or UBI, is an unconditional allowance or stipend that is paid out in cash to everyone in a society, out of the public purse, like a universal tax-free allowance, and regardless of income (in the same way as, for instance, child benefit is, or at least was, paid in the UK).[1]

I shall sketch the political reasons for instituting such a universal benefit at the start of this paper, as a kind of manifesto, and briefly consider the economic questions of affordability and whether it carries any net costs to the tax payers, before moving on to the philosophical issues that are the subject of my discussion in Sections 2 to 4.

So if we had a UBI what would change? Let us begin by thinking about which things matter most in our life. We might start with a list

---

[1] An accessible account of the idea, together with many of the practical and economic implications of introducing such a scheme, can be found in Standing (2017).

doi:10.1017/S1358246122000029   © The Royal Institute of Philosophy and the contributors 2022
Royal Institute of Philosophy Supplement **91** 2022

such as this, and see if we could put them into categories according to whether they are important for our lives and for our sense of well-being:

- Having lots of money to spend
- Love and friendship
- Caring for others, seeing family
- Creativity, music, art, sport, outdoor activities, inventing stuff, comedy
- Being out in the natural world, working with nature and animals
- Working hard to make money for the boss
- Doing a worthwhile or satisfying job
- Changing people's minds, campaigning, ending injustice.
- Time to study and improve oneself.

And then, having considered the things that seem important and valuable, we might think about which things are most costly to society and to its ability to provide us with the circumstances for a good life. Can we order them from worst to least? For sure, we might need some detailed information to be sure of which of the costly things are most costly, but here are some suggestions for our list:

- Mental health and depression
- Debt and loan sharks
- Drug addiction
- Stress-related illnesses (hypertension etc)
- Family breakdown
- Poor diet and fast food
- Child poverty and malnutrition
- Social stigma and bullying
- Benefit fraud
- Tax evasion
- Unfair taxation
- Subsidies to employers (i.e. in-work benefits to low paid workers)

Next we should ask why our society is so full of those terrible things, and why it proves so hard to improve the situation, no matter how much resource we throw at it. Why would we want a world so full of misery? Why not change it? Many of these things could be changed if we introduced a UBI, or so I shall suggest.

In the most recent available statistics for the UK, over £15 billion of means tested benefits went unclaimed by those who are entitled to them.[2] This is money that is not paid out because people never ask for it, perhaps because they are too proud, or too ashamed, or unaware that they qualify – resulting in the persistence of unnecessary poverty and hardship that the system is supposed to eliminate. Indeed far more is underpaid in this way than is overpaid to people who are not entitled to it (known as 'benefit fraud'), which was estimated at no more than about £2 billion in 2018/19.[3] Meanwhile, the tax gap (people avoiding tax, undeclared income etc, so not paying tax that should be paid) is officially said (by the government) to be 'only' £35 billion (much of it avoided by cash-in-hand self-employed people), though the real figure has been calculated by Richard Murphy to be more like £90 billion, if we include the avoidance schemes used by the super rich such as using offshore havens (Murphy, 2019). It is striking that such tax evasion seems to draw much less anger and attention in right wing media than the much smaller losses due to benefit fraud, and tax evasion is addressed with less assiduous staffing, while the pursuit of those suspected of benefit fraud represents a considerable cost in staff time and legal action.

Both the unclaimed benefits that leave needy people in poverty, and the misery and criminalisation that comes from sanctioning people guilty of benefit fraud, could be easily solved if the benefits in question were universal and unconditional. It would simplify the distribution, there would be no complex process or intrusive questions in order to qualify, and there would be no 'fraudulent claims' because the people collecting it would be properly entitled to it.[4] The simplicity of such a system would save many of the costs associated with the current system: not just the legal costs of prosecuting fraud and the personnel employed to detect and challenge potentially

---

[2]   This was the estimate reported by the UK government in 2020. It relates to figures no later than 2018/19, so it is far from up to date: see Jayaram et al. (2020) and for the methodology see Sorensen et al. (2020). In addition, the statistics concern only the take-up (or failure to take up) for some specific benefits (housing benefit, pension credit etc) but exclude the large majority of benefit claimants by not counting anything relating to Universal Credit (which has been excluded from the figures ever since it was introduced seven years ago) or council tax relief. For discussion and analysis see (on the 'Entitledto' blog) Entitledto (2021).

[3]   The basis of this estimate is explained by Boultwood (2019).

[4]   Difficulties are often raised about how the class of recipients is to be defined. We do not need to settle those questions here, though I think they are easily settled once we see what the rationale of the scheme is and once its intended outcomes and advantages are made clear.

fraudulent claims, but also the paperwork, the process of assessing people, determining whether they qualify, handling appeals, sanctioning those who fail to attend for interviews or struggle to comply with the conditions. The current system is designed to be miserable, intrusive and punitive, and as a result it is hugely costly, both in the endless work required for constant monitoring and sanctioning the recipients, and in the misery caused to the families who struggle to make ends meet and are oppressed with the demands of meeting the conditions. Our current system is not designed to deliver a happy society, but rather to shame and embarrass those who are in need, and force them to undertake penance. The result is that many would rather not claim, and would sooner choose to live in poverty than endure the indignities associated with asking for help.

So the first practical benefit of changing the normal economic support for those in need into an unconditional automatic payment to everyone is clear. It eliminates a vast army of bureaucrats, it eliminates fraud, it eliminates the misery of a shame-based system and it cuts costs – including the invisible costs that come with misery, desperation and anxiety. For sure, there would always need to be some additional support for specific categories of people with additional needs, especially those with costly needs in personal care due to disabilities. But most short term needs such as short breaks in employment due to illness, maternity, paternity etc would be automatically covered by the weekly universal payment, while retirement would be an option at any age since the state stipend would be there anyway. Students would be supported with an automatic maintenance grant with no need for questions about their parental income or any other intrusive discrimination, and with no need to disrupt their studies by taking a job alongside a full time course, just to pay the bills, and no loan repayments dragging their income down as they start their career. This would benefit both the students (better marks), the lecturers (better concentration and attendance), the country (better educated graduates), and the local economy where students currently take jobs and leave the local population unemployed, and where students would have more time to spend the money they did not have to earn.

A second practical and economic pay-off from such a system would be that there would be no penalty or deduction for earning a little, or a lot, of extra money on top of it. On the contrary, everyone is most welcome to earn, and encouraged to earn, and there is no disincentive to take employment or to engage in enterprising ways of making money, as there is in the current system. No one is forced to conceal additional earnings, to avoid the sanctions that currently prevent those on benefits from taking up employment. And because the stipend arrives automatically every month, whether you need it or not, there is no delay in getting help should the enterprise you were engaged in suddenly fall on hard times. It is abundantly clear why such a scheme would vastly help with ensuring the resilience of sectors such as the arts, music, culture, enterprise and self-employed activities in dire situations such as the epidemic we have been experiencing at the beginning of this decade. For everyone it would be best to earn a bit more, and always better to earn a bit more than that, to have more money to spend. And yet the fear of finding there was nothing in the bank and nothing in the larder, because no pay cheque arrived that week, would be removed.

This brings us to the third economic and practical advantage, which relates to mental health and happiness. For many the daily grind of going to a hateful job, and returning with not enough to live on, only to be obliged to apply for in-work benefits just in order to keep the family going, is the source of enormous misery and distress. Stress from the workplace and stress from money worries are blighting our society. A basic income to cover the bare necessities would rid us of some of the anxieties, the pressures to stay in an unsafe or oppressive workplace, the dependence on an abusive partner, the disputes over scarce household resources.

So in general, it might well turn out that providing what looks like a hugely costly movement of wealth from the top to the bottom of society could in fact deliver economic gains that more than cover its cost. Among the reasons to think that the effect of UBI would be a net benefit to the treasury, and a great boost to enterprise, the arts and local businesses are these: People spend money if they have it. People create businesses if they have the security to do it. People get themselves better educated if they have the time to do it. People can achieve things if they are not depressed or struggling to pay the bills. People can see their loved ones and give them the attention they need if they are free to work part time. When people are happy they do things to make the world a better place. They smile.

These benefits – which are hardly in doubt – span a huge range of the things that matter to us far more than money; but even if you were only concerned to count up monetary gains there are many indications that the outcome would be a net gain, not a loss, in economic terms. A careful economic analysis that models (for the USA) the economic effects of various levels of UBI scheme, to show that they would deliver net benefits, increased productivity and increased employment, can be found in Michalis Nikiforos et al. (2017). They model three different levels of proposed UBI and show that there are net economic benefits to the economy at all three levels. This is so whether you fund the scheme from government borrowing or by taxation. One might also address some doubts on this score by comparing the likely costs of a fully funded UBI scheme for the UK with the UK's recent hike in public spending in response to the Covid-19 pandemic. In the year 2020-21 the amount spent from the public purse for Covid-related costs amounted to somewhere between £315bn and £410bn (Brian and Keep, 2021). This is the equivalent of between £4,700 and £6,100 per person (counting people of all ages), which is roughly the cost of a UBI of £500 per month for adults and children alike. Some of that money was directed to procurement (e.g. PPE, test and trace systems etc), and some to schemes to support business and wages (such as the furlough scheme and support for self-employed workers). In effect, this amount of money was borrowed by the government and injected into the economy, either directly to businesses or to supporting people who were forbidden to go to work or to open their business. In effect much of that money paid people to stop being productive and to become idle (or, in many cases, to engage instead in creative and self-improvement activities and in home-making). Three things should be noted about the effect of this injection of funds from the public purse: first, that it was distributed unevenly so that those who earned more in normal times received more of it in times of crisis; it was therefore a regressive system as compared with the more progressive effects of a UBI.[5] Second, unlike a UBI, it was a scheme to reduce productivity (it paid people on condition that they must do no work) and was distributed at a time when it was also impossible to spend the money they were given in the local business economy because the local economy was closed for business, so

---

[5] The 'Corona Virus Job Retention Scheme' (CVJRS) was paid to employers, at a rate of 80% of the employee's full wage up to a limit of £2,500 p.m. so an employee paid at a higher wage received more than an employee paid at a lower wage, and only those in employment could access the money. There was no requirement for the employer to make up the missing 20%, so those on minimum wage were left with only 80% of the minimum wage. A scheme for self-employed people was later added which allowed them to claim on the basis of earnings from the previous year (resulting in extreme poverty for those with low or zero earnings in 2019, and extra support for those with unusually high earnings in 2019). Both schemes worked on the principle that those with more get more and those with less get less. This is regressive. While UBI superficially does not look progressive, in practice it is when combined with a progressive income tax.

the high street stimulus effect of injecting extra cash was suppressed and there was no knock on effect in improving takings, and thence wages and employment, as there would be in normal times. Third, despite the addition of an uplift in the Universal Credit benefit for low income households, the outcome was increased inequality, with the very rich becoming much richer during the pandemic and the middling to poor becoming poorer (alongside increased inequality of life expectancy), and a sharp rise in inflation (which was partly due to the high public spending, including procurement contracts, and partly due to non-covid-related price rises caused by other problems such as Brexit, energy shortages and so on). The increased inequality and inflation are a direct result of regressive policies, giving more to the wealthy than the poor and failing to recover it from the wealthy and super-wealthy in taxation, while instead increasing taxation on the low paid workers. Neither of these effects, nor the reduction in productivity or local business takings, would result from a normal UBI scheme in normal times, if it was accompanied by proper taxation of those who had no need of income support, to return the money to the treasury and ensure no devaluation of the currency resulted from a borrow – (or print money) – and-spend regime.

Many opponents of UBI say that there is no need to change the system from having a tax-free allowance to having a cash hand-out instead. If you think of the tax free allowance as an allowance ('Here, you can keep this money: we won't even tax it!') it looks as if it too is an allowance that everyone gets, including the wealthy and the super wealthy. Except, actually, that is not so. In fact the very wealthy get it, but the very poor do not. ('Here you could keep this money untaxed, if you had it. But sorry, you don't, so shucks'). UBI turns that round and says to everyone: 'Here, you can have this money, untaxed. Just pay tax on what you have in addition'. When you have nothing, when you lose your job, become ill or have to self-isolate, what you need is a cash hand-out, not an imaginary opportunity to earn some money and not pay tax on it. Your problem is that you don't have the money to not pay tax on. You don't even have a way to get it.

Only a UBI offers the ever-present safety net that sets you free. And while it is immediately recovered in tax from those with so much wealth that they have no need of it, so that it makes a real difference to the incomes only of those who are short of money, anyone who suddenly finds themselves without the income they used to have will be immediately supported, with no questions asked, and no five week delay while the claim is considered.

So much for the basic practicalities. My purpose here is not so much to explore the political, economic or practical advantages or the costs of such a scheme, though these are indeed interesting,[6] and suggest that the balance of cost to savings, combined with the gain in economic activity that would result, is such that a generous scheme, sufficient to cover basic living costs fully, would probably be cost-neutral or even a gain to the public purse – and indeed to the tax-payers. It is worth noticing that in our increasingly unequal society money trickles up, not down, and money added at the bottom is never lost to those at the top of the wealth scale.

But those are issues that would be addressed in economics. My task here is not to complete the work on those questions, but rather to examine the abstract issues, the philosophical issues. I shall divide these into three headings. First, issues about fairness and equality of opportunity. Second, a question about the values of our society, in particular in relation to what we think is a good life for a free citizen (and an exploration of what they thought about this in the ancient world). And third, some questions about freedom, slavery, exploitation and power.

2. The Philosophical Issues I: Fairness, justice, entitlement, and desert.

Naturally we are all in favour of making a system that is fundamentally fair and equitable. But people come to the question of what counts as fair with radically different preconceptions, many of them unquestioned until they encounter the philosophical challenge 'what exactly counts as making life fair?'. The notion of fairness is closely related to 'justice' and we could, for instance, take Plato's *Republic* to be at least partly a treatment of how to make a society fair (and just).

'Fair' and 'just' are the goals we want for a society. But what would a fair society look like? Do we live in a fair society at present? At the two extremes of preconceptions about fairness are these:

(a)   It's fair if people receive rewards according to what they deserve. It's unfair if some get something for nothing.

(b)   It's fair if initial disadvantages are remedied and reparations are made, to make good the unfairness of life-chances.

The first model tends to widen the inequalities in society, as those who fall into poverty or sickness find themselves less and less able to

---

meet the standard of 'deserving' anything, and those who are born lucky and have ample resources can acquire an expensive education and move into well-paid and secure jobs, or even live in complete idleness on inherited wealth and investments. The second model seeks to make society fairer by reducing the inequalities and giving everyone a fair chance to do something meaningful to the best of their ability.

Some advocates for universal basic income try to connect it with that idea of giving people only what they deserve. How can it count as fair in that way?

Maybe we could say that we all deserve something?

But why?

One argument for this tries to suggest that everyone, including the least productive members of society, are entitled to a share of the earth's resources, as if we owned our own little bit, and are entitled to reap the dividends from our share, even if someone else is actually extracting the resources.

This seems to me fanciful. It also buys into a problematic notion of private property and the right to proceeds from that property. And even if we did think we all own some bit of nature, who is to say that the dividend from that share would be exactly the right amount of income to cover the basics of a good life? Indeed this seems to me to conflict with a more plausible thought, that none of us is entitled to own any part of the earth or its resources, and that most of our problems stem from privatising the earth's resources and capitalising on them for the exclusive gain of those who have the ownership. The claiming of private income from what are essentially shared resources seems dodgy. That is what has led us into inequality, between citizens and between nations. Do we inherit our right to own the earth? If so, it seems that inheriting wealth is a way of becoming entitled. But then inherited wealth seems to bear no relation to deserving, and 'entitlement' bears no relation to any real entitlement or desert.

But on the second notion of fairness, which tries to remedy the inequalities in life, how can a UBI count as fair? It doesn't actually give more to those who have less, or less to those who have more. How is that fair? While fairness initially seems to be related to the notion of equality, what counts as equal can sometimes be a matter of proportional equality. Those who focus on deserving are presumably trying (and failing) to make the equality proportional to the deserving. But equality can also involve being proportionate to need. For instance, shoes: I need size 4, and you need size 11. It's no good giving everyone a size 9 to ensure that no one has a bigger share than anyone else, and it would be silly to demand a larger size just because it was larger or the same as someone else's.

Disability benefits are like that: to make life equal, a person needs whatever will bring their quality of life up to that of others without a disability. Similarly we don't necessarily all benefit from exactly the same type of education whether our talents lie in maths or in music. But when it comes to the basics of life, for those without significant disabilities or limitations that need special support, there is nothing substantial that differentiates us such that one of us needs more than another. The cost of a good life is roughly the same for all: everyone needs a room in a house, a bed of the same size, enough good high quality food, and a bicycle. Children need the same (or maybe a bit smaller). This is roughly true, no matter whether we are large or small, rich or poor, wise or foolish. So why not just give everyone the same?

For sure, this does not take account of the differential level of risk faced by someone with large savings compared with someone who just gets by. But as a blunt tool, it gives everyone the same protection in times of dearth and when savings have run dry. (And we should remember that if and when a person does have a substantial income, the handouts provided under a basic income scheme would be immediately returned in the tax deductions, so it is not in reality given to everyone regardless of need. Realistically it is only there on the day that you find yourself in need.)

In sum, a Basic Income scheme looks as if it is not *quite* fair by either model. It does not give people more resources, or less, based on desert. It does not make reparation by giving substantially more to the least well off. It does not (by itself) level up the poor or level down the rich, though combined with progressive taxation it can do that. But it does take everyone's basic needs and it says 'Don't worry about those: they're covered'. No one is left out – there is no moralising or judgement, no penalty for being rich, no penalty for being disadvantaged. So it is a kind of fairness that says that being human is the same for all, and no one is worth more or less than anyone else.

Is our current society, without UBI, fair by either standard?

Do the people who deserve more currently get more in our society?

We have a regressive tax system. Poorer people work long hours for low pay, and then pay a higher proportion of their income in taxes than the wealthy. The billionaires pay the lowest proportion of all.

This is partly because of the stealth taxes (e.g. VAT and duty on things like cigarettes, which are predominantly paid by the poor) and National Insurance taxes, which are paid by employers and employees – amounting to a tax that reduces the income of those who work, but not those with unearned income, and also increases the cost of employing someone – and partly because of the tax thresholds, aggravated by various loopholes that allow the super-rich to reduce their tax bills. So the poor pay more and earn less.

In terms of the contribution made by each sector of society in practical service and usefulness, again the situation is topsy-turvy. Many on low or middle incomes are servicing the fundamental provisions of a modern society (as we saw so clearly during the Covid-19 epidemic): teachers, nurses, health-care workers, those caring for the elderly, postmen, bin men, road maintenance, plumbing and heating engineers, doctors, scientists and police. Many of these jobs are 'vocation' careers: people choose to do them not for the pay but to do something good. This reveals a mismatch between the value of the work and the monetary rewards, or indeed the status of such people in society.

And besides, there is another huge body of work that is completely unpaid: nurturing relationships, caring for the elderly, nursing a sick child, not to mention political campaigning, standing for election, and all the other things that good citizens do for nothing.

When we look at this range of things and ask ourselves who is doing the most for our society, and to whom should we be most grateful, it is clear that the measure of their contribution is not their earned or unearned income, nor whether they are in a job that pays wages sufficient to meet or exceed their daily needs. The measure is whether they are doing something worthwhile and rewarding: something that we value. Forcing those people to stop doing those things and get a job 'to earn money' looks nonsensical, if by doing that we take them away from this care and attention to the things that need doing. And then again, suppose that they were doing something, and then through no fault of their own, the employer who needed their skills is forced to close? Nothing about that misfortune means that the person is no longer a useful member of society, or that they are deserving of being condemned to poverty.

When we ask who is doing the most for our society, and who is most highly rewarded, we see that there is no correlation. This tells us something about our values, and the mismatch between the good things we choose to do, and the monetary rewards, which do not track the good. Is a society that gives higher rewards to those who do nothing good and lower rewards to those who do the best and most important things making a mistake? How does it match with the idea that our priority should be to match rewards to desert, if the society is to be a fair one?

So even if we were tempted to think that fairness is about distributing things unequally, according to what people deserve rather than what they need, a genuine understanding of which people do and which people do not have more than they deserve would not leave us where we are now – not by a long way. Given the huge contribution made by those who work for nothing or for very low pay, and the huge potential of those who could (if they had the resources) do creative things or access education, but are prevented from doing so because they have to take menial jobs, it is clear that giving a basic wage to everyone, and a basic stipend to every child, would result in a fairer and more equitable provision, where no one is working for nothing and no one is at a loss for the resources to better themselves or make their contribution meaningful.

3. The Philosophical Issues II: What is a good society, and what is eudaimonia?

Now consider the idea of sanctions. In our current system the department responsible for ensuring that people are supported in times of need devotes a huge amount of resource to taking money away from the needy, if they are thought to have tried to cheat the system or have not fulfilled some punitive conditions designed to humiliate them and discourage reliance on help. This is our system of 'sanctions' against those we think of as the lazy and undeserving poor. At the same time huge numbers of charities are run on volunteer time, trying to give to these needy and struggling people the things that are being removed by the employees of the state. So while the state is aiming to ensure that large numbers of people are made hungry or homeless, if they fail to do what that they have to do in order to be entitled to help, others, not employed by the state but relying on the kindness of donors, do their best to help those people and give them a chance to turn their lives round, or at least to cling on to life. The result of this bizarre and incoherent struggle is a huge increase in misery, homelessness, poverty and the widespread destruction of families. Our official system is designed to aggravate the miseries of those who are struggling to make ends meet, by putting extra hoops to jump through – in the expectation that many will fail, and apparently in full knowledge of the fact that that some of these will end up in prison or imposing additional demands on the mental health service, though it often appears such knowledge is never actually joined up, and no real connection is made between the humiliating and punitive benefits system and the crisis in mental health, domestic abuse and dysfunctional parenting.

This regime of sanctions for benefit claimants is supposed to be good because it gives the appearance of reducing the number of people on benefits and 'saving the taxpayer money.' By picturing this misery as a way of saving money, or preventing the undeserving poor from becoming scroungers and good-for-nothings, it gains the approval of the wealthy who have no personal acquaintance with any of the victims targeted by the system. The result is a society in which the wealthy congratulate themselves on their right to keep what they earned, while other members of the same community are literally starving to death with no money for food or rent at all.

Eudaimonia

At this point we should stand back and ask what kind of society we could be proud of. What are the goals of a good society? What is our ambition for our community, or, as the ancients would say, our '*polis*'? Do we, for example, prize freedom? Or culture? Or intellectual achievement? Or the leisure time to pursue these goals? Or do we prize conformity, drudgery, compliance, servitude? What is it to be a great and admirable human being, and in what kind of society is it possible for people to live well to the best that a human being can achieve?

When ancient philosophers asked this question, they would be asking about *eudaimonia*: enjoying the blessings of good fortune. How can we create a society that delivers that?

The Platonist asks 'What is the good, and how can we create a society oriented towards that?'. Or how could we, in practical terms, approximate the best that can be done here on earth – bearing in mind that we can never achieve perfection? What must we do to make something *close to perfect,* to approximate the ideal as nearly as possible? That would be the Platonic question (and I am a Platonist). We find that kind of thinking in Iris Murdoch for instance.

An Aristotelian would think similarly, asking 'What would allow human beings to achieve a life that approximates to that of the God, who just sits and thinks, and who has no need to work?'.

These are ancient questions; but they are also questions that we really should ask for our own time, and we really should answer them properly. There seem to me to be two answers from the ancient world that deserve attention, and two from the modern world that need to be rejected.

From the ancient world, first, the idea that the good life is the life of leisure (as distinct from the life of a slave), and second, the idea that what makes leisure important is the freedom to do the unslavish things that one can do only if one has the leisure to do them. The value of being free is here pictured in contrast to the life of a slave, though there is also a more positive model of a worker who is a self-employed craftsman or doctor, whose primary goal is to produce good work and be pleased with it, not in service to a master but for the inherent value of what is achieved.

By contrast in the modern world, at least in the protestant north, it is hard to resist the impression that the primary goal is to accumulate wealth (and we seem to think that this goal is successfully achieved if a small minority are very wealthy and the rest destitute: hence the use of generic GDP figures or rises in 'average income' to measure improvements); and our second priority seems to be to see that the rest of the people, the ones who have little, are gainfully employed in creating the wealth for the lucky few, and that no one is evading that duty.

Indeed it looks uncannily like a goal of enslaving the many to deliver wealth for the few, but with a total lack of any consideration of whether the resulting life (for anyone, either rich or poor) is a good one or worth having for anyone.

a) Jobs and the value of idleness

This focus on jobs is common to both communist and capitalist societies. In the UK, both the Labour Party and the Conservative Party always want people to be in jobs. But why? Let us look at some thinkers who have challenged that corrupting obsession, and tried to speak out against the peculiar values that underpin it.

In 1932 Bertrand Russell published a wonderful little essay called 'In Praise of Idleness'[7] in which he notes that both communism and the West have an excessive focus on work and the constant demand for long hours over and above what is necessary. Russell's proposed solution is to reduce the working week to four days a week. 'I want to say, in all seriousness, that a great deal of harm is being done in the modern world by belief in the virtuousness of work, and that the road to happiness and prosperity lies in an organized diminution

---

[7]   First published in Harper's Magazine (Russell, 1932) and then reprinted in his collected Essays *In Praise of Idleness* (Russell, 1935).

of work,' he says (Russell, 1935, pp. 10–11). After showing that the wartime period proves that the country can exist, and produce enough to live on, with a massively reduced workforce while the rest are diverted to fighting or making ammunition, he suggests that work should be more evenly distributed. In practice, in a market economy, the effect of making too much stuff is that some people work long hours and others end up out of work and destitute. He illustrates the problem with the example of the pin makers:

> Suppose that, at a given moment, a certain number of people are engaged in the manufacture of pins. They make as many pins as the world needs, working (say) eight hours a day. Someone makes an invention by which the same number of men can make twice as many pins: pins are already so cheap that hardly any more will be bought at a lower price. In a sensible world, everybody concerned in the manufacturing of pins would take to working four hours instead of eight, and everything else would go on as before. But in the actual world this would be thought demoralizing. The men still work eight hours, there are too many pins, some employers go bankrupt, and half the men previously concerned in making pins are thrown out of work. There is, in the end, just as much leisure as on the other plan, but half the men are totally idle while half are still overworked. In this way, it is insured that the unavoidable leisure shall cause misery all round instead of being a universal source of happiness. Can anything more insane be imagined? (Russell, 1935, pp. 13–14)

Russell's solution is a redistribution of work, together with a rejection of the idea that we should constantly increase demand, so as to make more work for ourselves. We could also see this proposal as a redistribution of leisure: rather than having some people out of work, with more than enough leisure, and others in work with not enough leisure, everyone has less work, and more leisure. Should we see this solution as *taking some work away* from the one group, to let everyone have some, as if work was a good thing? Or should we see it as taking away some leisure from one group to allow everyone to have some, because leisure is precious, and something to be earned and enjoyed? The latter view, it seems to me, makes us more happy with the outcome. And that is because in fact the opportunity for leisure, not the opportunity for work, is the thing we should and must prize for free human beings.

From the late twentieth century, the problem that Russell had in mind was partly solved by the throw away society and the role of advertising. Advertising can make us want more and more stuff we don't need, and encourage us to throw away more and more perfectly serviceable stuff, so as to keep buying ever more stuff and never have enough. Settling for enough would undermine the need to employ more and more people doing pointless things and selling wasteful products to make money for the rich.

This was the situation that Herbert Marcuse diagnosed in his *One Dimensional Man* (Marcuse, 1964), in which he showed how we have become trapped in a system designed to pretend that we must have more stuff, and then to have more stuff we must work longer hours and earn more money, as if happiness could be bought with material objects; he illustrated the ways in which this system, built up through advertising and propaganda, traps us into a cycle of unnecessary work, destroying our judgement and leaving us with no time, energy or inclination to resist.

In my manifesto here, I could have chosen to propose a shorter working week, as Russell suggested. That is also a Green Party policy. But that proposal seems to me to be still somewhat stuck in the notion that it would be good to ensure that there are always jobs for everyone, which is still in thrall to the old model that thinks that people should and must be employed, gainfully employed in some kind of drudgery, for at least part of their time. So his practical solution seems not fully to have taken on board his correct observation that idleness is better than drudgery.

Why might we be tempted to think that people *ought* to be employed in paid drudgery for all or some of their time? Here is Bertrand Russell again:

> The idea that the poor should have leisure has always been shocking to the rich. In England, in the early nineteenth century, fifteen hours was the ordinary day's work for a man; children sometimes did as much, and very commonly did twelve hours a day. When meddlesome busybodies suggested that perhaps these hours were rather long, they were told that work kept adults from drink and children from mischief. When I was a child, shortly after urban working men had acquired the vote, certain public holidays were established by law, to the great indignation of the upper classes. I remember hearing an old Duchess say: 'What do the poor want with holidays? They ought to work.' People nowadays are less frank, but the sentiment persists, and is the source of much of our economic confusion. (Russell, 1935, p. 14)

In this attitude we can hear an echo of Aristotle's idea of the natural slave, used to justify exploitation of the enslaved on the grounds that the slave lacks the rational part of the soul and is best fitted for manual work.[8] This is what allows the free man to free ride on the back of the labour of others. Only the master gets the leisure to pursue the good life, and his good life is supposed to suffice to make the slave's life a good one too, because he vicariously takes care of ensuring that the slave has no spare money or leisure time lest he spend it irrationally on unsuitable things.

Russell's defence of idleness has been followed by a trickle of similar advocates over the century.[9] There is also a parallel discussion concerning the idea of meaningful work, as opposed to useless toil (as William Morris put it).[10] Here the idea is that some work is worth doing, whereas some of it is work in bullshit jobs – a theme explored famously by David Graeber.[11] But it is worth noting that meaningful work need not necessarily provide a wage. If it is worth doing, and important, people want to do it anyway. Setting people free to do that, and to spend their precious time on what is actually meaningful and creative, would be an act of superb transformation. That, as I shall suggest, is what a universal basic income could do.

I am suggesting that the provision of leisure (and opportunities for good use of that leisure) should be a dominant goal for society. Our focus for creating the good society should be on how to ensure that as many as possible – ideally everyone, young and old – have as much access to leisure as possible, while still providing everyone with *enough* income for their basic needs, and the respect they need for a sense of self-worth. Currently this situation is enjoyed exclusively by the rich, who, for the most part, lack neither goods nor leisure, whereas the working population mostly lacks either the leisure to do meaningful things or the means to keep their family housed, clothed and shod – the basic animal needs, the things that even Aristotle's slave never went without.

4. The Philosophical Issues III: Exploitation and power.

Introducing a UBI would effect a moment of unparalleled transformation for society, not just in enabling that kind of free use of leisure by everyone, but also because it would undo a very destructive power

---

[8]   See Aristotle *Politics* Book 1, 1253b15-55b40.
[9]   Josh Cohen summarises his top ten list of works on this theme in *The Guardian* for February 2019 (Cohen, 2019), and see also Cohen (2018).
[10]   See Morris (1888).
[11]   See Graeber (2018).

system that makes our society deeply exploitative.[12] Most people are not free to leave their job even if it is a bullshit job, even if it is a job producing stuff that makes the world a nastier place for everyone. People have to stick with a job that keeps the wolf from the door. Employers have no incentive to make their workplace civilised, pleasant, or free of bullying and intimidation. Picture a society of utterly miserable people, commuting miles, to work in horrible jobs all day, getting home too late to see their children, because if they didn't go they wouldn't be able to pay the bills.

A universal basic income would reverse this situation. People would need some additional income for sure: it will always be desirable to add a little luxury to the basics that might be covered in a generous and sufficient basic income. So people would want jobs, or various kind of productive employment. But no one would be at risk of destitution if they turned down a job that was worthless or badly paid.

Beggars can't be choosers, but once you make them no longer beggars, you can make them choosers. And to have the choice of saying no to a job, if the work is appalling or distressing, is to be free. And to decide to take a break from the job and do something different; to have the means to better yourself, to take yourself to college and find a new skill; to start a business in a niche that you would love to fit – these are the things that make life worthwhile, and lead to a creative and inventive society instead of a society of drudgery and pointless toil. Our current focus on jobs – any old jobs, including the jobs that are destroying our own planet – creates a situation of exploitation. It makes people wage-slaves. And this is still true, whether the jobs are unionised or not. It still creates a dependence of the worker on the employer, and it gives the employer the power to extract labour and make a profit from the work of others.

5. How, if at all, would this address the ills of modern society?

If you change this situation from the bottom up, various things happen. Jobs that are crucial to society have to be paid at a level that reflects their importance and their working conditions. We are already seeing something of this kind in the UK, after creating a shortage of labour in a range of tasks that used to be covered by cheap imported labour from Europe. But if no one in the community actually *needs* a job, even to cover the cost of their basic subsistence,

[12] On the emancipatory power of a basic income see the evidence from the pilot study in India (Davala et al., 2015) and Howard (2017).

employers can no longer rely on exploiting a workforce so desperate that they will do horrible work for wages that are barely enough to live on. Some jobs would have to pay more than they do now, including some public sector jobs. Some jobs would get better, because working conditions would have to improve. And some jobs in really worthwhile occupations would be able to pay less. No minimum wage would be necessary, and people would take work that they enjoyed doing even if it paid less than it does now. The cost of things produced by real craftsmen would go down, and the products of bad factories and foul meat processing plants would go up.

As things stand we pay people too little so that they are unable to afford decent food. We then have to produce terrible food for those who can't afford to eat well. The UK minimum wage is not enough to enable anyone to eat well. This has two consequences: it is damaging to the planet and the ecosystem and it is costly to the health service.

As things stand people are stressed by hours of commuting, unpleasant jobs that they must go to every day, pressure from the stigma of poverty and the money worries that break up families and destroy relationships. The savings in mental health, physical health, stress related illness, family breakdown and domestic abuse would be considerable. But we should count those savings not just in terms of the monetary costs. If we go back to that question of what kind of society we want to live in, the real question is: why would we ever set up a set of values that delivers such misery for so many people? And how easy would it be to change that?

And then there is the environment. Maybe people would commute less far, take more interesting jobs close to home, set up a small business, do voluntary work in the neighbourhood, make their community a happier place. Automation makes many jobs that used to be necessary unnecessary, but no one gets to benefit from that if we keep making more tat in order to make more paid jobs. The tat, the fast fashion, the latest fad gadgets, the fossil fuels we use to make them, the waste from throwing the old ones away, and the energy used to transport it and sell it, – these are the things that are killing the planet.

To sum up, I would like to suggest that not only would this system constitute a much simpler solution to the conundrum that Simon Duffy and Jo Wolff address in another chapter of this volume, in connection with the poverty trap that criminalises those who earn a little extra money while on benefits – it would also have much greater and more meaningful transformative power. As we come through the worst years of peacetime any of us have known, we have been forced to realise how easy it is to find that the income has just dried up, and there is nothing. The devastating effects of the failure to provide any safety net for freelance workers, musicians and actors, for example, during the pandemic shows that some of the things that are most important to a free, creative and leisured society require a safety net that keeps them alive in times of crisis. Such direct support does not do anything to reduce the economic and creative activity that such people contribute; in fact it makes it possible for them to maintain their professional skills so as to return to professional work again when the troubles are over.

A widespread and pernicious myth about the way public finances work and where the money comes from has made people suppose that the poor must always pay the costs of whatever the state has to subsidise, and that state borrowing must be reduced by cutting the things it funds. But that is a confusion. Spending is an investment that reaps dividends, if it is spent on enterprising solutions to the things that are costly and destructive.

Austerity programmes increase hardship, put more workers onto benefits, and more people out of work. They generate a spiral of increasing misery and despair and a collapse in public revenue. In building back better, we need to think about what kind of better we want to build. The fact is that, so far from being unable to afford this Universal Basic Income system, it is pretty clear that the lack of it is the source of many of our costs, and of the uncosted problems that are destroying the planet and leading us to exhaust the entire resources of the planet. In reality we cannot afford not to change the model of what is costly and what is the affordable solution. And besides, as suggested above, there is real evidence that this kind of redistribution of wealth could actually increase economic activity and enterprise, as well as cutting costs in a range of public services, especially those related to solving the problems caused by the misery and stigma of debt, poor health, poor education and home life, and poor diet. Solving these damaging problems would pay dividends not just in the economy, but more importantly in every single measure of the good life. Meanwhile it would terminate the employment of a huge army of bureaucrats whose current task is to assess whether the poor have reached a sufficiently dire level of poverty to be worth saving.

University of East Anglia
c.rowett@uea.ac.uk

References

Sinéad Boultwood, 'There's no easy way to compare benefit and tax fraud.', *Full Fact*, (31st July 2019) <https://fullfact.org/online/comparing-benefit-and-tax-fraud/> accessed 23rd September 2021.

Philip Brien and Matthew Keep, 'Public spending during the Covid-19 pandemic', *House of Commons Library, UK House of Commons* (2021), <https://researchbriefings.files.parliament.uk/documents/CBP-9309/CBP-9309.pdf>.

Josh Cohen, *Not Working: Why We Have to Stop* (London: Granta Books, 2018).

Josh Cohen, 'Top 10 books about idleness', *The Guardian,* (6th February 2019), also available at https://www.theguardian.com/books/2019/feb/06/top-10-books-about-idleness.

S. Davala, et al., *Basic Income: A Transformative Policy for India.* (London: Bloomsbury, 2015).

Entitledto, '£15+ billion unclaimed means-tested benefits – but the sketchy take-up data makes it hard to say for sure', *Entitledto* (January 05, 2021) <https://www.entitledto.co.uk/blog/2021/january/15plus-billion-unclaimed-means-tested-benefits-but-the-sketchy-take-up-data-makes-it-hard-to-say-for-sure/≥ accessed 23rd September 2021.

David Graeber, *Bullshit Jobs: a theory* (London: Allen Lane, 2018).

Neil Howard, 'Basic income and the anti-slavery movement', *Etica & Politica/Ethics & Politics*, XIX (2017), 213–17.

Herbert Marcuse, *One Dimensional Man* (Boston, Mass: Beacon Press, 1964).

Nikiforos Michalis, Marshall Steinbaum, and Gennaro Zezza, 'Modeling the Macroeconomic Effects of a Universal Basic Income', *Roosevelt Institute* (2017), <https://rooseveltinstitute.org/publications/macroeconomic-effects-universal-basic-income-ubi/>, accessed 6th December 2021.

William Morris, *Useful work versus Useless Toil* (The Freedom Library; London: Reeves, 1888).

Richard Murphy, 'The UK tax gap is £90 billion a year', *Tax Research UK*, (June 19th 2019) <https://www.taxresearch.org.uk/Blog/2019/06/19/the-uk-tax-gap-is-90-billion-a-year/≥, accessed 23rd September 2021.

Russell, Bertrand, 'In Praise of Idleness', *Harper's Magazine* (1932); *In Praise of Idleness and Other Essays* (London: Allen and Unwin, 1935), 9–21

Scott Santens, 'The BIG Library: Books About Universal Basic Income (UBI)', <https://medium.com/basic-income/the-big-library-books-about-basic-income-b9763071b987, (2016, updated September 14th 2021), accessed 23rd September 2021>.

Neil Sorensen, Narayan Jayaram and Jonathan Howard, 'Background information and methodology 2018 to 2019', *Official Statistics*, <https://www.gov.uk/government/statistics/income-related-benefits-estimates-of-take-up-financial-year-2018-to-2019/background-information-and-methodology-2018-to-2019≥, (2020, updated 29th October 2020), accessed 23rd September 2021.

Guy Standing, *Basic income: and how we can make it happen* (Pelican Introduction; London: Pelican/Penguin, 2017).

No More Benefit Cheats

SIMON DUFFY AND JONATHAN WOLFF

Abstract

The concept of the 'benefit cheat' plays a critical role in political rhetoric and public policy and it has been deployed to justify changes to the benefit system that have had a very negative impact on well being and justice. The authors argue that the concept is dangerous, adding to the existing burdens of poverty and exclusion and that it must be eradicated by a reorganisation of the welfare system. Dignity and a spirit of equality must be the starting point for any system of welfare that aims to promote universal well being.

> 'I have heard that [true] leaders of states or clans ... do not worry about poverty, but inequity. ... For if there is equity, there will be no poverty'.
>
> Confucius Analects 16.1

1. Introduction

A regular theme in the British popular press is the exposure of 'benefit cheats': people who have claimed benefits to which they should have known they are not entitled, or have failed to inform the authorities of changes to circumstances that reduce their entitlement. A random internet search brings up a regularly updated *Daily Mirror* feature with numerous stories, the first four of which in November 2020 were:

> Bogus carer claimed £30,000 of benefits for looking after a dead man for 6 years.
> Benefits cheat who rode elephants and ran brothel said she was 'too weak to walk'.
> Gran who lied blindness to steal 1m in benefits 'was craftiest woman ever'
> 'Hard working and decent mum' jailed for £20,000 benefit fraud
> (Daily Mirror, 2020)

The idea that the country is full of benefit cheats has arguably permeated public consciousness, with government minister Iain Duncan

doi:10.1017/S1358246121000382   © The Royal Institute of Philosophy and the contributors 2022

Smith reported as saying 'it makes his blood boil' (Worrall, 2015). Such a strongly negative view is encouraged by the government which has set up a simple to navigate website to allow people to report on benefit fraud (GOV.UK undated a), which in turn has come under severe criticism for generating hundreds of thousands of complaints that are not investigated (Cowburn, 2018).

We accept that, no doubt, there are cases of serious, systematic, dishonesty, that constitute theft or fraud. However, many people who are classified as benefit cheats are trapped by the structural injustice of a welfare system that provides a cruel choice between living a barely human life, or breaking the law. Many will choose to stay within the law, living in or near poverty. Others will attempt to improve their standard of living by choosing to break the law, thereby experiencing several layers of disadvantage. First, having to exist purely on benefits puts most people in a highly disadvantaged position; second breaking the law risks severe consequences; third, unlike other disadvantaged or stigmatised groups, they are unable to speak out for fear of self-incrimination; fourth it is very likely that the stress of living in such a situation has adverse health consequences (Wolff and de-Shalit, 2007; Marmot, 2015).

What has society come to, if it offers the most vulnerable the choice between a barely human life and crime? How, starting from where we are now, can the system be changed? In this paper we use the issue of benefit cheats as a way of approaching welfare reform. When people in power ignore the real injustice of a deeply flawed system and target those who struggle to manage within that system for stigma, scorn and even criminalisation, we must be careful not to accept their framing of the issue. Our alternative will be to focus, not on all aspects of welfare and public policy, nor on all public policy goals, but on how to ensure people have enough to live on with dignity. Our task will be to explore the major policy options for welfare reform, and to consider both the long-term moral and political goals of a welfare system and the shorter-term measures that could alleviate some of the most debilitating aspects of the current system.

2. Aspects of the Benefit System in the UK today

Those who do not have direct experience of being an applicant for, and recipient of, benefits in the UK today may give little thought to what it would be like, or may rely on portrayals such as that of Ken Loach's film *I Daniel Blake*, but perhaps suspect that it is an exaggeration or treats exceptional cases as typical. That film, and related literature, however, shows that the welfare system has two main goals, both to provide welfare, but also to exert social control over people's lives, conditioning action to particular behaviours, such as incessantly applying for jobs, even when there is no real prospect of success, and attending all interviews offered. Such social control may ostensibly be justified by its role in training people for the workplace, but much is arbitrary, and punitive, perhaps with the goal of making some people forfeit, or not even apply for, benefits to which they are entitled (Watts and Fitzpatrick, 2018).

A humane society would attempt to put more resources into welfare and less into social control. But concentrating on the welfare side, what standard of living does a welfare complaint typically experience? We might start by comparing benefit level with the poverty line in the UK. Today, over 2% of the population are defined as destitute. That means more than 1 in 50 of us are not just poor, but extremely poor, unable to buy the 'absolute essentials that we all need to eat, stay warm and dry, and keep clean' (Fitzpatrick et al., 2017). The Joseph Rowntree Foundation (2020) has also worked with the general public to define a Minimum Income Standard (MIS): 'a minimum socially acceptable standard of living in the UK today' but these standards are far higher than benefit levels.

State pension is 93% of the MIS. Disabled people on the highest levels of benefits will have incomes that are less than 75% of the MIS. For people on the lowest benefit levels their income is little more than 25% of the MIS. (Benstead, 2019). For example, weekly payments on Job Seekers Allowance are:

Maximum for a single person under 25 is £58.90
Maximum for a single person 25 and over is £74.35
Maximum for a couple over 18 is £116.80 (i.e. £58.40 each)

Money is reduced as you start to earn and for single people if they become a couple. As Paul Spicker puts it: '...the rules on fraud are trying to eradicate behaviour which is normal, reasonable and desirable' (Spicker, 2011).

And, of course, if you fall foul of the benefit system your income may become zero. If you apply for a disability benefit, are rejected and challenge your rejection you will be given no income while you go through the long and complex period of challenge, despite the high success rates for challenges. Or you may be sanctioned, perhaps for reasons as trivial as these:

• You volunteer to sell poppies for Remembrance Day

- You have a heart attack during the assessment process, and so fail to complete the assessment
- You don't look for work on Christmas Day
- You can't afford the bus fare to the workfare job where you are being forced to 'volunteer'
- You attend your grandmother's funeral

The net effect of this is food poverty, energy poverty, social isolation and mental illness. 'I used to be on average 9 stone 7; I'm now just under 8 stone... all the stress and everything. The doctor weighed me. He said that's malnutrition.' (cited in Benstead, 2019).

The growth in poverty, and particularly in extreme poverty is reflected in the rapid growth of food banks. The creation of a food bank used to be a rare event in the UK, connected to a strike or some unusual crisis. However, since the beginning of the so-called welfare reform period food banks have grown in number every year. In the UK in 2019 there were over 2,000 recognised food banks, with an estimated further 3,000 venues distributing food aid (Peck, 2019). By 2021 the number of established foodbanks had risen to 2,200 (Tyler, 2021). This is associated with another fundamental feature of the current system; feelings of shame and persecution that have been accelerated by the move to a benefits system with more conditionality, control and dehumanised assessment systems. For disabled people in particular new assessment systems, built around the false assumption that disabled people are likely to faking illness or disability, have led to extremes of fear, self-doubt, mental illness and suicide. Analysing the impact of the roll out of one element of this system researchers stated:

> We found that those local areas where a greater proportion of the population were exposed to the reassessment process experienced a greater increase in three adverse mental health outcomes — suicides, self-reported mental health problems and antidepressant prescribing. (Barr et al. 2015)

People adapt to extreme poverty in many different ways:

> Bill used to disappear around December, and came back in March. When asked he explained 'I get myself locked up'. Prison gave him the support he needed to cope with the winter. 'It's warm, free meals and plenty of company'. (Duffy, 2014)

Despite the difficulties of living on benefits, there is little evidence of widespread benefit fraud. For example, there were about 10,000 cases in 2012-13 (Worrall, 2015), but the factors that define both entitlement and fraud include many aspects that in other contexts would simply be considered part of a normal life, and do not constitute dishonest behaviour, such as the following (all taken from official government guidance):

1. changing your name or gender
2. finding or finishing a job, or working different hours
3. your income going up or down
4. starting or stopping education, training or an apprenticeship
5. moving house
6. people moving into or out of the place you live (for example your partner, a child or lodger)
7. the death of your partner or someone you live with
8. having a baby
9. starting or stopping caring for someone
10. getting married or divorced
11. starting or ending a civil partnership
12. planning to go abroad for any length of time
13. going into hospital, a care home or sheltered accommodation
14. any changes to your medical condition or disability
15. changing your doctor
16. changes to your pension, savings, investments or property
17. changes to other money you get (for example student loans or grants, sick pay or money you get from a charity)
18. changes to the benefits you or anyone else in your house gets
19. you or your partner getting back-pay (sometimes called 'arrears') for salary or earnings you're owed (Gov.uk, undated b)

Essentially the fundamental logic of entitlement is that you should be in paid work, and if you are not you need a good excuse. If you cannot work, your family should take care of you if possible, and you should use up your savings before asking for help, though you can get help if you can prove you are really sick or disabled or a carer. This logic of self-help, or family-help, suggests a type of (false) nostalgia for a time when people took primary responsibility for themselves and those around them. There is certainly something appealing in this picture, but it romanticises something that never really existed. Families where the 'bread-winner' was out of work or in poor-paid work have always struggled with severe privation, and a family has to be reasonably comfortably off to be able to survive unemployment without severe hardship even for a short period. This picture also ignores the duty of the community to assist those who, for whatever reason, are for the moment not in a position to meet their own needs. Critically, it also ignores the fact, documented since Benjamin Seebohm Rowntree's pioneering work, that having a job is not always sufficient to avoid poverty (1901). Today's welfare system acknowledges this by supplementing the incomes of those on lower pay, and indeed there are many more people receiving Income Support than Jobseekers Allowance (Dept for Work and Pensions, 2020b). However, by far the largest group of people receiving benefits are those on a state pension, followed by disabled people and carers. Next are people getting tax credits or Housing Benefit because their work doesn't pay enough, as well as a group of people who are in insecure work and who may dip in and out of the benefit system. There are relatively few people in so-called long-term unemployment as it is typically understood, willing and able to work but unable to find a job. But many people are in precarious, low paid, work that doesn't offer stable living conditions.

The emergency steps induced by the pandemic may have put the benefit system under huge stress, and temporarily changed the possibly of false claims, deliberate or inadvertent, in substantial ways (Dept for Work and Pensions, 2021), but if we go back to the last pre-pandemic figures, despite the adverse publicity, genuine fraud overpayments are very low, bearing in mind that the definition of fraud in the list conflates claimant error and fraud; any failure to volunteer information to the DWP is treated as fraud with an ongoing and live obligation to provide information. Even so, the figure as reported was just 1.4% of the total benefit system (Dept for Work and Pensions, 2020a). Nevertheless, the inherent logic is inhuman and hostile to human dignity and is in stark contrast to the tax system, where you report backwards, take time to review your situation, can gather information, double-check your rights and responsibilities, and where there is a presumption of honesty.

Also, while the DWP itself admit underpaying people at a rate of 1.1% (i.e. almost exactly the same as the amount overpaid because of fraud) arguably the really fundamental fraud is to create a system where many people do not claim what they are entitled to or find themselves unfairly being assessed, re-assessed or failing faulty assessment processes. One estimate puts unclaimed benefits at £21 billion which is about 10% of all benefits, or about 20% of non-pension benefits. (Entitledto, 2018)

If people received benefits that brought them an acceptable standard of living, it would be easy to write off the small number of benefit cheats as greedy exploiters who are trying to swindle a humane society, to the cost of others who have to subsidise their lavish life style. And as we have accepted, there are a very small number of people who fall into this category. Our suspicion, however, is that most cases are not like this; either they concern people whose circumstances have changed in ways that affect their entitlements, but they have not notified the authorities, or are people who realise that they cannot live what they regard as a bare human life without breaking the law in some way, and opt to break the benefit laws. The categories can merge in that some people will deliberately put their head in the sand in changing circumstances, knowing that if their benefits fall the consequences will be stark.

Consider, for example, the 4th case identified by the Daily Mirror, of the '"Hard-working and decent mum" jailed for £20,000 benefit fraud'. This person correctly claimed benefits at first, but failed to notify the authorities when her partner moved in, at which point she was no longer entitled to single parent tax credits. According to the press report, her barrister told the court that the money was 'not used to fund a lavish lifestyle', adding, 'She accepts there is no excuse and she accepts fully her culpability. She at the time was struggling with two young children and holding down a responsible and stressful job. She was in debt' (Mutch and Dresch, 2020).

This is the mundane story of poverty. People on low incomes struggle to do very ordinary things, such as buying birthday presents for their children, paying for school trips, going out with friends even once a month, or buying acceptable food or hygiene products. Much of the poverty literature uses the extended metaphor of a human versus animal existence. Rowntree, for example, says that poor people cannot be expected to survive on a 'fodder basis' (Rowntree, 1937), and from what we have seen, many people living on benefits are excluded from what makes life human. As a society we should be ashamed that we consign so many people to such fates.

3. A Life With Dignity

We have suggested that the current benefit denies people a life with dignity, viewing claimants as potential fraudsters, who have to prove that they have a genuine claim (cf Wolff, 1998), and avoiding normal human relations, such as spending nights with an intimate life-partner, in case it invalidates benefits. What, then, is a life with dignity? It is worth starting with an evocative passage from the development economist Arthur Lewis, who set out the following as the aspiration of socialists:

A society in which every child shall grow up in pleasant homes and attractive surroundings and with good educational opportunities; in which every adult shall be provided for in sickness and adversity; and in which the pensioner can take untroubled ease. (Lewis, 1948, pp. 32-33).

There is much to hope for in this account, which encompasses the life-cycle as a whole, and not only that of an adult of working age, which is so commonly the case. Yet it also provides a surprisingly materialistic, individualist and passive picture of an aspirational life. It misses out the quality of relations to others outside the family; the role one has in contributing to political decisions that are fateful for one's life; the nature of the work that one does; and the assurance that it is possible to achieve all of this without stepping beyond the bounds of the law (Wolff and de-Shalit, 2007). This is not the place to set out a full account of a dignified life (see Duffy, 2006), but we assume that any account must encompass material, relational, experiential, political and legal factors. The description we have given of a life on benefits should make it clear that the current system fails in numerous ways and the concept of 'benefit cheat' is a rhetorical device for reducing the status of all people claiming benefits and serving to undermine the status of people on benefits and also reducing the level of benefits people receive. Systems like Universal Credit have the function of causing two kinds of harm: low incomes and low status.

We want to eradicate the concept of a 'benefit cheat' because the concept is a threat to the status of those regarded as potential benefit cheats. It is a threat even to people who obey the rules, or break them for humanly understandable reasons, for the possibility of accusation hangs over every claimant. Merely being a recipient of 'benefits' is enough to threaten self-respect in many, though not necessarily all societies (Wolff, 1998). It is worse in those societies where we have been trained by the tabloid press and by politicians to associate the term 'benefit' with the term 'cheat' as in the contemporary United Kingdom. Moreover, even if we were only concerned with the distribution of material (rather than social or spiritual resources) we should seek to eradicate the notion of a benefit cheat because the concept clearly serves to support the ongoing reduction in real benefit levels and reduces pressure to redistribute resources fairly. What can be done to improve matters?

4. Prospects for Reform

What can be done? We will outline the current models for social security, with specific reference to the United Kingdom, by describing both the current system and major competing conceptions of benefits. All these descriptions are of course still relatively abstract, but the aim is to try and outline the shape of the competing models, particularly focusing on the underlying design principles.

A The legacy model - National Insurance

A common assumption is that benefits are or should be delivered on what is sometimes called a 'contributory basis', which implies that you may only receive benefits if you have contributed into the current system and what you get out may be in some way reflect what you put in. In reality, this model has long been on the wane and has never really been as important as could have been thought. In a highly unequal society it is extremely unlikely that the poorest can contribute enough to then provide themselves with enough in the future. A benefit system is quite properly redistributive.

There are fragments of the contributory principle still in action, but they are not significant. For our purposes a contributory system is more akin to private insurance than to a benefit system as defined here. A system where people pay into a pool in order to protect their own long-term self-interest is not a system governed by principles of social justice, and to the extent that systems build in a contributory principle they can be seen as departing from reference to the principles of social justice.

As with private healthcare, there are even social justice arguments for eliminating or minimising private insurance and contributory based systems because they encourage the better-off or others to believe that they do not need to pay attention to the needs of others because they have safeguarded their own personal needs through some private or quasi-private system.

B Welfare services – Universal Basic Services

Benefits are only one kind of welfare system; in addition there are also welfare services, where the state provides people with healthcare, education or other services. Clearly these services can play a significant role in reducing poverty, by removing essential costs for services that otherwise people would have to pay for, and also providing economies of scale, and reducing the need for administration of financial accounting. Such services, especially if they are genuinely universal (i.e not poor law provision, but provision for everyone) also tend to be good for reducing stigma. Universality is here critical. We may think that any service will help reduce the costs of poverty, but means-tested services can simply add to the risk of poverty by increasing stigma and generating poverty traps. Means-tested social care for instance may increase, not reduce, poverty.

The more that public goods are properly delivered in the form of universal services then the less that is required for people to receive in the form of benefits. However there are good reasons to think that there are some limits to this process in so far as people have varying tastes and demands and in the case of some public services like social care and housing there are also social justice arguments for increasingly reflecting personal autonomy by making such services more flexible and personal (e.g. personal budgets).

Universal Basic Services are then an important limiting system. Again, they are not strictly a benefit system, but a complimentary system of provision the size of which will impact on the size of the benefit system. Opinions differ as to the idea size of a Universal Basic Services sector (Duffy, 2018)

C Targeted (means-tested) benefits – Universal Credit

In the UK today the system used to provide financial benefits to people of working age is known as Universal Credit. This system, originally designed with simplification in mind, is actually a very complex combination of different systems, which have been only somewhat rationalised as the UK went through a process of what is know as 'welfare reform'. However, with some degree of simplification we might identify the following components of Universal Credit:

1. A cash benefit is provided to households (usually the person deemed the 'head' of the household), but only to those families who have income or savings below set levels.
2. The level of the benefit changes month-by-month depending on household earnings.
3. If the household earns extra money then the cash benefit is reduced by a large percentage (but usually less than 100%) called the withdrawal rate, equivalent to a marginal rate of tax on earnings.
4. If not working (and Universal Credit largely goes to people in low paid work) then people must be looking for work (or looking to work for longer hours).

5.   Alternatively, if you are judged to be incapable of work by an assessment of disability you are excused from looking for work, but you must therefore not work.
6.   People who are looking for work, looking for longer hours of work or deemed unable to work are all subject to supervision, control (attending meetings, trainings, carrying out defined tasks etc.) and sanctions (from loss of benefits to imprisonment), controls or enforced actions.

The underlying assumption of this system is that work is good for us, and perhaps a moral duty if you are capable of working, but that many people do not want to work and although a minimally humane society will provide benefits to stop people from starving, any such benefits are liable to risk encouraging laziness and creating welfare dependency. These assumptions then drive the design of the system. First, benefits are set as low as possible, so that there is less temptation to rely on benefits as the difference between benefit levels and paid work should be significant. Second, there should be a positive financial incentive to do paid work and this means trying to reduce the marginal tax or withdrawal rate below 100%. However, it is difficult to reduce withdrawal rates without increasing eligibility rates, because a lower withdrawal rate implies people can combine earnings and benefits and this means people outside the system of benefits may see their income overtaken by those inside the system. Third, the system uses negative incentives, including the threat of sanctions, to frighten people into work. Fourth, in addition to sanctions there is a further framework of scrutiny which can lead people to be charged with benefit fraud. Benefit fraud, in addition to the few cases of deliberate criminality, as we have seen above also occurs when people make undeclared earnings, exaggerate a disability or enter into a relationship with someone with earnings that the DWP believes should be used to support you or your family. Cleary such a system brings a high degree of cost, complexity and interference with privacy and freedom.

D Universal benefit - Universal Basic Income

In contrast to targeted benefits universal benefits have no means-tests and the name Universal Basic income (UBI) is given to the idea that a non-means-tested system of social security is both feasible and fairer than a targeted system. However, it should be noted that non-means-tested benefits are quite common in the UK. The state pension is not means-tested (although there is a modest contributory qualification) and both Child Benefit and the Personal Independence Payment (PIP) are also non means-tested. This means that currently about 65% of all benefits are non-means-tested.

However, absence of means-testing is not the only important dimension to UBI and the whole definition of UBI provides a very useful contrast to Universal Credit. In a sense these two systems seem to be opposites. A common definition of Universal Basic Incomes might include these elements:

1.   A regular cash payment that is sufficient to live on with dignity.
2.   No means-testing of the benefit, instead people pay tax on income above the set level. This implies that it is much easier to create a progressive tax system that doesn't load the highest levels of marginal tax on the poorest people.
3.   A payment to all individuals, not to households or heads of household. This reduces the risk of dependence within families and is associated with reduced domestic violence.
4.   No conditionality or sanctions based on whether you are deemed to be doing enough paid work.
5.   Assessments for disability or other extra needs generate additional payments which are also non-means-tested and individualised.

It should be noted that the concept of a Negative Income Tax is conceptually very close to that of a Universal Basic Income and that whatever name is given to any system one of the practical features of these kinds of system is that they are likely to see some kind of integration of tax and benefits into one administrative system.

Universal Basic Income is often criticised for disincentivizing work, or for being too expensive to fund at a worthwhile rate, or creating significant problems of transition from one system to another. These are important debates which we cannot enter here (For the authors' somewhat contrasting views see Duffy, 2018; Wolff, 2020, pp. 194-214.)

E Other options

In public policy terms these four options do not completely exhaust all possible options. However, they do probably set out the boundaries and shape of the debate. For instance, some people are currently arguing for a Minimum Income Guarantee (MIG) and the Scottish Government, although it would like to test UBI, recently made a

MIG its short-term objective. However fundamentally this is a policy similar to the first defining feature of UBI – a payment that is sufficient to protect dignity. Likewise a recent disability group proposed reform of the benefit system that would include both a MIG, payments to individuals (not households) and the end of sanctions; but they retained means-testing.

5. Policy Goals

Although it is tempting to propose a favoured policy solution, we will resist the temptation to make a simple policy recommendation for two main reasons. First, there may be a number of ways of reforming policy so that a life for all with dignity becomes possible; and second, rushed implementation of policy, without considerable research and evaluation, has often led to sub-optimal outcomes and now is not the time to make these mistakes again. Yet it is possible to lay out the policy goals. First, and foremost, it is critically important to be able to offer a life of dignity for all, and we have identified material, relational, experiential, political and legal factors that contribute to a life of dignity. Second, and in a way the main the focus of this paper, it is critically important to remove the threat of criminality to people who are already in a vulnerable position. Compounding vulnerability with threats is the opposite of humanity. These two changes should bring two more; third a reduction of stress for claimants, and, fourth, possibly a reduction in stress-related illness. These goals come with a radical reshaping of the concept of responsibility. Part of the social contract is to expect people to act responsibly in return for humane treatment, but unlike the present situation, there is no intention to make following a set of arbitrary hurdles a test of responsibility.

By way of conclusion it is interesting to explore what justification can be attempted for the current stigmatisation of benefits and for reducing the value of benefits and for therefore inevitably increasing levels of inequality. Certainly, after the post-war boom and the growth of the post-war welfare state there was a period when many did argue that inequality was not something that should concern us and that using stigma and shame to motivate people to work was necessary. It seems to us that the dangers and limitation of these arguments should now be very clear.

Growing inequality has not led to greater economic success nor overall wellbeing; but it has created an array of problems that don't just harm the poorest. Overall utility, even if we accept this as useful goal, is clearly diminished by the levels of inequality that have now been normalised in the UK. Similarly, unleashing stigma and shame as tools for social policy quickly unravels and has not only caused immense harm to those who are stigmatised but also contributes to declining support for the necessary institutions of redistribution and social security. It is particularly worrying when you realise that even those groups who might be seen as the 'deserving poor' are inevitably punished in the crossfire of policy of stigma.

Better policies need better goals and should perhaps be designed in a spirit of equal citizenship and mutual respect that assumes people are generally responsible and respectful. It should be a priority to make sure that people are not stigmatised by the design of social security, particularly given the fact that we need such systems for society to function effectively. We should avoid any system that is so mean-spirited that it tempts people into criminal activity, particularly where doing nothing or failing to immediately report some change of circumstances makes someone culpable.

We might be guided more an awareness both of outward and inward cost of such policies. When someone's status is at risk so is their mental health and well being. Beginning with a basic assumption that the purpose of the welfare state is that all citizens should fare well and feel well it would be impossible to pursue the current strategy of criminalisation and stigmatisation.

Citizen Network
simon.duffy@citizen-network.org
University of Oxford
jonathan.wolff@bsg.ox.ac.uk

References

B. Barr, D. Taylor-Robinson, D. Stuckler et al. '"First, Do No Harm": Are Disability Assessments Associated With Adverse Trends in Mental Health? A Longitudinal Ecological Study', *Journal of Epidemiology and Community Health* 70 (2016) 339–45. doi:10.1136/jech-2015-206209

S. Benstead, *Second Class Citizens: The Treatment of Disabled People in Austerity Britain*, (Sheffield: Centre for Welfare Reform, 2019).

Ashley Cowburn, 'Benefit Fraud Witch Hunt.' *Independent* (2018). https://www.independent.co.uk/news/uk/politics/benefit-fraud-public-tip-offs-legal-action-police-no-evidence-dwp-work-pensions-department-a8144096.html [accessed 26 July 2021]

Daily Mirror 'Benefit Cheats' *Daily Mirror* (2020) https://www.mirror.co.uk/all-about/benefit-cheats [accessed 1 November 2020]

Dept for Work and Pensions. 'Fraud and Error in the Benefit System 2019/20.' (2020a) https://assets.publishing.service.gov.uk/government/uploads/system/uploads/attachment_data/file/888423/fraud-and-error-stats-release-2019-2020-estimates-revised-29-may-2020.pdf [accessed 26 July 2021]

Dept for Work and Pensions. 'DWP Benefits Statistical Summary' (2020b) https://www.gov.uk/government/collections/dwp-statistical-summaries [accessed 30 August 2021].

Dept for Work and Pensions (2021). Fraud and Error in the Benefit System 2020/21. https://www.gov.uk/government/statistics/fraud-and-error-in-the-benefit-system-financial-year-2020-to-2021-estimates/fraud-and-error-in-the-benefit-system-for-financial-year-ending-2021 [accessed 26 July 2021]

S. Duffy, *Keys to Citizenship*, 2nd Edition. (Sheffield: Centre for Welfare Reform, 2006).

S. Duffy, Listening Up to Poverty. (Sheffield: Centre for Welfare Reform, 2014). https://www.centreforwelfarereform.org/library/listening-up-to-poverty.html [accessed 30 August 2021]

S. Duffy, *Basic Income or Basic Services?* (Sheffield: Centre for Welfare Reform, 2018). https://centreforwelfarereform.org/library/basic-income-or-basic-services.html [accessed 27 July 2021]

Entitledto, 'Over £20 Billion Still Unclaimed In Means Tested Benefits' (2018) https://www.entitledto.co.uk/blog/2018/december/over-20-billion-still-unclaimed-in-means-tested-benefits/ [accessed 26 July 2021]

S. Fitzpatrick, G. Bramley, J. Sosenko et al., Destitution in the UK. (York: Joseph Rowntree Foundation, 2016). https://www.jrf.org.uk/report/destitution-uk [accessed 30 August 2021]

GOV.UK *Report Benefit Fraud* (undated a) https://www.gov.uk/report-benefit-fraud [accessed 26 July 2021]

GOV.UK *Benefits: Report a Change in Your Circumstances* (undated b) https://www.gov.uk/report-benefits-change-circumstances [accessed 26 July 2021]

A. Lewis, *The Principles of Economic Planning* (London: George Allen and Unwin, 1948).

M. Marmot, *The Health Gap*, (London: Bloomsbury, 2015).

M. Mutch and M. Dresch, "Hard Working Decent Mum' Jailed' Daily Mirror (2020). https://www.mirror.co.uk/news/uk-news/hard-working-decent-mum-jailed-22163499 [accessed 26 July 2021]

L. Peck, 'Food Banks in 2019' (Sheffield: Centre for Welfare Reform, 2019). https://centreforwelfarereform.org/library/uk-food-banks-in-2019.html [accessed 30 August 2021]

Joseph Rowntree Foundation, 'UK Poverty 2019/20' (York: Joseph Rowntree Foundation, 2020) https://www.jrf.org.uk/report/uk-poverty-2019-20 [accessed 30 August 2021]

B.S. Rowntree, *Poverty: A Study of Town Life* (London: Macmillan, 1901).

B.S. Rowntree, *The Human Needs of Labour* (London: Longmans Green & Co, 1937. Revised edition).

P. Spicker, *How Social Security Works*, (Bristol: Policy Press 2011)

G. Tyler, 'Food Banks In The UK' (House of Commons Library, 2021). https://researchbriefings.files.parliament.uk/documents/CBP-8585/CBP-8585.pdf [accessed 24 July 2021)

B. Watts and S. Fitzpatrick, *Welfare Conditionality*, (London: Routledge., 2018).

J. Wolff, 'Fairness, Respect, and the Egalitarian Ethos'. *Philosophy & Public Affairs* 27 (1998), 97–122.

J. Wolff, *Ethics and Public Policy*, (London: Routledge, 2020, 2nd ed.)

J. Wolff and A. de-Shalit, *Disadvantage* (Oxford: Oxford University Press, 2007).

P. Worrall, 'Benefit Fraud vs Tax Evasion', Channel 4, (2015). https://www.channel4.com/news/factcheck/factcheck-benefits-fraud-tax-evasion [accessed 25 July 2021]

A Reconciliation Theory of State Punishment: An Alternative to Protection and Retribution

THADDEUS METZ

Abstract

I propose a theory of punishment that is unfamiliar in the West, according to which the state normally ought to have offenders reform their characters and compensate their victims in ways the offenders find burdensome, thereby disavowing the crime and tending to foster improved relationships between offenders, their victims, and the broader society. I begin by indicating how this theory draws on under-appreciated ideas about reconciliation from the Global South, and especially sub-Saharan Africa, and is distinct from the protection and retribution theories that have dominated the Western philosophy of punishment for about 250 years. Then I argue that it neatly avoids objections to them and is prima facie plausible in its own right. I conclude that this reconciliation theory of state punishment should be taken seriously by philosophers of law and policy makers.

1. Introducing Theories of Punishment

I propose a theory of punishment that is informed by under-appreciated ideas about reconciliation from the Global South, especially sub-Saharan Africa, and conclude that it should be taken seriously as an alternative to dominant Western theories. A theory of state punishment is a comprehensive answer to four major questions about the justice of burdening or depriving someone in response to a legal transgression that appears to have been committed. One question is when the state may rightly punish people, with there being debate about whether it may punish, e.g., those who have broken the law but did so without fault. A second question is why the state may punish anyone at all; given that kidnapping is unjust, why think that imprisonment – which looks an awful lot like it – is just? A third question is how severe a penalty ought to be for a given person, e.g., a slap on the wrist, the death penalty, or something in between? A fourth question (for some reason less frequently addressed by philosophers) is which kinds of penalties the state should mete out, and here we might ask whether fines and

doi:10.1017/S1358246121000400   © The Royal Institute of Philosophy and the contributors 2022

Royal Institute of Philosophy Supplement **91** 2022

imprisonment should be the default modes of punishment or whether some other kinds of punitive burdens would be more appropriate.

For about 250 years in the West, there have been two dominant ways of answering this cluster of questions, which are the protection and retribution theories. As discussed below, the former answers these questions by appealing to respects in which society would be protected from crimes in the future by using penalties principally to incapacitate and deter. In contrast, the latter invokes considerations about the past, contending that just penalties are those that fit the nature of the crime that was already committed, regardless of whether they are likely to bring about any good.

Drawing on some ideas about reconciliation that have been prominent particularly in African cultures and philosophies, I spell out a novel alternative and argue that it neatly avoids objections to the protection and retribution theories and is prima facie plausible in its own right. According to this reconciliation theory, the state normally ought to have offenders reform their characters and compensate their victims in ways the offenders find burdensome, thereby disavowing the crime and tending to foster improved relationships between offenders, their victims, and the broader society. Elsewhere I have addressed the many who have suggested that reconciliation is best understood as an alternative to punishment; I have argued that in fact a *punitive reconciliation* is coherent and also more attractive than forgiveness or restorative justice models of it (Metz, 2022). Although I do draw on some of that reasoning, what I mainly strive to do here is instead to show that a *reconciliatory punishment* is a strong rival to, if not preferable to, much more familiar and influential theories of the justification of state punishment in respect of at least the English-speaking world.

In the following I begin by spelling out the protection and retribution theories, to remind readers of their basics and note some objections to them that have been common to make in the literature (section 2). Then, I spell out the essentials of the reconciliation theory, along the way indicating how it is grounded on ideas about criminal and compensatory justice salient especially in the African tradition but also present in some others in the Global South (section 3). Next, I show that the reconciliation theory avoids the problems facing the protection and retribution theories (section 4). I conclude by noting the need to address some prima facie problems with and gaps in the reconciliation theory that critics are likely to raise, suggesting that this new approach warrants further reflection (section 5).

2. Protection and Retribution Theories and Their Problems

In this section I recount the essentials of the two broad approaches to state punishment that have dominated Western thought for at least two centuries as well as point to well-known problems with them. I do this not merely to highlight the distinctness of the reconciliation theory (in section 3), but also to show that it straightforwardly avoids their problems and so merits consideration as a replacement of them (section 4).

2.1. Protection Theories

The protection approach to state punishment harks back at least to the work of Jeremy Bentham (1830), who argued on utilitarian grounds that penalties ought to be used to prevent crime. Utilitarianism is the view that an action or policy is right insofar as it is expected to produce happiness and reduce happiness in the long run, taking the interests of everyone into account. Bentham argued with care that, while punishment always causes some unhappiness, e.g., for harming the one punished and costing society some resources, it is often justified on balance by virtue of the greater unhappiness it precludes, particularly in the form of preventing crime, but potentially also by virtue of pleasing victims and their families.

How severe the punishment should be is whatever would maximize happiness and minimize unhappiness, with the right types of penalties being whatever would do the same. On this score, imprisonment is often recommended as what would effectively both incapacitate and deter would-be offenders. Ideally a penalty such as prison also ought to reform those disposed to commit crime. However, Bentham thought the most good that a penalty could normally do for society would be to deter the general population from committing crime (1830, chap. 3, bk 1), which means that prison would often be justified even if it would not rehabilitate, as it tends not to do (at least as it has typically been employed in the West). Utilitarians might well hold that current forms of imprisonment are unjust because of conditions such as overcrowding and gang life. However, in principle for them there is probably a way to imprison that would routinely best promote the general welfare.

Utilitarianism is just one instance of a broader protection model of state punishment.[1] According to the latter, a necessary condition for

---

[1] Additional consequentialist, even if not invariably utilitarian, theories include: Braithwaite and Pettit (1990); Smart (1991); Husak (1992); and Shafer-Landau (1996).

state punishment to be justified is that it would have the desirable consequence of preventing crime, centrally by means of deterrence, incapacitation, and reform (again, in practice Western states tend to neglect the latter). By this approach, the right penalty on a given occasion is whichever amount and kind would prevent the most crime with the least degree of harm imposed.

It is important to see that, unlike the utilitarian, one could believe in basic moral rights and also hold a version of protection theory. For example, one might think that punishment is justified by the principles that make sense of using force in self-defence or defence of innocent others (as per Farrell, 1990; Murphy, 1992; Montague, 1995). When a criminal aggresses against others, perhaps he forfeits his rights not to be harmed, at least when inflicting harm on him, such as by putting him in prison, would do the long-term good of protecting innocent parties from becoming victims of crime. Prison would instil fear in would-be offenders, would prevent the actual offender from re-offending, and could (even if in practice it does not) rehabilitate his character. The maximum penalty that would be justified is whatever is no greater than the crime committed, analogous to the way one may not in self-defence shoot someone trying to steal one's toaster oven, while involving the least harm necessary to serve a protective function.

Another way to think of a protection theory of state punishment is in terms of it being a 'forward-looking' account of which penalties are justified and why. In order to know whether to punish a given individual, one must consider what the effects of doing so would be. Specifically, the penalty must be expected to render the one punished unable to commit crime that he would have been inclined to do or to scare off him and other potential offenders from committing crime. In addition, to know precisely how to punish him, one must again look into the future, to ascertain which quantity and quality of penalty would be the least amount required to perform those functions to a maximal extent (perhaps without being any greater than the crime already committed).

Protection theories face at least the following three major objections in the philosophical literature. First, they are known for entailing that it can be just to punish persons who have not culpably committed any crime when it appears unjust to do so. Utilitarianism in principle justifies punishing an innocent person if the long-term results of doing so would be for the greater good. Sometimes that is thought to take an extreme form in which an innocent is framed for a crime so as to deter even worse crimes. Other times it is claimed that utilitarianism justifies what is often called 'strict liability', punishing those who break the law even though it was not at all their fault, e.g., serving alcohol to a minor who produced convincing fake identification, the thought being that such stringency would be likely to deter law-breaking.

The point probably applies to the defensive force version of protectionism, too (even if that is not as frequently recognized). After all, the logic of defensive force is usually taken to allow it to be used against 'innocent threats', those who pose harm to other innocent people for no fault of their own. If someone temporarily loses his mind and is attacking you, for most ethicists you may respond with the least force necessary to protect yourself, despite his innocence. However, so the objection goes, when it comes to punishment, it is nearly always unjust to inflict it on those who were not at all responsible for their actions.

A second objection to protection theories is that they tend to entail that certain overly harsh penalties can be just. That is again a stock problem with utilitarianism, which in principle could approve of, say, torture or the death penalty for those who commit traffic offences such as failing to indicate or speeding, if that would deter people from committing them and thereby save lives in the long run or even if that would promote much less significant benefit, such as convenience, for a much larger number of people.

The logic of defensive force also suggests that certain severe penalties are justified when they in fact seem not to be. If torturing a torturer would prevent more torture, then it would on grounds of defensive force be permissible, supposing that the logic of defensive force indeed justifies punishment. However, the state simply should not be in the business of torturing anyone, at least not as a penalty. Some defensive force theorists are willing to 'bite the bullet' when it comes to the death penalty, contending that, if it would indeed prevent more deaths, it is justified when inflicted on murderers (e.g., Montague, 1995, pp. 135–36, 155; Farrell, 2004). However, it is difficult to accept the natural extension of the point to torturing torturers or raping rapists.

A third objection commonly made to protection theories is the converse of the second, viz., that sometimes they prescribe penalties that are intuitively too light. Both utilitarianism and defensive force theory require minimizing the harm inflicted with punishment, whenever one can prevent no less crime that way than with a greater penalty that is more comparable to the gravity of the crime. For example, if five years in prison were all that it took to prevent a first-degree murderer from killing again as well as to deter others from killing, then no greater penalty would be justified on grounds of protection. Indeed, if no penalty at all were necessary to prevent murder to the degree that some penalty would, then no penalty would be justified. The deep reason that the second and third objections both apply is that a protection theory ties the justification of punishment to the prevention of crime through deterrence, incapacitation, and (ideally) reform, where the results of penalties vary depending on the circumstances.

2.2. Retribution Theories

Since it seems easily able to avoid these three problems with protectionism, many have opted for the other major theory of state punishment, i.e., retributivism or a 'pay back' account. Broadly speaking, a retribution theory maintains that penalties are justified on 'backward-looking' grounds. One is to look into the past to see whether a crime was committed by a responsible agent and how grave it was. If there was a crime culpably done, then there is moral reason for the state to punish the criminal, and the right penalty is whatever is proportionate to the nature of the crime, where that includes the degree of responsibility for it. Hence, if there was no crime or no one responsible for it, no penalty is justified on retributive grounds, and if penalties do not fit the crime (including level of responsibility), either for being disproportionately severe or light, they are also unjustified.

There have been three prominent forms of retributivism. The most influential version is the desert theory, according to which state punishment should serve to give offenders what they deserve for having culpably done wrong. In the way one can positively deserve a reward for having been heroic or a well-paying job for having obtained qualifications, so one can negatively deserve to suffer harm for having mistreated other people. What one deserves is whatever is proportionate to what one did. Desert theory goes back some millennia, with 'an eye for an eye' appearing explicitly in the Hebrew Bible and, amongst classic philosophers, advocated at times in the work of Immanuel Kant.[2]

More recently, philosophers of punishment have articulated and supported backward-looking theories that are not grounded on desert. One is the fairness or fair play theory, according to which criminals gain an unfair advantage relative to law-abiding citizens such that state punishment must be imposed to remove it (e.g., Murphy, 1979; Sadurski, 1985; Davis, 1992). The idea is not that

---

[2]   See Kant (1797/1996, pp. 472–77). More recent works include: von Hirsch (1986); Moore (1997); and Kershnar (2001).

criminals gain financially or materially from their crime, but rather that, in the act of committing a crime, they take a liberty that others have restrained themselves from taking upon obeying the law. Punishment is justified insofar as it removes the extra liberty the criminal took, with the greater the liberty taken, the greater the justified penalty.

A third backward-looking theory that contemporary philosophers have advanced is expressivism or censure theory, which is the view that the state ought to punish offenders so as to convey certain disapproving attitudes or judgements. For instance, upon punishing one who has broken just laws, the state thereby stands up for the victim who should not have been wronged and treats the offender as a responsible agent who misused his moral capacities. For the state not to punish the guilty would constitute a failure to respect the agency of both parties, where the greater the wrong done, the greater the disapproval that must be expressed and hence the greater the penalty should be (e.g., Feinberg, 1970, pp. 95–118; Hampton, 1988; Duff, 2001).

For all three of these retributive theories, punishment need not do any good in the future to be morally justified. Instead, for all three, it is sufficient that the penalty is proportionate to a crime that was (culpably) committed in the past, in stark contrast to the protection theories. However, like the protection theories, the retribution theories are natural allies of imprisonment as a mode of punishment. Even if jail would do nothing in terms of incapacitating the offender (say, because he would commit crimes against other inmates) or deterring others, it could be an appropriate penalty because the harm or restriction of liberty involved would fit the nature of the crime that the offender was responsible for having committed.

Although retributivism appears attractive in virtue of avoiding problems facing protectionism, it is not clear it can avoid all of them and it also faces some problems of its own. One concern common to both broad classes of theories is that they end up justifying penalties that are too harsh. Of course, for the retributivist the punishment must fit the crime, such that it would be wrong to take two eyes for one. However, it still seems to license literally taking a person's single eye if he has wrongfully gouged out someone else's. It is true that this mode of punishment would not be required, so long as some other penalty, say, a length of prison time, were equal in amount of harm. The point, though, is that there is nothing in the logic of retributivism to *forbid* maiming offenders who have maimed others, for that would be one way of imposing a proportionate penalty. Similar remarks apply to torture, rape, whipping, and death; these, too, could well be proportionate to crimes involving those activities, but the state would intuitively be wrong to mete them out.

A second objection to retributive theories is that they seem insufficiently responsive to the character of the offender, in their standard versions focusing exclusively on an offender's actions as opposed to attitudes. On the one hand, it appears that retribution accounts are forced to prescribe the same penalty for a first time offence and for the same offence undertaken a second time after having undergone the initial penalty. If the same crime is performed a second time, the same, proportionate penalty is warranted. However, many have the intuition that a stronger penalty is often appropriate the second time, and not merely because, say, the level of responsibility is greater; for it could in theory have been just as high on the first occasion. On the other hand, sometimes the character of an offender is such as to ground, not an enhanced penalty, but a reduced one. Here, consider those who are remorseful for their misdeeds. There is nothing they can do to change what they wrongfully did, with the fact of having done wrong being all that matters for standard versions of the retribution theory. A person's present attitudes are not relevant to the justification of punishment, and only their past actions are. However, many have the intuition that a somewhat lighter penalty, i.e., mercy is appropriate for someone who accepts the error of his ways, feels bad for what he has done, and would not do it again.

A third objection to retributivism is that, even if it can entail plausible judgements of who should be punished, how much, and in what manner, it offers an incomplete explanation of why state punishment is justified. Surely one major point of a criminal justice system is to reduce crime, so goes the criticism, while retribution theories counterintuitively maintain that the aim of punishment has absolutely nothing to do with that. A criminal justice system is extraordinarily expensive in terms of money and also requires substantial labour from people, where it is difficult to believe that these costs would be worth the mere 'gain' of imposing suffering merely for its own sake and without any expected long-term good.

In the following sections I spell out an alternative theory of state punishment's justification. Although I expect many readers to find it somewhat intuitive in its own right, my principal defence of it will consist of showing that it neatly avoids all the problems mentioned above with the long-standing protection and retribution theories.

3. The Reconciliation Theory

My favoured approach to punishment is grounded on ideas about how people should resolve conflict that have been salient amongst

sub-Saharan African peoples and have informed their moral philosophical thought. Their watchword has been 'reconciliation', which
characteristically involves hearing out those involved in conflict and
then offenders apologizing, making compensation, committing not
to do wrong again, and afterwards rejoining society. Reconciliatory
approaches of various kinds have been used to respond to large-
scale social conflict in African countries such as Sierra Leone,
Rwanda, and South Africa. The latter's Truth and Reconciliation
Commission (TRC) has been particularly influential, famously
having listened to victims' stories, awarded amnesty from criminal
and civil prosecution to offenders if they fully disclosed their apart-
heid-era political crimes, and directed the government to compensate
victims. Although the TRC advanced reconciliation as an alternative
to punishment, and it is often associated with forgiveness, in this
section I suggest that the best sort of reconciliation would be punitive
(while in the next section I provide reason to think that the best sort of
punishment would be reconciliatory).

To begin to see the plausibility of my approach, consider that many
of South Africa's victims of human rights abuses during apartheid
were not satisfied by the TRC and wanted perpetrators to face something that was routinely labeled 'justice' (Hamber, Nageng, and
O'Malley, 2000, pp. 30–32, 37–39; Hamber and Wilson, 2002,
p. 48). After all, torturers and murderers went scot free if they confessed their wrongdoing (they did not even have to express
remorse), a bitter pill to swallow even for those cultures that prize a
reconciliatory approach to resolving conflict. What was missing, I
suggest, was not obviously retribution, but rather a sort of reconciliation that included a proper disavowal of the injustice that had been
done. A desirable kind of reconciliation would be one not merely
aiming to repair relationships by hearing out victims, healing their
wounds, and providing reason to think they would not be revicti-
mized. It would also include offenders feeling bad and placing
burdens on themselves to express their guilt, or at least a public organization expressing the judgement that what they did was wrong
by holding them accountable (beyond the discomfort of recounting
their crimes).

Consider that in cases of conflict between family, friends, and
lovers, that is what many of us want to see – we would like those
who have wronged us to experience some guilt and to atone (cf.
Metz, 2022). And we also typically want those who care about us to
express the judgement that we were mistreated and to distance themselves from those who mistreated us, at least until the wrongdoers
have fully expressed their remorse. Forgiveness should often ideally

come, but only after wrongdoers have undergone some burdens. Something analogous is apt in the sphere of criminal justice. There, too, offenders should accept burdens as a way to show regret for how they behaved and the state should impose burdens as a way to disavow the way they treated their victims.

In the light of these reflections, I submit that the sort of reconciliation the state should promote in the sphere of criminal justice is one that expresses disapproval of the offender's crime by imposing burdens, albeit burdens that are productive in the sense of improving relationships (first advanced in Metz, 2019). Punishment is justified if it serves these dual functions. On the one hand, penalties should be ways for the state to stand up for victims, if not also for offenders to express their misgivings, while, on the other hand, penalties should be of a kind that have offenders compensate their victims and reform their characters so that they will not revictimize anyone, consequent to which it would be reasonable for them to rejoin society.

Something like this approach to sentencing has evidently been adopted at times by the Yoruba people in what is today Nigeria. One philosopher whose ideas are grounded on Yoruba beliefs and practices remarks that 'the reconciliatory factor is lacking in Western theories of law and penology where the offender is punished without making restitutions; and emerging from prison, he is reconciled neither to himself, his victim, nor to society....(W)hen a culprit is punished, such is done with the view to fine-tuning the character of the said offender in line with the communalistic ethos of the Yoruba culture' (Balogun, 2018, pp. 246, 311). Another philosopher doing similar work also reports, apparently approvingly, that those who had committed crimes that 'do not threaten the existence of society' were often punished in Yoruba communities by 'being forced to labor on community projects or those of their victims in reparation/restitution for the loss caused' (Bewaji, 2016, p. 164).

Rwanda is another African country in which a broadly reconciliatory and punitive approach has been adopted, specifically in response to the 1994 genocide. The country had flirted with the idea of a *Fonds d'indemnisation* (FIND), a compensation fund into which those convicted of genocide were supposed to pay (Bornkamm, 2012). Although that did not materialize, the famous Gagaca courts did sentence more than 100,000 offenders to perform community service (Penal Reform International, 2010).

Colombia is a third society in the Global South that has considered a reconciliatory approach to sentencing. Like Rwanda it has not done so in the context of everyday crimes but instead as a measure of transitional justice, specifically in response to the long-standing conflict between the government and the FARC guerrillas. As part of what was titled the 'Final Agreement' of 24 November 2016 (Government of the Republic of Colombia, 2016), which was meant to provide a definitive framework for peace between the Colombian state and the rebels, victim compensation is central. As to who is to do the compensating, the agreement proposes that it should be offenders in the first instance, with use of the compelling phrase 'restorative sanctions' (Government of the Republic of Colombia, 2016, p. 175): 'In the context of these (reparation) plans, stress will be laid on acknowledging the responsibility of the state, the FARC-EP, paramilitaries and any other group, organisation or institution that caused harm or injury during the conflict' (Government of the Republic of Colombia, 2016, p. 191; see also pp. 137, 145, 189). Restorative sanctions are to advance 'the overall aim of realising the rights of victims and consolidating peace. They will need to have the greatest restorative and reparative function in relation to the harm caused' (Government of the Republic of Colombia, 2016, p. 174). Included amongst a list of such penalties are repairing infrastructure, building houses and schools, engaging in waste disposal, growing crops, fixing roads, and improving access to water/electricity (Government of the Republic of Colombia, 2016, pp. 183–84).

Now, so far as I am aware, no contemporary society has been implementing the reconciliation theory systematically in the context of criminal justice. The 'traditional' Yoruba had also adopted deterrence and incapacitation measures (Bewaji, 2016, pp. 44, 175; Balogun, 2018, pp. 311–12), while the more 'modern' Nigerian state has not adopted anything reconciliatory. Rwanda used community service systematically only as a transitional justice measure, not for day to day criminal justice. And then Colombia also has proposed restorative sanctions only in the context of transitional justice, and has not even implemented them; so far as I have been told,[3] they remain at the level of policy, not practice. Furthermore, there has been no thorough philosophical exposition and defence of a reconciliatory approach that would prescribe it as the central, if not sole, justification of state punishment in a 21st century society. That is my aim.

To continue the articulation of my favoured reconciliation theory of state punishment, note that it includes a 'backward-looking'

---

[3] By Colombian participants in the Conference on Transitional Justice and Distributive Justice: Comparative Lessons from Colombia and South Africa; see note 6 below.

condition, and specifically appeals to elements of the expressive theory sketched above. However, reconciliation differs from that form of retribution in two important ways.

First, where it is possible for the burdens placed on an offender to do some good in the form of repairing relationships, they should. Recall that the retributive model does not 'look forward' in any respect; all that matters is that the penalties match the crimes that were committed, which tends to justify having people waste away in prison. In contrast, for the reconciliation theory, if penalties could compensate and reform, they must take that form.[4]

For examples of burdensome compensation, perhaps someone who has cheated on his taxes should be made to perform some dull tasks for the state revenue service. Maybe a person who has robbed a household should wear a uniform and serve as a neighbourhood-watch guard for a time. Possibly someone who has unjustifiably taken the life of a breadwinner should farm with his hands, providing sustenance to the victim's family. For examples of burdensome reform, a court should often prescribe mandatory therapy to get to the root of what caused the mistreatment of others, something that would be time-consuming and psychologically difficult. Consider as well penalties meant to instil empathy and an awareness of the consequences of actions, such as a judge sentencing drunk drivers to work in a morgue. Finally, there are the points that sometimes the hardship of punishment can itself be a way for offenders to appreciate how they have mistreated their victims, as well as that the guilt consequent to moral reform would also be a foreseeable burden that offenders should undergo.

There are admittedly some situations in which compensation would be impossible to effect, say, where an offender has killed his victim; no burden placed on him would be sufficient to make up for the harm done. There are also cases where reform would happen on its own, with the offender having had a proverbial 'come to Jesus' moment; no burden placed on him would be necessary to change the offender's character and thereby prevent him from doing any further harm. Even so, by the present account, the need of the state – and ideally of the offender – to disavow the crime would remain, continuing to justify punishment. That being said, where punishment would do some good in the forms of compensation or reform, it should, thus making a reconciliatory approach different from a retributive model.

---

[4] The following examples have been cribbed from Metz (2019, pp. 126–27).

A second respect in which reconciliation differs from retribution concerns which degree of burden constitutes an appropriate disavowal.[5] For standard versions of retribution, whether the desert theory, fairness theory, or the expressive theory, punishment must be proportionate to the crime that was committed. For those theories, there is some amount of harm or wrong done to victims, perhaps discounted by the degree of the offender's responsibility for it, and punishment should exactly match that amount. In contrast, my approach to reconciliation prescribes penalties that track the crime, in the sense that the worse the crime, the greater the penalty, but without involving the same degree of harm/wrong as the crime. Instead, it recommends a range of penalties somewhat below that amount. For example, suppose we assigned cardinal numbers to the gravity of a first-degree murder with 1000 (in the case of full responsibility), a theft with 100, and jaywalking with 1. Then, instead of punishing such a murder with a penalty weighted 1000, the appropriate penalty would be in a range of, say, 750-500, and theft would similarly be punished with 75-50 instead of 100. Offenders would invariably receive a sentence that is less than retributivists think is deserved or fair, for instance.

Although my aim in this section is to spell out the reconciliation theory, and not so much to defend it, I do note here one major motivation for favouring backward-looking penalties that track the crime but are not proportionate to it. It is that almost no societies in fact impose proportionate penalties. In jurisdictions that base punishment at least in part on the nature of the crime, none so far as I know seeks out a penalty equal in severity to, say, torture.

Having discussed similarities and differences between the reconciliation and retribution models, I now do the same for the reconciliation and protection models. Like the forward-looking theories, the reconciliation model has us look into the future to consider which penalties are justified. Like them, it holds that one reason to impose punishment is normally to prevent crime.

However, it differs from the protection theories in some crucial ways. As noted above, the reconciliatory approach does not take crime prevention to be a necessary condition for a penalty to be justified. Where no sort of punishment is expected to mend broken relationships, the reconciliatory approach deems punishment to be justified nonetheless because of the need to disavow the fact that relationships were broken in the first place.

---

[5] Here I do a bit more to flesh out a brief suggestion from Hampton (1988, p. 137).

Another salient difference between reconciliation and protection is the sort of good that should come from the imposition of penalties. While they both seek to prevent crime, the protection model makes deterrence and incapacitation central, whereas the reconciliation model does not. Instead, insofar as the latter prescribes doing what is likely to prevent further wrongdoing, it would have a court do what is expected to reform the offender's character, which is only one (and often secondary) element of the protection theory.

For a third key difference, remember that the good the reconciliation model seeks to promote is not merely to prevent crime (specifically in the form of offender rehabilitation), but also to make up for crime that has already taken place. A central reason for imposing one penalty rather than another is that it is expected to help compensate victims. The best sort of burden to place on an offender is often labour that would improve his victim's quality of life. Of course, it would be time consuming to oversee that kind of punishment; it is much easier simply to put someone in jail. However, that does not make imprisonment just, let alone the ideal.

Summing up, note how considerations of reconciliation are relevant to answering the cluster of four questions pertaining to the justification of state punishment. First off, who is it that should be punished by the state? In the first instance, the answer is those who have failed to relate to other people or the state in the right sort of way, requiring them to make amends. Second, why should the state be in the business of inflicting penalties on people? Roughly speaking, the answer is to express disapproval of the crime by getting the offender to *clean up* his own mess, *contra* imposing punishment for reasons of retribution or incapacitation, and to clean up *his own mess*, in contrast to doing so for reasons of general deterrence. Third, how severe should a penalty be? The answer is that it must track the crime in the sense of be a function of how grave it was, but that it should not be proportionate to it. Fourth, which kinds of penalties should the state mete out? The answer is usually not prison and fines, if a state has the resources to avoid them, since these are unlikely to compensate victims and reform offenders; instead, the norm should be productive burdens such as labour that is expected to improve victims' quality of life and offenders' character.

Although I hope that the reader finds this theory to be prima facie attractive, it is in the following section where I really make the case for it. I now show that the objections to protection and retribution theories are plausibly avoided by the reconciliation theory, giving us reason to consider it as a replacement.

4. Advantages of the Reconciliation Theory

I have in other work argued that the reconciliation theory should be found attractive by those who think that we have a dignity at least in large part because of our relational nature (see Metz, 2019). If what gives us a superlative non-instrumental value is substantially our capacity to relate positively or cohesively (an idea salient in the African philosophical tradition, but having a greater resonance, in at least the Global South), then it is natural to hold that the aims of punishment should be both to express disapproval when that value is degraded and to mend broken relationships. In contrast, I here aim to show that even those without such foundational moral commitments should find much attractive about a reconciliatory approach to sentencing, insofar as it avoids widely recognized problems with the rival protection and retribution models. In this section I demonstrate that the reconciliation theory articulated in section 3 avoids the objections to the theories discussed in section 2.

Recall the problems facing protection theories such as utilitarianism and defensive force accounts. One was that they seem to justify punishment of the innocent, roughly since, for these views, responsibility for wrongful harm is not necessary for one to be liable for punishment. Utilitarianism naturally supports strict liability, while the logic of defensive force permits it to be used against innocent threats. In contrast, there is intuitively no need to reconcile with someone who has not culpably broken a just law. If someone is truly not responsible for having caused or threatened harm to another, then no disavowal and moral reform are warranted. While compensation could be called for, the state need not force an offender to make it in a manner that is intentionally burdensome for him, which would be apt only in the case of someone responsible for wrongdoing.

A second problem with the protection theories is that they tend to prescribe certain extremely severe penalties that seem impermissible. That is a standard problem for utilitarianism, which is well known for entailing that severe burdens should be placed on an individual if it would produce trivial benefits for many others. In addition, given that the logic of defensive force permits one to kill in order to save innocent life, say, because the aggressor has forfeited his right to life, it appears also to permit the state to torture a torturer in order to prevent the innocent from being tortured. However, the reconciliation theory does not permit penalties that are overly harsh. On the one hand, disavowing crimes requires penalties for them to be within a certain range that tracks, but is less than proportionate to, their gravity.

That would forbid the death penalty for traffic infractions, on the one hand, and also normally rule out killing killers and torturing torturers, on the other. Furthermore, death and torture are not instances of productive burdens; they are not forms of labour that would serve the functions of compensating victims or reforming offenders' character. Hence, the backward-looking and forward-looking elements of reconciliatory sentencing do not seem to permit intuitively extreme penalties.

The third problem with implementing punishment in order to deter or incapacitate (or even reform without consideration of the need to disavow the past crime) is that sometimes overly light penalties, or no penalties at all, for serious crimes would be sufficient to produce the relevant consequences. All protection theories require minimizing the amount of harm inflicted on an offender, if sufficient to protect society. However, the principle that the more serious the crime, the more severe the penalty should be looks compelling. That need not entail a system of proportionate sentencing, but instead is consistent with one that tracks the nature of the crime in the manner of the reconciliatory approach spelled out here. Disavowing unjust ways of treating victims with a penalty that falls within a certain range that is pegged to what would be proportionate but is less than that sidesteps the problem of insufficiently harsh sentences as it applies to protection theories.

Turning to retributivism, it is open to its adherents to maintain that anything less than a proportionate penalty is unjust, i.e., to argue that the reconciliation theory retains the problem facing protection theories regarding overly light penalties for serious crimes. However, I believe in fact that retributivism must be jettisoned if we want to avoid the implication that killing, torturing, raping, and maiming are just penalties when imposed on (certain) killers, torturers, rapists, and maimers. Recall the objection that retributivism permits a literal eye for an eye. Weighty disavowal of egregious behaviour seems possible with penalties that are somewhat less than proportionate, whereas it would also be apt for those guilty of such horrific crimes to labour in strenuous ways expected to make their victims better off. Furthermore, consider the point that imposing such sentences arguably expresses, not just disavowal of the offender's misdeeds, but also that he is without a dignity, which is an unjust kind of treatment (see Hampton, 1988, pp. 136–37).

Turn, now, to the second objection to retributivism I had mentioned, that it is utterly unresponsive to an offender's character. Retributive theories have little leeway for prescribing differential penalties to a first-time offender and a second- or third-time offender;

supposing he has committed the same crime, the same proportionate penalty is required. The natural thing to say, however, is that the second- or third-time offender has not learned his lesson, and so merits a greater penalty, which the retributive theory cannot easily make sense of but which the reconciliation theory can. Working within the range of tracking penalties, it would be open to a judge adopting the reconciliatory model to prescribe ones more severe for those who have demonstrated recalcitrance.

The flipside of the retributive focus on a penalty proportionate to a past misdeed is the inability to impose a lighter penalty in the face of moral reform that has taken place after the crime but before the imposition of a sentence. For many, some kind of penalty remains appropriate, again in the ballpark of the severity of the crime, but one that is less than what would be apt for a shameless offender who lacks remorse. Again, working within the range of tracking penalties, it would be open to a judge to prescribe lighter ones for, and hence display mercy to, those who have atoned on their own.

Finally, the third problem with retributivism above is that it cannot account well for the intuition that one proper function of a criminal justice system is crime prevention. Some kind of expected benefit to society seems essential to justify the enormous expense and time of a criminal justice system, but retributivism is a strictly backward-looking theory; for it, the only reason to punish is to impose a penalty proportionate to the crime that was committed in the past (and hence is deserved, fair, etc). In contrast, the reconciliation theory includes forward-looking elements, prescribing the placement of burdens on offenders that, when possible, will do some good in the form of rehabilitating offenders so that they do not re-offend and of compensating victims so that in the ideal case the effects of the crime are nullified. Those benefits plausibly make it worth setting up a punishment institution, beyond the admitted importance of the state distancing itself from crimes that have occurred and expressing support for victims.

5. Conclusion: Disadvantages of the Reconciliation Theory to Be Considered

My aim is not, with a single essay, to convince anyone to change her mind about the justification of state punishment, but rather to articulate a plausible alternative to the two approaches that have dominated Western thinking for more than two centuries. Drawing on ideas about reconciliation that have been prominent in parts of the

Global South, I have advanced a novel theory of who should be punished by the state, why, how much, and in what ways that I submit should not be dismissed as a rival to the protection and retribution theories. In a nutshell, the right candidates for punishment are those who should atone for their misdeeds by undergoing burdens that disavow the way they treated their victims by tracking the crime and that in the best case have the effects of compensating the victims and rehabilitating the offenders.

Being a new approach, it naturally could use further development and consideration. For example, while I have provided reason to think that the logic of reconciliation rules out punishing someone for the sake of general deterrence, i.e., instilling fear amongst would-be offenders in society, does it permit punishing someone for the sake of special deterrence, that is, instilling fear in him so that he would not commit the crime again? Is the only justifiable mechanism to prevent crime the imposition of a burdensome sort of rehabilitation, or can scaring the offender also be a way to get him to 'clean up his own mess'?

For a second topic that deserves reflection, what should the state do if an offender refuses to engage in the requisite sort of punitive labour? Suppose he will not attend the prescribed therapy or do the work that would direct funds to his victim. What resources does the reconciliation theory have to address this problem? Here is one strategy worth considering. It might be that issuing threats and, if necessary, imposing hardships on this recalcitrant offender would be justified, not as a form of punishment, rather as a form of defensive force. In failing to submit to the appropriate penalties, the offender would be committing a new offence, where a threat of, say, indefinite detainment until he complies might be justified as a kind of non-punitive coercion. If the reader is inclined to hold that it would count as a kind of penalty, that need not mean that the reconciliation theory is incoherent for including two different sorts. After all, no one charged the TRC with incoherence when it offered human rights violators amnesty from any punishment if they fully confessed, but retributive penalties if they did not.

A third issue that arises is how well the reconciliation theory of how a judge should sentence offenders fits with our best understanding of which kinds of criminal laws a legislator should pass. The kind of thing that should be criminalized by a Parliament should naturally be the kind of thing that should be punished by a court of law. Now, which sort of behaviour merits a reconciliatory response? Presumably not purely self-regarding actions, i.e., those that do not directly harm or interfere with others and that instead harm or degrade the person performing them alone. If there is no victim, then there is no need to inflict a penalty that would compensate a victim or would disavow the way she was treated. I, for one, find it a welcome implication of the reconciliation theory that actions such as drug use, which need not be discordant in respect of others, should be legal, even if they merit other responses from the state such as education and treatment centres. However, those who believe it can be justifiable to punish people merely because of the way they have treated themselves will disagree.

Fourth, there are admittedly real concerns about how practical it would be to implement the reconciliation theory on a daily basis. Although, as I pointed out, something like it appears to have been accepted by some Yoruba clans in Nigeria and as a transitional justice measure in Rwanda, that is different from using it routinely in a mass society. However, perhaps those currently employed as corrections officials, parole officers, and counsellors could be repurposed to ensure that offenders do the work of changing their beliefs, desires, and emotions that led to the crime as well as the work of doing what would make their victims better off. Where that kind of shift is not feasible, and plea bargaining combined with prison time are unavoidable due to the enormous numbers of criminals in the system, at least the reconciliation theory would plausibly tell us that a certain measure of injustice is present, providing a picture of to what a state should aspire.[6]

University of Pretoria
th.metz@up.ac.za

[6] Thanks to Julian Baggini for having shared written comments on a previous draft of this essay. For their oral input on some of these ideas, I am also grateful to participants in three gatherings: the Conference on Transitional Justice and Distributive Justice: Comparative Lessons from Colombia and South Africa, organized by the South African Institute for Advanced Constitutional, Public, Human Rights and International Law in 2018; a KJuris: King's Legal Philosophy Workshop, organized by the King's College London Dickson Poon School of Law in 2020; and the London Lectures Series: A Philosophers' Manifesto, organized by the Royal Institute of Philosophy in 2020. I have not been able to answer in this draft all the important queries I received from these colleagues, but look forward to continuing the debate in future work.

References

Oladele Balogun, *African Philosophy: Reflections on Yoruba Metaphysics and Jurisprudence* (Lagos: Xcel Publishers, 2018).

Jeremy Bentham, 'The Rationale of Punishment', (1830), https://www.laits.utexas.edu/poltheory/bentham/rp/.

John Ayotunde Bewaji, *The Rule of Law and Governance in Indigenous Yoruba Society* (Lanham, MD: Lexington Books, 2016).

Paul Christoph Bornkamm, *Rwanda's Gacaca Courts: Between Retribution and Reparation* (Oxford: Oxford University Press, 2012).

John Braithwaite and Philip Pettit, *Not Just Deserts* (Oxford: Clarendon Press, 1990).

Michael Davis, *To Make the Punishment Fit the Crime* (Boulder, CO: Westview Press, 1992).

R. A. Duff, *Punishment, Communication and Community* (Oxford: Oxford University Press, 2001).

Daniel Farrell, 'The Justification of Deterrent Violence', *Ethics* (1990) 100, 301–17.

Daniel Farrell, 'Capital Punishment and Societal Self-Defense'. In William Aiken and John Haldane (eds), *Philosophy and Its Public Role* (Charlottesville, VA: Imprint Academic, 2004), 241–56.

Joel Feinberg, *Doing and Deserving* (Princeton: Princeton University Press, 1970).

Government of the Republic of Colombia, 'Final Agreement to End the Armed Conflict and Build a Stable and Lasting Peace', (2016), http://especiales.presidencia.gov.co/Documents/20170620-dejacion-armas/acuerdos/acuerdo-final-ingles.pdf.

Brandon Hamber, Dineo Nageng, and Gabriel O'Malley, '"Telling It Like It Is…."; Understanding the Truth and Reconciliation Commission from the Perspective of Survivors', *Psychology in Society* (2000) 26, 18–42.

Brandon Hamber and Richard Wilson, 'Symbolic Closure through Memory, Reparation and Revenge in Post-conflict Societies', *Journal of Human Rights* (2002) 1, 35–53.

Jean Hampton, 'The Retributive Idea'. In Jean Hampton and Jeffrie Murphy (eds), *Forgiveness and Mercy* (Cambridge: Cambridge University Press, 1988), 111–61.

Douglas Husak, 'Why Punish the Deserving?' *Nous* (1992) 26, 447–64.

Immanuel Kant, 'The Metaphysics of Morals', Mary Gregor (trans.). In Mary Gregor (ed.), *Immanuel Kant: Practical*

Philosophy (Cambridge: Cambridge University Press, 1996), 353–603 (originally published in 1797).

Stephen Kershnar, *Desert, Retribution, and Torture* (Lanham, MD: University Press of America, Inc, 2001).

Thaddeus Metz, 'Reconciliation as the Aim of a Criminal Trial: *Ubuntu*'s Implications for Sentencing', *Constitutional Court Review* (2019) 9, 113–34.

Thaddeus Metz, 'Why Reconciliation Requires Punishment but Not Forgiveness'. In Krisanna Scheiter and Paula Satne (eds), *Conflict and Resolution: The Ethics of Forgiveness, Revenge, and Punishment* (Cham: Springer, 2022).

Philip Montague, *Punishment as Societal-Defense* (Lanham, MD: Rowman & Littlefield, 1995).

Michael Moore, *Placing Blame* (Oxford: Oxford University Press, 1997).

Jeffrie Murphy, *Retribution, Justice, and Therapy* (Dordrecht: D. Reidel Publishing Company, 1979).

Jeffrie Murphy, *Retribution Reconsidered* (Dordrecht: Kluwer Academic Publishers, 1992).

Penal Reform International, *Eight Years on...A Record of Gacaca Monitoring in Rwanda*, (2010), https://cdn.penalreform.org/wp-content/uploads/2013/05/WEB-english-gacaca-rwanda-5.pdf.

Wojciech Sadurski, *Giving Desert Its Due* (Dordrecht: D. Reidel Publishing Company, 1985).

Russ Shafer-Landau, 'The Failure of Retributivism', *Philosophical Studies* (1996) 82, 289–316.

J. C. Smart, 'Utilitarianism and Punishment', *Israel Law Review* (1991) 25, 360–75.

Andrew von Hirsch, *Past or Future Crimes* (Manchester: Manchester University Press, 1986).

How Should Liberal Democratic Governments Treat Conscientious Disobedience as a Response to State Injustice?: A Proposal

BRIAN WONG AND JOSEPH CHAN

Abstract

This paper suggests that liberal democratic governments adopt a *reconciliatory* approach to conscientious disobedience. Central to this approach is the view – independent of whether conscientious disobedience is always morally justified – that conscientious disobedience is normatively *distinct* from other criminal acts with similar effects, and such distinction is *worthy* of acknowledgment by public apparatus and actors. The prerogative applies to both civil and uncivil instances of disobedience, as defined and explored in the paper. Governments and courts ought to take the normative distinction seriously and treat the conscientious disobedients in a more *lenient* way than they treat ordinary criminals. A comprehensive legislative scheme for governments to deal with prosecution, sentencing, and imprisonment of the conscientious disobedients will be proposed, with the normative and practical benefits of such an approach discussed in detail.

1. Introduction

Recent years have seen many large-scale political protests in different parts of the world. They have taken place not just under authoritarian regimes such as Belarus and Myanmar, but also in states conventionally deemed to be liberal democracies. From the Black Lives Matter protests remonstrating police brutality in the United States throughout 2020, to the Extinction Rebellion protests that took Britain by storm in 2019, to the Gilets Jaunes protests in France that began in 2018, it is clear that liberal democracies have seen their fair share of protests, directed towards problems ranging from public apathy towards climate change and police brutality. None of the above protests strived for revolutionary regime change as such. They had a limited goal of changing a supposedly unjust decision, policy or practice, reforming a flawed institution, and/or transforming public attitudes. Although many of these protests were largely peaceful and civil, they occasionally turned violent – but even so, the participants involved in violence were not, in a majority of instances, armed with tools of destructive force.

Political protests not only trigger huge political tensions and controversies in societies; they also generate many moral questions for both protestors and governments alike. Much of the contemporary literature on political disobedience in recent decades has focused mainly on the ethics of disobedience, exploring the questions of what the individual protestor may or may not do in protests. A few exceptions in recent years aside[1], relatively little attention has been paid to the question of government action: How should governments treat who those who transgressed the law in political protests? In particular, what should governments do with regard to prosecution, sentencing, imprisonment in cases of legal transgression?

Our paper confines legal transgression to what we call *conscientious disobedience*, which can manifest in both civil and uncivil forms. Disobedience is understood to be a violation of law, often resulting in disruption to law and order. Disobedience is *conscientious* if it is motivated by what the disobedients perceive as state injustice, which includes the state's *direct* violation of basic rights or freedoms, such as racial injustice, policy brutality, or political disenfranchisement, as well as *indirect* injustice such as the state's failure to rectify long-term social injustice.

Our paper recommends that liberal democratic governments adopt a *reconciliatory* approach to conscientious disobedience. Central to this approach is the view that there is a *normative distinction* between the conscientious disobedients and those who commit ordinary crimes.

For the purpose of this paper, we take 'normative distinction' to denote a morally significant difference – one that affects the way we should appraise the moral quality of the actions and/or characters of the agents involved. More generally, normative statements involve value judgments or rules of behaviour – they make claims about how people or institutions should act, and whether their actions are appropriate or justified.

The disobedients have experienced substantial injustice under the coercive state apparatus or systematic structural injustice. If the disobedients turn to unarmed violence, more likely than not they do so as a last resort to resist the police's actions to disperse them away

---

[1]   For examples of such works, see Smith (2013); Lefkowitz (2007); Shock (2015); Scheuerman (2020) and Smith and Brownlee (2017).

from the streets they occupy for the purposes of protest. The disobedients often wield force not disproportionate to the injustice they have suffered. Of course, there must be violent acts that must not be given sympathetic treating. Our paper does not need to presuppose that conscientious disobedience is always morally justified, still less to argue that citizens have a *right* to it. We are sympathetic to, but will not defend, the view that conscientious disobedience is sometimes justified. Instead, we argue only for a weaker claim: justified or not, conscientious disobedience is normatively *distinct* from other criminal acts with similar effects, and such distinction is *worthy* of acknowledgment by public apparatus and actors.

Governments and courts ought to take the normative distinction seriously and treat the conscientious disobedients in a more *lenient* way than they treat ordinary criminals. We propose a legislative scheme for governments to deal with prosecution, sentencing, and imprisonment of the conscientious disobedients. In our proposal, the scheme is to be adopted by the government based on a legislation debated in society and passed in the legislature, so that the scheme has a political mandate so to speak. One strong advantage of this scheme is that it will take the heat away from the court room as it were, in the sense that judges can avoid as much as possible making judicial decisions on the basis of their own controversial political or moral beliefs. The prosecutors are the officials to decide whether or not to initiate prosecution using the scheme. The adoption and implementation of the scheme is thus not a purely legalistic process but also a political and moral one.

We shall explain the scheme and its philosophical rationale in the main sections. In the second section, we explain why conscientious disobedience is normatively distinct from ordinary crimes. In the third section, we explain why governments and courts should take seriously the normative distinctness of conscientious disobedience. In the fourth section, we outline a legislative scheme for governments to treat the conscientious disobedience in legal proceedings. In the fifth section, we consider two objections to our approach. The sixth section concludes.

Before we move on, we want to note here that the considerations that might motivate governments to adopt the reconciliatory approach apply *primarily* to liberal democracies, as opposed to authoritarian regimes. Liberal democratic governments under the pressure of public opinions do occasionally admit that they have made serious mistakes. They understand that their legitimacy is partially based on the people's willing endorsement, and that a mass political protest of a prolonged period of time might signal a kind of government's failure that eventually erodes their legitimacy. In addition, in liberal democratic states, the rule of law must be based on respect for human rights and civil liberties, and so governments would have incentives to prefer reform to repression as a response to political protests. More often than not, a stringent legalistic approach to punishment would harden political divisions and tensions, making reforms difficult to carry out within parliamentary or civil society settings. All these considerations seem to motivate liberal democratic governments to consider a reconciliatory approach to handling the conscientious disobedients. These prudential considerations, however, cannot easily apply to authoritarian states, which typically refuse to admit state injustice or tolerate citizens' serious political challenges through open and unfettered competition at the electoral and sub-electoral levels.

2. Why conscientious disobedience is normatively distinct

We follow Smith and Brownlee in defining *conscientious disobedience* as 'nonconformity with a law, injunction, or formal directive for principled motives to communicate convictions to particular addressees' (Smith and Brownlee, 2017). This term serves as an umbrella term that encompasses *civil disobedience and uncivil disobedience*, and conscientious objection.

2.1 Civil Disobedience

To see the normative distinctness of conscientious disobedience, we shall first look at its more common and widely discussed form, namely, civil disobedience. Let us begin with Rawls' relatively comprehensive, archetypal definition of civil disobedience. An act of civil disobedience is a (1) *public*, (2) *non-violent*, (3) *principled*, (4) *political* act (5) *contrary to the law*, (6) *with the aim of bringing about a change in the law or policies of the government* (Rawls, 1971, p. 364).

(1)   denotes the *publicity* condition – an act of civil disobedience must be fundamentally capable of communicating a clear and unambiguous message to *the public*, with apparent visibility and publicisation of the act in question.

(2)   constitutes the *non-violence* condition: civil disobedience must refrain from force, violence, and physical forms of disruption and undermining to the wellbeing of third parties. Per Rawls'

original interpretation, civil disobedients ought to be cognizant of the 'civilly disobedient quality of [their] acts, [which would be undermined by...] any interference with the civil liberties of others' (Rawls, 1971, p. 321).

(3)   comprises the *principledness* condition. Individuals who partake in civil disobedience must do so with the intention of challenging unjust laws, structures, and tenets on the basis of sincere commitments (Delmas and Brownlee, 2021). Principled disobedients are driven by collective, societal interests, as opposed to individual, ego-centric gains. Recent discussion has raised the view that civil disobedience need not be selfless – *per* Delmas (in Ferzan and Alexander, 2019, pp. 167-88), oppressed groups could derive much from their continued resistance against injustice, though we are of the view self-centric gains should by no means be the *dominant reason* for which individuals carry out their acts.

(4)   consists of the *political* condition in civil disobedience. Disobedience must be political in kind – *grounded in the political values in the society*, individuals employ civil disobedience as a means of securing political and institutional reform, with an apparent focus on the distribution of resources, rights, and power under existing sociopolitical structures. In contrast, conscientious objection – as a refusal to conform with a legal prerogative or stipulation – tends to be more *private in kind*: *grounded in the individual's personal values or faith*, individuals conscientiously object in order to avoid the requirements or associations with particular roles.

(5)   constitutes the *transgressive* condition. Trivially, civil disobedience requires *some* law to be broken, in order for it to be differentiated from mere acts of public protest or criticisms. Legal violations – of unjust protocol, rules, and regulations – are part and parcel of civil disobedience Some theorists include additional stipulations – that only laws whose transgression is *absolutely necessary* for *effective* and *proportionate civil disobedience* should be broken. Under this view, individuals are obliged to accept both a) the consequences and penalties associated with their legal violations (Rawls, 1971, p. 322) and b) the importance of (accepting and abiding by) laws that are not targeted by their critique, to the extent that such laws exist. Call this the *thin* variant of 5).

On the other hand, others are skeptical of both the moral imperative of agents to respect the legal system in which they carry out their disobedience (Lyons, 1996, pp. 33-34), as well as the extent to which accepting the legal system at large is mandated on grounds of political legitimacy (as opposed to prudential reasons) (Sharp, 2012). In other words, agents are permitted to evade their legal responsibilities under this view. Call this the *thick* variant of 5). We will return to whether the *thin or thick* variants are to be preferred, in subsequent sections.

Under the *transformative* condition (6) – civil disobedience should seek to introduce transformations to governmental structures and official policies, with the operative description being one of *reform*. As Singer describes it, civil disobedience is a 'plea for reconsideration' (Singer, 1973, pp. 84-92). Habermas terms it a 'symbolic [...] appeal to the capacity for reason and sense of justice of the majority' (Habermas, 1985, p. 99).

There exist plentiful defenses of civil disobedience that we shall not relitigate in detail here. Some accounts invoke the principle that disobedients are offering an active critique of the law, which paves the way for the law to improve upon its fidelity to principles of procedural and substantive justice underpinning it (Dworkin, 1978). Others argue that the selfless and publicly oriented motivation of civil disobedience ought to render it morally permissible, especially if conducted under systems engaged in systemic, sustained violations of human rights and civil liberties (Delmas in Ferzan and Alexander, 2019, pp. 167-69). We are sympathetic to the view that civil disobedience as understood above is normally justifiable from a moral point of view. Yet our present aim is to support the weaker position that civil disobedience is normatively distinct from ordinary crimes committed with non-civil disobedience-related motivations. It is easy to see that ordinary crimes do not meet criteria of (1) publicity, (3) principledness, (4) politically grounded, and (6) aiming at political transformation. All these features convey significant values commonly shared in liberal democracies.[2]

2.2 From civil to uncivil disobedience

The question is thus as follows – what are we to make of disobedience that is *uncivil*?

---

[2] We do not, however, grant that individuals have a right to civil disobedience Individuals may possess strong reasons to wish to engage in civil disobedience – though they must also be open to a range of potential consequences and sanctions that subsequently bind them.

Given we accept that civil disobedience is indeed normatively distinct from criminal behaviours performed with ulterior motives, could we extend this *normative distinction* to apply between criminal acts and acts of *uncivil* disobedience? To offer a broad preview of the argument we shall make, we do not seek to *justify uncivil disobedience*, nor is such *justification* necessary for our account to hold. We are of the view that not only *civil disobedience*, but also *some forms of uncivil disobedience* are worthy of distinction from ordinary, criminal acts. More specifically, acts that satisfy criteria (1), (3), (4), and (6), whilst failing to meet the *non-violence* criterion and engaging in legal transgressions that extend beyond those deemed justified under the thin variant of 5), should and can still be deemed as *normatively distinct* from other acts of violent legal transgressions: they amount to instances of uncivil disobedience.[3]

Prior to delving into the exposition of why uncivil disobedience is distinct from ordinary criminality, let us establish the characteristics of the cases we are discussing here. Recall that these cases satisfy the *publicity, principledness, politically grounded*, and *transgressive* conditions outlined above, though they *may* fail to be a) *non-violent* and b) *transformative* in nature.

On the former, uncivil disobedience may feature *violence* – here, taken to denote the use of physical force causing or likely to cause injury to the *physical persons* and *property* of individual agents. Instances of violence in disobedience could range from mild physical confrontations and altercations to arson and destruction of public property. Such violence may arise as a part of more general episodes and movements undergirded by and conforming largely with tenets of civil disobedience. Alternatively, however, disobedience-centric violence may also be enacted on a standalone basis – e.g. limited violence is employed by disobedients as the sole and predominant means of securing their end goals.

As for the latter, we posit that uncivil disobedience can also be *non-transformative*. To be clear, there exists a range of actions that can be undertaken with transformation in mind – even if transformation is not realistically achievable within the short- to medium-term – that is, uncivil disobedients may adopt acts that seem to be practically futile in generating results, yet nevertheless be *aimed* at transformation. With that said, we would suggest that uncivil disobedience *can* also be aimed purely at registering discontent towards unjust laws – transformation need not be an objective that undergirds such actions. Delmas notes that, 'But even where there is no hope

---

[3]   Lim terms this the 'Differentiation Demand' in Lim (2021).

of socio-political reform or moral suasion, uncivil disobedience may still have intrinsic value insofar as it constitutes a meaningful expression of political solidarity and assertion of agency in the face of injustice' (Delmas, 2018, p. 63).

The argument that disobedience must be directed towards the securing of reforms from within the system, presupposes that the legal and political institutions are indeed open to the processes of protest and appeal invoked by disobedients. Yet where such institutions remain unmovable and intransigent in face of persuasion, disobedience may be warranted as a form of passive resistance against injustice. Democratic regimes, too, could be obstinate in face of movements seeking empowerment and rectificatory justice – consider, for instance, the violence championed by Malcolm X and adopted by forces such as the Black Panther Party against white-supremacist groups and the political disenfranchisement confronting African-Americans in 20th century America (Shelby, 2005); or alternatively, the violence embraced by vigilante groups such as the Gulabi Gang (Richards, 2016, pp. 558-76) against sexual predators in India. These entities' actions should not be reduced into mere protests and articulation of disavowal of the state – instead, they straddle the amorphous terrain beyond civil disobedience, yet is short of a full-fledged revolution or rebellion.

In advancing the view that uncivil disobedience is *distinct* from criminality, we are answering to the negative against those who insist that uncivil disobedients are nothing more than merely 'thugs', or are comparable to violent criminals who employ force as a means of securing selfish gains. However, we are *not* concurrently defending the view that there exists *no morally salient difference* between civil and uncivil disobedience; it would be entirely plausible, indeed most likely the case, that differences *also exist* between civil and uncivil disobedience. Nor are we defending the proposition that uncivil disobedience is *justifiable* or *always permissible*.

We advance three possible lines of defence as for why uncivil disobedience should not be equated, all else being equal, with general criminal violence. The overarching strategy here is to identify unique explanatory factors that exist – and only exist – in instances of uncivil disobedience, as juxtaposed against violent crimes at large.

Firstly, there is the view that uncivil disobedients are wielding force that is *roughly proportionate* as a response to the egregious structural violence that they endure. Some unpacking is warranted here. The presupposition is that the disobedients themselves, or the group on which they are resisting and fighting, have been experiencing substantial transgressions under the probably coercive state apparatus. Injustices ranging from systemically engrained police brutality, structurally hard-wired racism and alienation of particular groups, and socioeconomic deprivation at the hands of inept, unresponsive bureaucrats and politicians, may fall into the category of such transgressions.[4]

Indeed, such injustices could amount to what Galtung (1993, p. 106) terms *structural violence* – 'avoidable impairment of fundamental human needs'. We would add that the scope of relevantly egregious deprivation could extend beyond the scope of violation of core human rights, and apply equally to civil and political liberties deemed and agreed upon as morally urgent in the spaces where the violence is perpetrated. Lest we be accused of excessive stretching of the concept, we do not posit that structural violence is wholly equivalent to physical violence; this is why the physical force deployed by disobedients can only be *roughly* proportionate. We would nevertheless also note that certain forms of structural violence inflicted by the state could well harm individuals in manners more intense, long-lasting, and substantial as compared with physical infringements – consider, for instance, the harms inflicted by electoral disenfranchisement and denial of access to freedoms of assembly as compared with the mild pain posed by piercing someone's fingers. Physical violence is not innately more severe than structural violence[5]; this is also why uncivil disobedience may be *appropriate*, even if non-justified all-things-considered, as a response to egregious violations by the state that would amount to a systemic inducing of avoidable impairment of human needs. The circumstances to which disobedients are responding to, as well as the moral urgency attached to remediating their occurrence, render the uncivil disobedience sufficiently distinct from incidental violence.

Secondly, there a salient distinction between the use of violence as a last resort for self-protection under circumstances of significant duress (as in the case of uncivil disobedience) and resort to frivolous violence for flippant reasons in other criminal cases. In the case of

[4]   It would be incredibly difficult, albeit certainly a direction for possible future research, to determine what would constitute transgressions of such kind and to such degree. We suggest that injustices such as persistent gerrymandering, rigging of welfare services to exclude or penalise particular groups, and the systemically engrained suppression of reasonable dissent would comprise 'clear examples' of such transgressions, though the definitions and boundaries of the subset are, as with most questions in politics, debatable.

[5]   Where severity is measured by the extent to which the individual is personally affected in permanent, intense, irreversible, and significant ways.

uncivil disobedience, the disobedients often have few options to turn to other than violence, as a means of transforming and/or engaging (non-transformatively) with political structures writ large. In other words, the violence adopted constitutes a *last resort* – in at least one (if not both) of two ways: a) *objective constraints* – there actually exists no closely accessible alternative method through which disobedients can accomplish their political objectives; b) *reasonable belief* – under the circumstances, the disobedients can reasonably believe, on the evidence the disobedients can reasonably obtain, that there exists no alternative method through which they can accomplish their political objectives. The upshot here is that under conditions of great duress, the extent to which the motivation stems from a place of despair and exhaustion of alternatives does and should matter in shaping our judgment concerning the character of the act and agents involved.

Thirdly, there is often a temptation to engage in excessively ideal-theoretical evaluation of the dynamics and mechanics of social movements, to the point where *realistic considerations* and *sensitivity* to the complex empirical circumstances in which individuals find themselves are eschewed in favour of monistic moralisation (Srinivasan, 2018, pp. 123-44). This ignores the fact that activists, protesters, disobedients may be caught up in conditions in which they subjectively opine that there exists no option but to turn to the deployment of force as a recourse. Indeed, the very nature of sites of protests being active locations for struggles and contestations for power manifesting through physical altercations that are at times violent, renders the act of instantaneous, impromptu violence one that is, more likely than not, driven by impulse and impetuous whims, as opposed to well-thought-out reasons. Now, does this justify uncivil disobedience? Plausibly not. Yet would the dearth of measurement and restraint – induced by the mass frenzy of social movements – render the manifest behaviours of individuals normatively distinct from those who engage in criminal conduct in a private and non-social movement-related manner? We would suggest the answer lies to the affirmative.

In his recent discussion on differentiating uncivil disobedients from ordinary criminals, Lim (2021, p. 129) makes the meta-observation that theories of disobedience should be willing to '[accommodate] imperfect beings like ourselves.'; that the failure to meet one or more of the strictly stipulated conditions concerning what conscientious disobedience (outlined above) looks like, should not be taken as automatic disqualifiers in terms of judging whether individuals are in possession of 'conscientious convictions'. Delmas

(2018, p. 68) makes the observation that '[...] those who shoulder the burdens of oppression cannot reasonably be expected to satisfy the demands of civility, since these demands aim to preserve civic bonds that do not extend to them and even serve to maintain their oppression'. Without weighing too much into the more contentious debate of whether such incivility is, all things considered, justified or permissible, it is evident that uncivil disobedients should be differentiated from those who partake in flippant or egregious violence for motives and under conditions that are disanalogous from those characterising conscientious disobedience – civil or uncivil.

3. Why courts should take seriously the normative distinctness of uncivil disobedience

The subsequent question, then, is this: why should courts take seriously the difference between uncivil disobedience and violent criminality at large? Whilst most debates on conscientious disobedience have revolved predominantly around questions of *justification* and *justifiability* (public or private), an emerging strand in the existing literature features a reflection upon the appropriate responses specifically the court should, and should not, undertake – that is, the judges, jury, and other co-participants of the judicial process (Smith, 2011, pp. 145-50).

Consider the dualist view that whilst a) conscientious disobedience can be justified (or individuals may have pro tanto rights to commit such actions), b) conscientious disobedience should also remain punishable by the courts. As Farrell (1977, pp. 165-68) notes, the affirmation of these two propositions reflects the view that the law serves as a rule-based system that should not forego punishing disobedience. A primary explanation cited here is that in foregoing punishment, the law would encourage undesirable downstream consequences, by setting the wrong precedents. Let us term this the *consequentialist* objection.

This objection opines that any principle officials employ to differentiate between illegal acts committed as a matter of civil/uncivil disobedience, and those committed for non-disobedience-related reasons, could well open the floodgates to further criminal behaviours from private citizens. Individuals may infer from some judgments – rightly or wrongly – that their criminality would go unpunished, thereby undermining the instrumentalist role of the law in deterring transgressions in the future (Greenawalt, 1987, p. 273). There are two subsets of individuals that are particularly worth highlighting here – first, those who see themselves as engaging in (justified) conscientious disobedience, even where they are not; second, those who would interpret the lenience of the law as a feature to take advantage of in enabling them to commit non-disobedience-related crimes of their own. Both groups' transgressing the law would be deeply undesirable from the perspective of *ordre public*.

Further variants of this claim include the charge that disobedience would 'challenge the state's supreme right, through law, to take decisions on behalf of a whole community' (Horder, 2004, p. 224), or that an attempt at differentiation would weaken the authority and credibility of the courts in the eyes of those who feel aggrieved by the court's failure to punish accordingly.

Our response is three-fold. Firstly, the normative link between *differentiating* between uncivil disobedients and violent offenders at large, and the *tacit endorsement or encouragement* of uncivil disobedience (and hence violence), is not as potent as it may seem. Courts can rule that there exists a difference between criminal violence and uncivil disobedience, *without* expressing or adopting the view that the latter is thus *justified*. This is also amongst the reasons for which we have emphasised repeatedly that the justificatory question must be separated from the differentiation question.

Secondly, as effective remedial measures, the court could also offer elucidating comments in its sentencing and ruling, in noting that whilst there exists a normatively salient distinction between criminal violence and uncivil disobedience, this does not thereby render the latter something that others ought to emulate – especially if conducted with flippant or improper motives. This could be done through precise, targeted communicative strategies whose contents are beyond this paper's scope.

Thirdly, a partial concession could be adopted – we could acknowledge that there are instances where the instrumentalist case against recognition of such differences is so potent, that the court ought to refrain from granting any consideration to the normative distinction raised above. Indeed, as Ceva proposes (albeit in the distinct context of political and legislative processes), 'the concession of conscientious exemptions is [...] an issue whose case-by-case evaluation must be open to consequence-sensitive considerations concerning the impact that any given exemption could have on the rights of others' (Ceva, 2015, pp. 26-50). A case-by-case, context-sensitive judiciary approach both precludes the undesirable slide down the slippery slope, as well as ensures more accurate appraisal of the situation in the judiciary process. The upshot of the above, however, is that the consequentialist argument holds little water in precluding courts from adopting the proposed distinction.

Is there a *positive argument,* then, for the courts to take seriously the distinction raised? We believe so. Our suggested argument is one centred around *quality of intentions.* Intentions matter. A core tenet undergirding criminal law is 'the act is not culpable unless the mind is guilty'; *actus reus non facit reum nisi mens sit rea.* In engaging with the specific question of the mental state of the agent, we must take into consideration the values and beliefs the agent espouses. Indeed, dispositions, motivations, beliefs, and values, in turn, can determine not only the charge they are presented with in the first place, but also the extent to which the agent should be deemed worthy of condemnation and/or partial clemency (considerations that feed directly into the sentencing process). Consider, for one, an individual who tosses a Molotov cocktail at a shop out of *sheer ennui* could be charged with *assault* and *arson*; on the other hand, if the said individual does so as a part of a destructive, semi-organised political gang of a number of people, this would transform the act of tossing the cocktail into one of *rioting,* too. Alternatively, if the agent partakes in the act out of genuine and reasonably grounded fears that the shop harbours individuals who may threaten their wellbeing (e.g. terrorists), the charge in question may be dropped entirely, on grounds that the act *could* comprise reasonable self-defence.[6] None of this is to say that the violence is at all justified, but that the specific reasons for which the agent acts could determine the nature of their crimes – especially given that courts bear the responsibility of arbitrating not only whether the act in question is committed, but also the mental and psychological circumstances surrounding the said act. The court bears what we term the *context-sensitivity prerogative,* to be sufficiently discriminate and judicious in detecting and processing the mental states of the defendant *at the time of the act in question.*

Mental states are often opaque; at other times, they are difficult to arbitrate without a comprehensive understanding of the past and broader behavioural patterns of the agent (Lim, 2021, pp. 133-35). As such, judgments concerning culpability may – on grounds of incomplete or inconclusive evidence – require background evidence (e.g. testimony from character witnesses) on the character and integrity of the defendant, which could act as tipping-point factors in determining the precise charges laid against the individual. Furthermore, even if a defendant is deemed to be guilty, a comprehensive assessment of their character would be necessary in ensuring

---

[6] For more literature on this, see Cohan (2007); Cameron (2020).

that the penalties (e.g. sentencing, orders, and whether their criminal record would be spent) are commensurate with whom they are as *individuals* in relation to both the law and the public at large. An agent who – out of vigilante impulse – inflicts grievous bodily harm at another person they deem to be guilty and who has wrongly escaped the law, should be differentiated from an agent who maims others, purely out of their sadistic motives. Noting the potential impediments to an accurate assessment of an individual's character purely on the basis of their *past* behaviours (Rhode, 2019, pp. 378-385), it is all the more important that – as far as is possible – the court takes seriously testimony and circumstantial evidence concerning the individual's mental state *at the time* of their committing the disobedient act, in order to calibrate and come to the most fitting judgment that is cognizant of both their past and present moral profiles. We term this the *character-sensitivity prerogative*, to be as accurate as possible in gauging the overall character of the defendant both prior to and at the time when the act is committed.

4. A legislative scheme for treating conscientious disobedients

If governments and courts should take seriously the normative distinctness of conscientious disobedience, including its uncivil form, how should they do it in practice? We recommend a *reconciliatory* approach, in the sense that a measure of *leniency* is to be applied throughout the legal process of handling the civil disobedients. We flesh out this approach in terms of a legislative scheme with the following features:

1. The scheme is to be adopted by the government, via a piece of legislation debated in society and passed in the legislature, such that the scheme has a political mandate and popular legitimacy.
2. The scheme covers all stages of a legal process, from arrest, prosecution, and sentencing to imprisonment and post-imprisonment.
3. One strong advantage of this scheme is that it will take the heat away from the court room as it were, in the sense that judges can avoid as much as possible making judicial decisions on the basis of their own personal political or moral beliefs.
4. The discretion is to be given rather to the prosecutors: they decide whether or not to put a case of prosecution under the scheme.
5. The adoption and implementation of the scheme is thus not a purely legalistic process but also a political one.

The scheme consists of guidelines regarding (a) the eligibility conditions; the roles of (b) the police, (c) prosecutors, and (d) judges; (e) the treatment of the convicted during imprisonment; and (f) post-release treatment.

a. Eligibility conditions: Offenders eligible to be treated under the scheme are those who participated in a protest, expressing serious discontents over perceived state injustice, and calling for policy or institutional changes. There has to be a rational connection between the aims of the protests and the actions undertaken. Looting, for example, would generally be regarded as failing to satisfy this requirement. Furthermore, the protesters' response must be *roughly proportionate* to the injustice of the threat posed to them during the protest. This proportionality requirement may appear rather indeterminate. Yet generally, we could divide cases into three kinds: (1) *ineligible cases* in which responses are quite clearly disproportionate, such as killing, serious violent attack on a policy officer or another person; (2) *eligible cases* in which responses are quite clearly proportionate, such as unlawful assembly or demonstration, obstruction of road traffic and minor violence such as burning of things on the streets to prevent police's dispersal of protesters, physical confrontation of a minor kind with police officers; and (3) *intermediary cases that lie in between*, whose eligibility can only be determined by prosecutors on a case-by-case manner.

b. The police: For unlawful assembly or demonstration of a peaceful kind, the scheme recommends that the police tolerate it as circumstances allow. If dispersion of protesters is necessary to restoring law and order, it should be done peacefully and without arrest. For other kinds of protests that go beyond peaceful demonstration, leading to significant disruptions of public order and safety, the police might judge that arrests be necessary. After arresting a protester, the police could then consider *the option of diversion* for minor offenses, which means the case in question will not be brought forward for prosecution, but put it in an alternative scheme, such as *warning*, or *bind-over*[7], which *in this stage* is not a conviction

---

[7] Binding-over is an exercise by criminal courts in certain common law jurisdictions to deal with issues that are usually low-level public order offenses; individuals are required to enter into an agreement to keep the peace and be of good behaviour, in exchange for a waiver of sentence after conviction, or a withdrawal of prosecution. See Feldman (1988).

or punishment, but an agreement of the offender to engage in good behavior within a specified period of time. The government may even consider offering not just legal aid but counselling service to the offender during police investigation.

c. The prosecutors: If a case is brought forward for prosecution, the government prosecutors will decide in light of the spirit of reconciliation whether or not to place the case under the scheme.

d. The court and judges: The court (by judges or juries) will decide whether the defendant is guilty or not. If found guilty, judges will make judgments about sentencing according to the leniency spirit of the scheme. Bind-over and compulsory social service are preferable to imprisonment, and if the latter is necessary, a lighter sentencing than similar crimes falling outside of the scheme is to be encouraged.

e. Custody: There exists a trend amongst liberal democracies, where social movements and protests are increasingly helmed by young people still in school or college. During imprisonment, their education would inevitably be affected – if not come to a grounding halt. The scheme will provide enhanced educational opportunities and services for this special category of the convicted. Another category of convicted protesters is those who are educated, white-collar, or professional. Standard work opportunities for inmates in various countries tend to be low-skilled or manual labor. The scheme will offer diverse and tenable work opportunities for educated in-mates. Such opportunities should also serve a rehabilitative role, in facilitating in-mates' re-integration and rekindling of normal ties and connections with their community at large.

f. Post-release treatment: In many countries, a criminal record itself would pose significant constraints on discharged prisoners in relation to job opportunities, travel and immigration, and eligibility of board membership and political representation. To reduce these constraints for the discharged prisoners falling under the scheme, it is recommended that for imprisonments under three years, no criminal record will be given for the discharged. For imprisonments from three to five years, deletion of criminal record after three years of absence of offense after release should be implemented. If a criminal record is to be given in any case, it should note that the discharged prisoner was treated under the special scheme for conscientious disobedients. Unlike ordinary criminals, discharged prisoners of this category will not be prevented by law from standing for elections or appointment in boards, councils, and political bodies; they can also be invited to sit on consultative bodies concerning prison governance.

We believe that this scheme is *not utopian* and can be implemented without excessive difficulties in resources and administration. After all, many similar provisions such as alternatives to imprisonment and educational opportunities for inmates are already in place for other occasions in many jurisdictions. The *adoption* of this scheme is rather a matter of political judgment and will. A crucial factor is whether liberal-democratic governments will see not only the *normative rationale* of a reconciliatory approach to conscientious disobedience, but also its *prudential value*.

There are a few reasons for thinking that a liberal democratic government may see the scheme's prudential values and thus have *incentives* to adopt it. First, adopting the scheme means that the government acknowledges dissents and discontents are not uncommon in a liberal democratic society, and part of the value of liberal democracy is precisely its willingness to recognize and accommodate them as best as it can. Secondly, adoption of the scheme expresses the government's goodwill to reconcile with protesters and win back the support from them and their sympathisers, paving the way for cross-partisan consensus and convergence. Thirdly, the scheme helps minimize the likelihood of further radicalization of protests. Prosecution and imprisonment of protesters will likely result in further serious loss of trust in democratic politics and erosion of government legitimacy in the eyes of the protesters, leading to radicalization of the aims and means of political action on the part of the disaffected. Fourthly, and from a narrowly defined self-interest-centric perspective, because of the above benefits, the scheme would enable the incumbent administration to cultivate political goodwill and get re-elected. It would correlatively help the new administration to make peace with protestors who were disaffected with the previous administration.

5. Possible Objections

Objection #1: A right to conscientious disobedience?

A primary objection to our account is that we don't go far enough in recognising the purported right of conscientious disobedients to engage in their transgressive acts; in other words, our account is defective because it *presumes* the court's right to *punish* disobedients.

Grounding his account on citizens' right to engage in disobedience – even when in doing so they fail to act in accordance with bringing about the *right* state of affairs – Lefkowitz argues that the moral right to political participation entails a *right* to civil disobedience (Lefkowitz, 2007, pp. 205-208). Noting that the right to political participation entails both individuals' rights to a) participate in decision-making processes, and b) continue to contest the decision reached through the decisive procedure, Lefkowitz submits that individuals may reasonably disagree with the law and courts' interpretation over the morally best *means* and the particular *ends* served by public policymaking. In cases of such disagreements, then, individuals should be *permitted* to express their discontents and disagreements through concrete actions, as opposed to merely abstract speech.

In explaining why this right to disagree should extend to and justify the employment of illegal means (e.g. civil disobedience), Lefkowitz invokes four tentative reasons: firstly, it would take *too long* for individuals to articulate their demands, should they *not* break the law – violating the law is hence an *effective means to* an end, pace Lefkowitz; secondly, disobedience *works* – it raises salience and highlights the problematic dimensions of a particular policy; thirdly, that disobedients are willing to risk the imposition of various costs upon them attests to the *strength of their convictions*, which in turn suggests that their disobedience is at least founded upon relatively praiseworthy intentions, and should not be unreservedly condemned; fourthly – and perhaps most substantially – Lefkowitz (2007, p. 215) is of the view that, 'The best understanding of the moral right to political participation is one that reduces as much as possible the degree to which it is a matter of luck whether one attracts majority support for one's reasonable views regarding what justice requires.'

What is the upshot of this? Here, Lefkowitz draws a distinction between *penalty* and *punishment* – whilst the former refers to the imposition of costs, fines, and other negative disincentives associated with the transgression in question, the latter features *not only such costs*, but also the *expressive component* that the individual in question is worthy of resentment, indignation, disapproval, and reprobation. The former is warranted, as a prudential means of ensuring resolution of collective action problems; the latter, on the other hand, is unwarranted – on grounds that individuals do possess the right to engage in civil disobedience. Term this the *punishment-penalty cut*.

Conscientious Disobedience and Democratic Governments

In our view, Lefkowitz's view, as intriguing as it is, does not work. Firstly, the explanatory move from the right to political participation/ disagree, to the *right to break the law* in order to express *disagreement*, is unwarranted. The first three explanations Lefkowitz provides – concerning efficacy and lack of expedient remedies – suffice in explaining why civil disobedience *differs* from non-disobedience transgressions of the law, i.e. what we have surmised above. Yet they do not, without further qualification, justify the existence of a *permission* to break the law, which entails the imposition of costs (both symbolic and actual) upon others in the community.

The implicitly *moral luck*-grounded fourth argument is more promising (e.g. individuals should not be faulted for whether one attracts a majority of society's support for one's reasonable views), but even then, it appears unclear why the particular *means* of violating the law is permissible – we can accept that individuals should be compensated and offered adequate opportunities to express their discontents about the law, but this neither suggests that they have the right to *act out accordingly* (in ways that affect others in their community), nor that the specific *method* of legal violations is thereby justified. In any case, Lefkowitz's argument from *expression* and *participation* to *transgression* – seems too quick a move for the substantiation of a *right to civil disobedience*.

Secondly, Brownlee (2018, pp. 291-96; 2008, pp. 711-16) offers a further critique – that to the extent that Lefkowitz attaches a significant value to the non-instrumental right of individuals to autonomously participate in the political system, such value should render it thereby impermissible for the state to seek to impose any penalty at all against practitioners of such disobedience. To prescribe any forms of penalties, costs, or orders restricting the agents' future actions, would also undermine their respective autonomy – as such, the alternatives to sentencing that Lefkowitz advances are equally compromising when measured against the overarching objective of preserving individuals' ability to register and express their disapproval of collective decisions. Brownlee (2008, p. 716) suggests that Lefkowitz's *punishment-penalty cut* is untenable, for '[the] status of public disobedience as a legitimate form of political engagement considerably weakens the symbolic grounds for penalisation'.

We share Brownlee's concerns, and offer a further reason as to why the punishment-penalty cut does not hold. To the extent that Lefkowitz believes penalties are *necessary* in enabling the state to facilitate, as is necessary, effective decision-making processes and deter undue violations of the law, it is unclear why he would not *also* support the imposition of *punishment* upon the disobedients.

Recognise that the communicative value of punishment – in expressing the moral wrongness in the actions conducted by the disobedients, in appraising them as blameworthy – would in fact play a pivotal role in deterring disobedients from committing such offences in the future. This is because the sheer costliness of penalties alone will not suffice in dissuading individuals – fully convinced of the *rightness* of their *behaviours* and potential sacrifices – from committing the disobedient acts in question. The communication that there is something *wrong* with what they are doing, is thus necessary in precluding them from partaking in such behaviours in the future. This also explains why a fine may suffice in deterring illegal parking, but not in preventing future disobedience. Hence, following on from Lefkowitz's logic, if courts are truly concerned about preventing the disorder and instability sowed by individuals viewing disobedience as a *carte blanche*, they should not stop at purely penalty – but must also impose communicatively embedded punishment upon the perpetrators.

If Lefkowitz is serious about his instrumentalist and prudential reasons in favour of punishment, he must also resist waiving the penalty imposed upon offenders. To push back against this, Lefkowitz must explain why the *correct compromise/balance* is struck at the precise point of *penalty without punishment*. This strikes us as rather implausible. A more reasonable view, we suggest, is a *continuum-based* approach: where disobedients, both civil and uncivil, *can* be punished for their actions, but the extent of penalty-cum-punishment exacted should be determined in accordance with a basket of variables, including but not limited to:

a)   the individual's precise quality of will at time of the act in question;
b)   their broader background and upbringing;
c)   the socio-political circumstances that precipitated their transgressive act;
d)   the punishment (or lack of)'s impact on others' likelihood of offence;
e)   the punishment (or lack of)'s impact on the individual's likelihood of re-offence.

These parameters reflect, more broadly and fundamentally, the range of considerations that ought to be pertinent in shaping the state's precise response to conscientious disobedience. The legislative scheme outlined in IV aptly encapsulates this continuum-based view – whilst for an extreme minority of individuals, it would be appropriate to forego any and all negative sanctions against uncivil disobedience altogether,

in most cases, the prudential justification for sanctioning uncivil disobedients would require the government to adopt *some* negative treatments
against such transgressors. Where this is indeed the case, Lefkowitz's
punishment-penalty cut would be irrelevant – indeed, the state
should punish *and* penalise these individuals, albeit not without
applying discounts commensurate with the aforementioned considerations a) – e). Note, such sanctions should go hand-in-hand with the
specific treatments proposed in IV – e.g. deletion of records, implementation of bind-overs and diversion, and/or the provision of assistance
with re-integration upon the completion of the sentence.

A further pushback to our rejoinder here, is that perhaps there
exists no positive case for the punishment of conscientious disobedience in the first place. This pushback operates as follows: given that
we grant that disobedience *can* be justified, it seemingly follows
that *where* such disobedience is justified, the state – e.g. the courts,
police, and related apparatus – ought not sanction those engaged in
such actions. This is because the punitive exacting of costs upon
these individuals requires there to be something worthy of *condemnation* on the part of such agents – they must have acted *wrongly* in order
to merit punishment (Tadros, 2011). To the extent conscientious
disobedients have not acted wrongly, they should not be punished.

In response, note that whilst there may be *some* instances where
conscientious disobedience can be justified, there are also many
where conscientious disobedience is *not* justified – civil or uncivil.
This may be because such acts of transgression are *unacceptably
disproportionate* (e.g. inducing mass disruption to civilian life over
relatively minor infringements by the law), clearly *not committed
as a last resort* (e.g. there are other alternatives available to the
participants with regard to advancing institutional changes), or
driven by a significant (though not predominantly so) preoccupation
with *self-interest*; whilst these acts may technically qualify as
disobedience per the definitions stipulated in section 3, they are not
justifiable disobedience, all things considered. Alternatively, it may
be because the robust normative reasons for punishing disobedience
– again, well-litigated in existing literature[8] – outweigh contextually
the reasons against such. Given our primary aims, we have not
allocated as much space to arguments in favour of punishing
disobedience – this is by no means to say that we disagree with the

---

[8]   To see two established examples of such arguments, consider Moore
(1997) and Feinberg (1994); the latter offers a specific account centered
around the community's disapproval of law-breaking disobedience.

reasoning adopted by these accounts. Conscientious disobedience – civil or uncivil – can be unjustified.

A further thought – worthy of further, separate exploration – is this: even where acts of disobedience are indeed justified, this does not imply that the individuals involved are not deserving of at least *some* condemnation. Indeed, one specific way in which this may play out is this: disobedients – even if justified in their acts of transgression – can be deemed worthy of condemnation for the downstream consequences induced by their actions. For instance, if justified acts of disobedience result in heightened perceived permissibility of lawbreaking, or undercuts the credibility of the state's threat in upholding law and order in instances where such legal requirements are both justified and binding, we may have powerful prudential grounds to sanction disobedients for having *foreseeably brought about* such consequences, even if they are justified in doing so. It is beyond this paper's scope to flesh out a complete theory of *justifiable yet punishment-worthy* disobedience.

Objection #2: 'Bad Apples' – Proving too Much?

A second objection is as follows. Suppose one grants the validity of our account – and that the distinction between uncivil disobedience and ordinary criminal violence must be taken seriously. It appears that there are instances where the implementation of our model would be unreasonable, if not downright absurd. Consider, for example, the mob of extremist protesters who stormed the Capitol Hill on January 6, 2021, in dispute of the results of the 2020 U.S. presidential election results (*Capitol Hill*) (Heine, 2021), or, indeed, individuals who took to violent protests in Martinique and Guadeloupe over the French government's decision to implement a COVID-19 vaccination mandate (*Anti-Vaxx*) (France 24, 2021). In both *Capitol Hill* and *Anti-Vaxx*, we may have tentative grounds to believe that what unfolded were episodes of uncivil disobedience: protesters were opposing what they construed to be unjust laws or policies (e.g. the ruling that Donald Trump lost the 2020 elections; the vaccination mandate to be issued by France) through means that were violent, albeit perhaps not to the degree of terrorism and/or civil war.[9]

If our argument on uncivil disobedience does indeed hold, must this behove courts to treat with *leniency* those engaged in

[9] Some may dispute this assessment for the Capitol Hill riots.

disobedience across both instances? Granting this conclusion seems problematic – and it is on such an 'unpleasant' implication that our account may be challenged by sceptics. The *bad apples* seem to pose a problem for our model.

We offer several responses. The first is to suggest that some of those involved in *Capitol Hill* and *Anti-Vaxx* do not meet the necessary criteria to qualify as participating in uncivil conscientious disobedience. It would not be unreasonable to speculate that some of the many protesters across both cases were not driven *predominantly* by a desire to serve public or communal interests – anti-vaccination protesters saw the vaccine mandate as jeopardising their own wellbeing, and/or the riots as a convenient opportunity for them to express frustrations towards the government at large; many Capitol Hill rioters opposed the outcome of the vote not out of a sense of grievance or public justice, but because they held personal grudges against the Democratic Party and the political establishment.

Yet such a speculative rejoinder is only partially successful, for we possess neither the empirical evidence nor the contextually grounded perspectives to judge. This is why our model places a heavy premium upon procedures of arbitration, determination, and investigation, where it falls upon the judiciary and disciplinary forces to pursue the truth and establish the facts of the matter, as much as is possible. For some of the protesters involved – more than others – the state may have strong evidentiary grounds to believe that they acted out of genuine concern for others, as well as fulfilling the criteria (1), (3), (4), and (5) necessary for the acts in question to qualify as *conscientious disobedience*. In these cases, we would gladly bite the bullet, and argue that our reconciliatory approach should indeed be adopted. Countervailing intuitions – in absence of potent moral justifications – should not be accepted as necessarily normatively binding. We could well be prey of partisan biases that skew us erroneously in favour of particular moral judgments.

Finally, we do not rule out the existence of independent reasons – stemming from the downstream detriments and structural harms posed by (some of) the anti-vaccination and Capitol Hill protesters – that render their actions worthy of punishment. Indeed, these reasons' entailment that they be punished, and punished stringently, are perfectly compatible with what we advance here: a plurality of factors must be considered in determining the nature of treatment most befitting and suitable for those who engage in uncivil disobedience. This has always been our stance.

6. Conclusion

Liberal democracies are supposed to be able to effectively pursue several tasks at the same time: to encourage free political expression and popular participation; to co-opt diverse political views and interests into workable governing platforms and policies, thereby containing disagreements and dissents within a political and legal framework acceptable to all, and to uphold a minimum level of political order. However, with the ever widening economic inequality, the rise of populism, and the increasingly frequent occurrences of protests and riots in liberal democracies in recent decades, many individuals have begun to seriously question liberal democracy's ability to deliver upon its promises.

So long as liberal democracies have yet to emerge with proper diagnoses and creative solutions to such malaise, these large-scale, mass protests will not disappear, and governments and citizens in liberal democracies must ponder over the question of how to cope with them. Repression is inconsistent with the fundamental values of liberal democracy. A *draconian* approach may achieve short-term results, but will not ensure long-term stability and peace. A *permissive* approach that takes no legal action against legal transgression of protesters, on the other hand, would only encourage undue transgressions and undermine the rule of law.

Our paper steers a middle way between these two extremes by proposing a *reconciliatory* approach to handling the conscientious disobedients. According to this approach, while the government and police may take legal action against protesters in order to prevent further disruption and deterioration of the law and order, a measure of *leniency* is to be applied throughout the legal process of handling the civil disobedients. We have tried to justify this approach by arguing that there is a normative distinctness of *conscientious* disobedience that separates it from other crimes committed in a non-conscientious disobedience situation. We have further argued that such distinctness applies to both the civil and uncivil form of conscientious disobedience.

This is not to say that conscientious disobedience is always morally justified. Yet even if it is not justified – in reality, there must be many such instances – we have argued that the normative distinctness of conscientious disobedience ought to be given serious consideration in legal proceedings against the conscientious disobedients. This consideration, we have argued, is best fleshed out in a legislative scheme that implements a measure of *lenience* in treating the conscientious disobedients throughout the legal process, from arrest, prosecution, and sentencing, to imprisonment and post-release treatment.

We believe that this legislative scheme has appropriate flexibility to handle the complexity of judging about conscientious disobedience. It is not an easy task to determine whether a law-breaking act is as an instance of conscientious disobedience. Still more difficult is to decide whether an instance is morally justified all things considered. Judgments must be highly context-sensitive and case-by-case. The scheme thus places a heavy onus upon the judiciary and disciplinary officials to pursue the truth and establish the facts of the matter. In particular, the prosecutors – given the discretion to decide whether to place a particular case under the scheme for further legal action – and the courts should jointly determine the extent of penalty-cum-punishment in accordance with a basket of variables.

Irrespective of whether an act of conscientious disobedience is morally justified, we believe that this scheme, with its reconciliatory spirit and an emphasis of context sensitivity, is realistically the best path forward for liberal democratic governments.

Oxford University
yue.wong@politics.ox.ac.uk
Princeton University
jcwchan@hku.hk

References

Kimberley Brownlee, 'Penalizing Public Disobedience', *Ethics* 118 (2008), 711–16.

Kimberley Brownlee, 'Two Tales of Civil Disobedience: A Reply to David Lefkowitz', *Res Publica* 24 (2018), 291–96.

Rob Cameron, 'The Case for Black American Self-Defense', *Foreign Policy* (September 24, 2020), https://foreignpolicy.com/2020/09/24/case-black-american-self-defense-protests/.

Emanuela Ceva, 'Political Justification through Democratic Participation', *Social Theory and Practice* 41 (2015) 26–50.

John Alan Cohan, 'Civil Disobedience and the Necessity Defense', *The University of New Hampshire Law Review* 6 (2007) 111–75.

Candice Delmas and Kimberley Brownlee, 'Civil Disobedience', *The Stanford Encyclopedia of Philosophy* (Winter 2021 Edition), Edward N. Zalta (ed.), URL=https://plato.stanford.edu/entries/civil-disobedience/.

Candice Delmas, *Duty to Resist: When Disobedience Should Be Uncivil* (New York: Oxford University Press, 2018).

Candice Delmas, 'Civil Disobedience, Punishment, and Injustice', in K. K. Ferzan and L. Alexander (eds.), *The Palgrave Handbook of Applied Ethics and the Criminal Law* (London: Palgrave Macmillan, 2019), 167–88.

Ronald Dworkin, *Taking Rights Seriously*, 5th ed. (Cambridge, MA: Harvard University Press, 1978).

Daniel Farrell, 'Paying the penalty: Justifiable civil disobedience and the problem of punishment', *Philosophy and Public Affairs*, 6 (1977), 165–84.

Joel Feinberg, 'The Expressive Function of Punishment' in A. Duff and D. Garland (Eds.), *A Reader on Punishment* (Oxford: Oxford University Press, 1994).

David Feldman, 'The King's Peace, the Royal Prerogative and Public Order: The Roots and Early Development of Binding over Powers', *Cambridge Law Journal* 47 (1988) 103–106.

France 24, 'France postpones vaccine mandate after violent unrest in Martinique and Guadeloupe', (November 26 2021), https://www.france24.com/en/europe/20211126-france-postpones-vaccine-mandate-after-violent-unrest-in-martinique-and-guadeloupe.

Johan Galtung, 'Kulturelle Gewalt', *Der Burger im Staat* 43 (1993).

Kent Greenawalt, *Conflicts of Law and Morality* (Oxford: Clarendon Press, 1987).

Jürgen Habermas, 'Civil Disobedience: Litmus Test for the Democratic Constitutional State,' J. Torpey, trans. *Berkeley Journal of Sociology* 30 (1985).

Jorge Heine, 'The Attack on the US Capitol: An American Kristallnacht', *Protest* 1 (2021) 126–41.

Jeremy Horder, *Excusing Crime* (Oxford: Oxford University Press, 2004).

David Lefkowitz, 'On a Moral Right to Civil Disobedience', *Ethics* 117 (2007), 202–223.

Chong-Ming Lim, 'Differentiating Disobedients', *Journal of Ethics and Social Philosophy* 20 (2021), 119–43.

David Lyons, 'Moral Judgment, Historical Reality, and Civil Disobedience', *Philosophy and Public Affairs* 27 (1996) 31–49.

Michael Moore, *Placing Blame: A General Theory of the Criminal Law* (Oxford: Oxford University Press, 1997).

John Rawls, *A Theory of Justice [TOJ]* (Cambridge, MA: Harvard University Press, 1971).

Matthew Richards, 'The Gulabi Gang, Violence, and the Articulation of Counterpublicity', *Communication, Culture, and Critique* 9 (2016), 558–76.

Deborah Rhode, 'Character in Criminal Justice Proceedings: Rethinking Its Role in Rules Governing Evidence, Punishment, Prosecutors, and Parole', *American Journal of Criminal Law* 45 (2019) 353–406.

William Scheuerman, 'Can Political Institutions Commit Civil Disobedience?', *The Review of Politics* 82, (2020), 269–91.

Gene Sharp, *Sharp's Dictionary of Power and Struggle: Language of Civil Resistance in Conflicts* (Oxford: Oxford University Press, 2012).

Tommie Shelby, *We Who Are Dark: The Philosophical Foundations of Black Solidarity* (Cambridge, MA: Harbard University Press, 2005).

Kurt Shock, *Civil Resistance Today* (New York: Polity, 2015).

Peter Singer, *Democracy and Disobedience* (Oxford: Clarendon Press, 1973).

William Smith and Kimberley Brownlee, 'Civil Disobedience and Conscientious Objection', *Oxford Research Encyclopedia of Ethics* (2017).

William Smith, *Civil Disobedience and Deliberative Democracy* (Abingdon: Routledge, 2013).

William Smith, 'Civil Disobedience and the Public Sphere', *The Journal of Political Philosophy* 19 (2011), 145–66.

Amia Srinivasan, 'The Aptness of Anger', *Journal of Political Philosophy*, 26 (2018) 123–44.

Victor Tadros, *Ends of Harm: The Moral Foundations of Criminal Law* (Oxford: Oxford University Press, 2011).

Irregular Migration, Historical Injustice and the Right to Exclude

LEA YPI

Abstract

This paper makes the case for amnesty of irregular migrants by reflecting on the conditions under which a wrong that is done in the past can be considered superseded. It explores the relation between historical injustice and irregular migration and suggests that we should hold states to the same stringent standards of compliance with just norms that they apply to the assessment of the moral conduct of individual migrants. It concludes that those standards ought to orient migrants and citizens' moral assessment of how their states handle questions of irregular migration and to inform political initiatives compatible with these moral assessments.

> *We did not cross the border, the border crossed us.*
> (Mexican saying)

1.

Suppose that at some point in the past a gang of Mafiosi managed to fence off a chunk of land and through sheer violence and oppression convinced everyone around that it had acquired legitimate property. Does a group of this sort have the right to exclude newcomers who want to have access to the same land? And what, if anything, justifies their descendants' right to exclude given the tainted origins of first acquisition?

While the answer to the first question is likely to be uncontroversially negative, one way to respond to the second one is to invoke the supersession of prior injustice. With the passage of time, one might say, a change in circumstances progressively mitigates the initial injustice, if certain conditions about supersession hold. A claim that was established through wrongdoing in the past could then be considered justified going forward.

Theories of supersession are often invoked to discuss the rights of irregular migrants to naturalise in states in which they reside as a result of some prior wrongdoing. The alleged wrongdoing may take a number of forms, from unauthorised boundary crossing, to entering with false passports, to overstaying visas. Of course, those

doi:10.1017/S1358246122000066   © The Royal Institute of Philosophy and the contributors 2022

Royal Institute of Philosophy Supplement **91** 2022

implicated in these actions often have good reasons for committing them, and we may find additional resources to question categorising these actions as wrongdoing. But I want that to be the conclusion rather than the opening assumption of the paper. Let us agree, at least *ex hypothesi*, that irregular migrants commit a wrong in settling without official permission. What could justify granting them amnesty and a right to stay, regardless of that initial wrong?

To answer the question, the literature on amnesty in immigration invokes theories of supersession. Irregular migrants, it is often said, might acquire a right to stay in host states, provided certain conditions about supersession hold: a sufficient period of time has elapsed, no new wrongdoing has occurred and the claims have not in the meantime been contested (Shachar, 2009, pp. 185–189; see also Waldron, 1992; Bosniak, 2016).

The purpose of this paper is to explore the justification and implications of theories of supersession for states' rights to exclude irregular migrants in light of their own tainted history of territorial jurisdiction. In the first part of the paper, I look at some prominent criticisms of supersession theory applied to the case of irregular migration. I suggest that if the criticism of supersession theories leads to rejecting irregular migrants' right to stay, it also fails to justify the rights of states to exclude. The same critique of supersession that is often endorsed to reject clams to amnesty by irregular migrants can be deployed to reject the jurisdictional right of states and their related right to exclude.

In the second part of the paper I ask whether supersession theories can justify both the right of states to exclude and the rights of irregular immigrants to stay. A supersession trilemma then emerges. If the theory of supersession is sufficient to justify the rights of irregular migrants to stay, it is sufficient to justify the states' right to exclude too. But if states have a right to exclude, they can decide on which terms to accept or turn down illegal immigrants. That would mean that immigrants don't have a right to stay. But if they don't have a right to stay, why does the theory of supersession favour states' right to exclude and not the immigrants' right to stay? It looks as if either we should abandon arguments from supersession altogether, or that we have to find a way of reconciling how it applies to irregular migrants and to the right of states to exclude.

In the final part of the paper I explore what that reconciliation might look like. I suggest that we should hold states to the same stringent standards of compliance with just norms that *they* apply to the assessment of the moral conduct of individual migrants. I further argue that those standards ought to orient migrants and citizens' moral assessment of how their states handle questions of irregular migration and to inform political initiatives compatible with these moral assessments. This has important implications not just for how to think about irregular migration (e.g. with regard to practices of deportation, amnesty and naturalisation) but also on what kind of measures, if any, are acceptable to prevent irregular migration, and what role the theme of migration should play in theories of global justice more generally. I conclude the paper by sketching some of these implications.

2.

Let me start with a clarification and a reminder. The clarification is that when I speak about claims and rights, I mean moral claims and moral rights, not legal ones. States do all sorts of things as a matter of legal practice. They are within their right to do so in so far as that right is grounded on legal recognition backed up by the coercive use of force. But the international order may well be made up of many 'impostor' states who, much like the 'impostor' property-owners in Rousseau's *Discourses on inequality*, find people simple enough to believe their claim 'this is mine' and 'to forget that the fruits of the earth belong to all and the earth to no one' (Rousseau, 1997, p. 161). So, rather than taking the claims of states at face value, the task of political theory is to scrutinise that legal order and ask what its moral foundation might be.

The reminder concerns my use of the terms 'right to jurisdiction' and 'right to exclude'. Modern states, it is often said, are territorial agents. The right to jurisdiction is typically understood as a justified claim to make law within the particular territory a state occupies. The right to exclude is typically understood as a justified claim to control the movement of people and to establish the terms under which outsiders are permitted to enter and exit. Both are prerogatives of modern states as we know them, and both are the result of how sovereignty emerged and was consolidated.

But the history of how states came to bundle up these claims matters. And the history, as most would readily acknowledge, is not a happy one. Few would contest today that, as a matter of fact, the shaping of modern sovereignty involved the evolution of an international order in which projects of domestic repression and international colonization were pivotal to the development of state prerogatives, including the right to jurisdiction and the right to control the movement of people. Modern sovereignty was historically established against the background of thoroughly immoral and un-justified practices involving the colonization of distant others and the exploitation and/or displacement of internal dissident minorities for purposes of self-enrichment (Keal, 2003; Anaya, 2004; Pagden, 2007). Historically, the modern state was analogous to the gang of Mafiosi who manages to fence off a part of land and through the use of violence and oppression convinces everyone around that they have acquired legitimate claims to rule.

The tainted origins of territorial sovereignty are obvious if we focus on at least two dimensions. First, many states that now claim and enforce the right to exclude, states like the USA, Australia and Canada, emerged as a result of colonial settlement in areas occupied by indigenous groups, and through the unilateral coercion and estab-lishment of institutions and forms of rule that violated fair terms of association with members of such groups. Secondly, the territorial boundaries of many modern states were consolidated in a period of accumulation of wealth that involved a massive appropriation of labour and resources from oppressed minorities within and from the purchase and sale of slaves and other valuable resources outside (Ypi, 2013).

3.

All this is, of course, well-known. But while few would doubt that modern states really were like gangs of Mafiosi, many would object that this is no longer the case. Some might insist that we are now dealing not with the perpetrators but with their descendants, many of which include members of groups that were previously oppressed, whether within the territory or outside. What if anything can ground a claim to supersession of that initial injustice? What could justify the right to make laws in a particular territory and to keep others from claiming the same right?

Given the unjust past, that question now needs to be further quali-fied in light of our argument about the tainted origins of first acqui-sition. To justify the claim of wrongful occupants, we could appeal to theories of supersession. Think about the analogy with squatting. A squatter acquires a right to stay in a building that was initially wrongfully occupied provided a sufficient period of time has lapsed, nobody claims the occupied property and the squatter has es-tablished strong relevant ties to it in the meantime. Some authors have suggested that as a squatter can appeal to some version of super-session theory to turn a wrong into a right, wrongful occupants of land (or territory, in this case) might establish a right to that land after a sufficient period of time has elapsed, provided that the property has not been contested. As one author puts it, 'there must be a point in time when the authorities are stopped by their own inaction; in other words, the unauthorised entrants ought to gain immunity from deportation and removal, in addition to being offered an eventual route to legalising their status' (Shachar, 2009, pp. 185–87).

But when invoked in that context, critics of irregular migration tend to express reservations. They argue, for example, that the theory of supersession only works if it combines a claim to continuous enjoyment of access to land by the current illegitimate occupier with indifference from others whose rights are violated by such wrongful and unilateral acts. The latter, they emphasise, is clearly not the case in contemporary cases of conflicts over irregular migration since citizens of host states are very obviously worried about the impact of irregular migrations in their societies. Therefore, a version of supersession theory is insufficient to provide irregular migrants with a justification of the right to stay (Miller, 2016, pp. 122-23).

Let me return to my initial concern in light of this objection. Take the case of a country like the USA, or like Australia or like Canada, who all claim the right to deport irregular immigrants. These are all countries of irregular (or unauthorised) immigrants whose current claim to exclude is grounded (like that of the Mafia) on the violence, exploitation and displacement of indigenous people. If the theory of supersession does not give illegal immigrants a right to settle in the territory they occupy even after some lapse of time, it also does not justify the territorial rights of states whose claims to jurisdiction and the related right to exclude is built on an analogous (and in fact much worse) form of unilateral occupation of territory.

One could argue here that the 'ongoing contestation' clause matters. In the case of irregular migrants, unless there has been an amnesty, their legal residence is still contested. But in the case of states, their territorial rights can no longer be considered up for grabs, since the states' holding on to illegitimately acquired property can no longer be considered contested once they have been recognised by most other states.

But it is not clear here that the only recognition that matters is that of other states. Recall that I am concerned with the moral right to exclude, not the legal recognition of that right. To say that the right of states to exclude is recognised by other states is the same as saying that the claims of the Mafiosi are recognised by other Mafiosi. Surely what matters is not the Mafia itself but its victims. And surely what matters in the case of places like Australia and

Canada is not just what other states think and argue but also what members of indigenous groups whose lives and practices were disrupted by colonialism, think and argue. And if we turn to them, it is not clear that the moral authority of their state's right to jurisdiction is entirely uncontested, as the next pages go on to illustrate.

4.

One argument that critics of supersession claims often emphasise in the case of irregular migrants is the relevance of social membership ties. The argument from social membership ties is that the bonds that migrants develop to a host society over time justify their right to stay even if the modalities of access were unauthorised to begin with. As one prominent scholar puts it, since 'social membership does not depend on official permission', the 'moral right of the state to apprehend and deport irregular migrants erodes with the passage of time' (Carens, 2009).

But that argument has also been challenged. As one critic puts it, the social membership argument 'creates a strong presumption' in favour of allowing irregular immigrants to stay but it is one that 'can be legitimately set against the other goals that immigration policy is intended to achieve' (Miller, 2016, p. 124). Yet if we apply that very same argument to the descendants of the Mafiosi and their alleged right to exclude, we would say that although with the passing of time they have acquired a presumption to stay and claim a right to jurisdiction where they are, such presumption would also have to be set against 'the other goals that immigration policy is intended to achieve'. Therefore, if the argument from social membership ties can be criticised as inconclusive to authorise the right to stay of irregular migrants, it is also inconclusive to establish a right to jurisdiction in the case of the citizens of liberal democracies whose right to exclude we fail to problematise.

5.

One objection to the story I have told so far is that the disanalogies between the case of recent irregular immigrants and that of the descendants of the Mafiosi might weaken my case. But in so far as there are disanalogies, I think they support rather than undermine the overall argument. One important disanalogy concerns the role played by the amount of time that stands between the original wrong and the point in which the demands of supersession are triggered. Surely, someone might say, it is a long time since white settlers abused aboriginal people in Australia but people overstay their visas all the time in current circumstances.

Yet, it is hard to be convinced that timescale should matter more than what one does in the time that has passed. Surely what really matters is not how much time has passed but whether the agents who are responsible for wrongdoing have in the meantime rectified the wrongs they are responsible for. In the case of amnesty for recent irregular migrants it matters for example that, except for the original wrongdoing, migrants can show a history of compliance with the norms of the host community, and that the initial offence involving breaking the law has not been repeated. But the same cannot be said for colonising states. Their body of laws and their public attitudes more often than not reinforce the norms of the colonial past rather than departing from them. The history of interactions with indigenous communities in Australia and Canada illustrates that often the same colonial arrogance that pervaded relations in the past characterises the way in which demands by these groups are met in the present too. As, Luke Pearson, the founder of @Indigenous X, an online platform for sharing the perspectives of indigenous communities in Australia put it, 'Do you really think that we are upset over what happened "200 years" ago, or what started 200 years ago? [...] Remote Aboriginal communities in Western Australia are facing forced dispossession of their land right now. Aboriginal children are locked up or removed from their families every single day, as they have been for generations. [...] You cannot get over a "colonial" past that is still being implemented today'.[1]

Irregular migrants can usually prove that the alleged wrong of unauthorised crossing of boundaries or the wrong involved in overstaying visas (even *if* one considers these to be wrongs) is limited to these individual instances. But the colonial wrongs of the past are continuously reiterated and pervade the norms of formerly colonising states even in our days. Bygones are by no means bygones.

A second objection concerns the identity of those on whose behalf the theory of supersession is invoked. In the case of migrants, those who have committed the wrong and those who claim the right to stay are the same people. In the case of states those who have committed the wrong and those who claim the right to exclude are different.

[1]   https://www.theguardian.com/australia-news/commentisfree/ 2016/apr/02/dont-tell-me-to-get-over-a-colonialism-that-is-still-being-implemented-today.

If the perpetrators are long dead and gone, the wrong fades over time. But in the case of migration, wrongdoers are still alive and the analogy seems to break down.

To answer this objection, it pays to think more about the agent on behalf of whom the claim to exclude is being made. The state is an artificial agent; its identity is a legal one. In the absence of revolution, the state preserves its identity just as any corporate agent does, through the replication of rules, practices and regulations applied by various officials. That such officials are individual people with finite lives makes no difference to the social positions they occupy, and to the rules they are asked to enact. It is only when the state's laws, practices, and regulations take a radically different form that the identity of the state as an artificial agent is fundamentally altered. The identity of the state is not explained with reference to the identity of the people that enact its rules, but with reference to the identity of the fundamental social institutions that shape its legal profile over time.

This is where colonial history becomes relevant. The corporate identity of the most powerful states is the direct result of their colonial past. There have been no revolutions in the international legal order: the effect of decolonisation has been to consolidate imperial legacies rather than undermine them.[2] Both the way in which liberal Western states currently police their boundaries, and the way in which they make decisions on who to admit and who to exclude is shaped by their contribution to colonial projects and by the way in which the movement of people has been regulated following processes of decolonisation (for an insightful history see Torpey, 2000). While it is true that in the case of states, the identity of citizens at any given point in time is different, the claim to exclude is made on behalf of a corporate agent whose legal personality is maintained over time. That the individual identity of citizens is different, matters very little when different citizens are responsible for complying with the same exclusionary laws.

Another disanalogy that a critic might invoke is that in the case of recent immigrants, the cost of exclusion is deportation and deportation, however nasty, implies that immigrants have another place to return to. But in the case of citizens of formerly colonising states there would be no other place to settle and no deportation is at stake. In response two points can be made. The first is that even

---

[2]   For the most recent evidence on the reproduction of the contemporary legal order, see the excellent discussion in Parfitt (2019). See also the essays in Bell (ed., 2019).

though citizens of host states have nowhere to move into, the most advantaged among them have ample scope of levelling down to make available some of their land and resources to newcomers. Secondly, notice that deportation is only the visible expression of what is thought to be a prior wrong, namely the fact that irregular migrants take advantage of the benefits of a host community whilst not being entitled to do so. Deportation is the price to pay when you have no right to stay, and no justified claim to join a particular territorial group in making specific political rules, in this case rules about who is in and who is out. But this is also true if we focus on the case of the descendants of formerly colonising states, since the challenge we are mounting is precisely that the forms of political association they find themselves involved in do not have the moral legitimacy that they claim they do when it comes to shaping the precise boundaries of who is in and who is out. The conclusion to draw is that regardless of whether deportation is available, the right to make political rules with regard to the boundaries of a self-governing political body in the case of citizens of formerly colonial states can be challenged in the same way it is challenged in the case of irregular migrants and for much the same (moral) reasons.

One might object here that the force of my argument is limited because it only shows that there is something wrong with the right to exclude as practiced by former colonial states but does not extend beyond them. It is limited because it does not challenge the right to exclude as such, and it does not protect all irregular migrants from the abuses of all states (including those with no colonial history). This is undoubtedly true. But while I remain open to alternative ways of challenging the right to exclude, my analogy captures the most problematic examples of exclusion, in the majority of liberal democratic states, indeed it targets precisely those states who are at the forefront of current exclusionary policies with regard to irregular migration. It targets states built on settler societies who have consolidated their institutions on the basis of the exclusion of indigenous populations (think about the USA, Australia or Canada). But it also targets former colonial states whose wealth and institutions have emerged partly as a result of the exploitation of labour and resources in other parts of the world (like the UK, France or the Netherlands). Wherever we look in contemporary liberal democracies, the states adopting the harshest exclusionary practices and setting the standards of hostile immigration policy when it comes to irregular migration are also those carrying the heaviest colonial debt. This debt is still outstanding and makes current generations of citizens of many wealthy liberal democracies look much like the descendants of the Mafia in the example with which I started. While other states can and should also be held into account (perhaps on different grounds) the tainted link between the claim to jurisdiction and the right to exclude in the cases I have examined is an important source of moral critique. This critique ought to shape how citizens of liberal states think about who they are, and in what terms they engage with the problem of irregular migration.

6.

Let me consider now a more general criticism to the argument presented so far. If the right to jurisdiction of former colonising states can be challenged when it comes to issues of amnesty in migration, what about other laws? Does the tainted history of states' jurisdiction mean that everything any given state does or purports to do, every claim it makes on those subjected to its authority loses its force? To answer this question, it is important to return to the distinction between a legal and a moral claim to rule with which we started. My critique of many liberal states' treatment of immigrants is a moral critique, and the point of such critique is not to challenge all aspects of law-making but to scrutinise its moral foundation with a view to informing political judgment on its most problematic aspects. Not all areas of law are a contentious political issue, and colonial history may or may not be relevant even to those that are. Traffic laws, for example, are only mildly controversial and the history of how they emerged may or may not be relevant to their current moral assessment. If it is, as with cases of segregation of particular groups, then it should inform debate in that policy domain too. More generally, it seems plausible to say that there may be prudential or moral justifications for particular laws and policies that are compatible with denying moral standing to the institution that makes those laws and policies. If an apartheid state makes laws that prohibit murder, it is a good idea to respect those laws, however unjustified many, perhaps most, of its other laws are (see on this last aspect also Simmons, 2001, pp.155–57).

But let me return to the case of political debates around irregular migration that is the focus of this paper. The history of how states came to enforce the right to exclude, and against whom, is – as I tried to show – crucial to the current assessment of their moral authority when it comes to the enforcement of border controls. That history ought to feature much more prominently in our assessment of the claims of irregular migrants and in debates surrounding amnesty in immigration. Instead, in the current debate historical considerations only matter when we assess the biographies of individual migrants and when we appeal to supersession theory to reflect on the potential case for mitigating the wrong of, say, unauthorised boundary crossing or unlawful visa overstay. The point of the comparison with colonial injustice is to orient our judgment when setting out relevant criteria for deciding around issues of amnesty. Some may find supersession theory a controversial point to start with. But let us assume, as many seem to do, that it is a plausible way of seeking philosophical orientation when answering pressing contemporary questions. Consistency requires that we extend the comparison beyond the case of individual migrants to the case of agents on whose behalf assessments of compliance or noncompliance are made. Therefore either we should be much more concessive when assessing the case for amnesty in immigration or uphold strict standards but direct them to a more radical critique of the states' moral claim to exclude. The former colonial state, as we know it, can either defend a moral right to jurisdiction or a moral right to exclude, but it cannot defend both.

7.

Suppose however that a critic bites the bullet at this point. Suppose, that critic argues, that supersession theory justifies *both* the right of states to exclude and the rights of irregular immigrants to stay. This would give rise to what we may call the supersession trilemma. If supersession theory is sufficient to justify the rights of irregular migrants to stay, it has sufficient plausibility to justify the states right to exclude too. But if the states have a right to exclude, they can decide on which terms to accept or exclude illegal immigrants. That would mean that immigrants do not after all have a right to stay – they depend on state regulation for that. Therefore it looks like supersession theory, the justification of the right to exclude and the rights of irregular immigrants to stay cannot all be maintained at the same time. Either we drop supersession theory, or we have to think of a way of reconciling its requirements with regard to the states' right to exclude and the immigrants' right to stay.

I think it would be unwise to drop supersession theory altogether. The origins of most claims to territory and property are tainted, the arguments they give rise to are contested. Thinking about the *current* use of land and resources in settling difficult disputes related to these claims seems like a reasonable way to proceed. But what the implication of supersession theory vis-à-vis the right to exclude shows is that there are important asymmetries to take into account when balancing the different claims.

One important implication of this point concerns the claim to indifference. Recall how supersession theories maintain that an agent may be entitled to keep certain goods that have been unjustly acquired, provided sufficient time has passed from the original wrong and provided that other people are indifferent to their current use. Migrants are not indifferent to the territorial rights of states. They are also not indifferent to the process through which such rights came to be established. Colonial history for them is not just history, it is one of the most important (often *the* most important) reasons that they are forced to migrate. As the Mexican saying goes: 'we did not cross the border, the border crossed us'. The migrants currently drowning in the Mediterranean or subjected to dehumanising treatment in detention camps in Libya all come from states that were former European colonies. They are a victim of European Union border enforcement practices, as well as of the asymmetrical, manipulative processes of negotiation between the EU and its former colonies and satellite states (Mezzadra and Neilson, 2013). The abusive colonial history of European states in the past is the premise of their predicament in the present.

Looking at it from the other perspective, current inhabitants of former colonial states are not indifferent to the fact that states should retain the right to exclude. They are also not equally responsible for their states' past wrongdoing. It would be wrong to ask domestic oppressed minorities or the more vulnerable citizens of these societies to bear the cost for the past and present failures of their ruling elites to endorse radical change. This is perhaps what motivates liberal defenders of states right to exclude to only frame debates on supersession as a debate about amnesty in immigration. This answer is insensitive to the injustices that cause irregular migration in the first place, and obliterates the power asymmetries that pervade both the political institutions of liberal states and the global international order that they contribute to shape. This is not how to do justice to immigrants, but it is also not how to do justice to the claims of vulnerable citizens in host states.

8.

The liberal solution to the supersession trilemma burdens immigrants disproportionately and lets liberal ruling elites off the hook. To reconcile the claims of migrants and those of the most vulnerable citizens of liberal states, we need to readjust our image of the contemporary liberal political community as one that acts in the interests of all its citizens. We ought to apply to states, the same criteria for supersession of injustice that they apply to individual immigrants. The first such criterion, recall, is the recognition of previous wrongdoing. The second, the analogue to individual good character, is evidence of compliance with norms of global justice. On this account, the justification of the states' right to exclude is conditional on the rectification of historical wrongs and the elimination of the structural injustices that turn migration into a problem in the first place. Once we apply to states the same criteria of rectification and compliance with the just norms of a global society of states as they apply to immigrants, we can address the supersession trilemma with a weak, permissive, justification of their territorial rights.

This theory has been discussed in greater detail elsewhere and it is not necessary to repeat the argument here (Ypi, 2014). What matters to this paper is acknowledging that the global order we currently have is continuous with that which led to the emergence of colonialism and the structural reproduction of exploitation and injustices of both domestic minorities and vulnerable groups and populations in other areas of the world. Until the political institutions of dominant Western states make a clean break with such past patterns of unjust accumulation and exploitation, their right to exclude should not trump irregular immigrants claim to stay. When I talk about a clean break with the past, I do not mean a mere change of leadership, or the support for policies tweaking the old system here and there. This is just what we have now. What I mean is a fundamental transformation of the corporate identity of the state, the abolition of the legal and political regimes that reproduce colonial dependence and replicate structural injustice, and their replacement with political institutions promoting social justice and radical democracy at every level, both domestic and international. While explaining how exactly all this would work takes us too far from the topic of this paper, here I want to end with just three implications of my approach for the question of irregular migration as it affects us here and now.

One important implication is that until these changes are in place, there should be not only amnesty in immigration but also access to citizenship rights for irregular migrants. Both should be automatic and unconditional (De Schutter and Ypi, 2015). The second is that practices through which liberal states take advantage of the colonial past by outsourcing border control to third parties, or by involving client states in the enhancement of border controls (e.g. in the form of border walls) should be condemned as a matter of not just international but also domestic justice. A political community that has not settled accounts with its own problematic past cannot be considered internally just since the current shape of its political institutions is premised on the exploitation and domination of vulnerable minorities both within its borders and outside: the one cannot exist without the other. The third is that the creation and consolidation of detention camps within the territories of liberal state should be considered akin to political apartheid, and the states enforcing such policies should be the target of international condemnation, boycotts and civil disobedience campaigns as has been the case with apartheid regimes in the past.

Some of this reiterates ongoing calls of pro-immigration theorists and activists all over the world. But the justification is new and more radical. What motivates my argument is neither a prudential argument that explains how immigration is after all in the interest of host societies nor an abstract moral defence of the human right to freedom of movement. It is an argument that applies to states the same standards for supersession of injustice that they apply to individual immigrants, emphasising how domestic and international justice are interdependent. There is no real conflict between the demands of vulnerable citizens within liberal states and those of irregular immigrants. The same system that enables the exclusion of the latter shapes the conditions for the exploitation of the former. Powerful elites benefit from both kinds of exclusion and shape political institutions that give them discretion over how far to share these benefits and with whom. Historical and structural injustice mutually support each other, and the conditions for the supersession of the one, are the same as those that require the elimination of the other. Colonialism and immigration are entrenched. If we fail to explore the implications of that entrenchment for our assessment of justice and injustice, and of whether they belong to the present or to the past, all efforts to solve the conflicts to which they give rise will be short-lived and ill-directed.

LSE
l.l.ypi@lse.ac.uk

References

S. James Anaya, *Indigenous Peoples in International Law* (Oxford: Oxford University Press, 2004).

Duncan Bell (ed.) *Empire, Race and Global Justice* (Cambridge: Cambridge University Press, 2019).

Linda Bosniak, 'Wrongs, Rights and Regularization', *Moral Philosophy and Politics*, 3, (2016) 187–222.

Joseph Carens, 'The case for amnesty', *Boston Review*, (2009).

Paul Keal, *European Conquest and the Rights of Indigenous Peoples: The Moral Backwardness of International Society* (Cambridge: Cambridge University Press, 2003).

Sandro Mezzadra and Brett Neilson, *Border as Method or the Multiplication of Labor* (Duke University Press, 2013).

David Miller, *Strangers in Our Midst* (Cambridge Harvard University Press, 2016).

Anthony Pagden, *Peoples and Empires, A Short History of European Migration, Exploration and Conquest from Greece to the Present* (Random House Publishing, 2007).

Rose Parfitt, *The Process of International Legal Reproduction: Inequality, Historiography, Resistance* (Cambridge: Cambridge University Press, 2019).

Helder De Schutter and Lea Ypi, 'Mandatory Citizenship for Immigrants, *The British Journal of Political Science*, 45 (2015), 235–51.

Ayelet Shachar, *The Birthright Lottery: Citizenship and Global Inequality,* (Cambridge: Harvard University Press, 2009).

John Torpey, *The Invention of the Passport* (Cambridge: Cambridge University Press, 2000).

A.J. Simmons, *Justification and Legitimacy. Essays on Rights and Obligations* (Cambridge: Cambridge University Press, 2001).

Jeremy Waldron, 'Superseding historic injustice', *Ethics*, 103 (1992), 4–28.

Lea Ypi, 'A Permissive Theory of Territorial Rights', *The European Journal of Philosophy*, 22 (2014), 288–312.

Lea Ypi, 'What's Wrong with Colonialism', *Philosophy and Public Affairs*, 41 (2013) 158–91.

Radical Democratic Inclusion: Why We Should Lower the Voting Age to 12

MARTIN O'NEILL

Abstract

Democratic societies such as the United Kingdom have come to fail their young citizens, often sacrificing their interests in a political process that gives much greater weight to the preferences and interests of older citizens. Against this background of intergenerational injustice, this article presents the case for a shift in the political system in the direction of radical democratic inclusion of younger citizens, through reducing the voting age to 12. This change in the voting age can be justified directly, with reference to the status, interests, and capacities of younger citizens, and it can also be justified as a remedy to existing forms of intergenerational injustice. This change in the voting age would require a parallel transformation in the role of secondary schools as part of the 'critical infrastructure' of a democratic society, which would be part of a broader shift towards a more genuinely democratic political culture. The proposal is defended against less radical alternatives (such as votes at 16) and more radical alternatives (such as votes for younger children). The article concludes with some reflections on democracy and intergenerational justice in light of the Covid pandemic and the climate emergency.

1. Introduction: Radical Democratic Inclusion and Votes for Young Citizens

This essay presents an argument for a deep transformation of our democratic societies, so as to make them more inclusive of younger citizens. On the view I present here, the borders of full citizenship should be extended to include those, from the age of twelve upwards, who are in secondary level education. This is obviously a radical proposal in more ways than one, and is far from the real-world political agenda of any current political society, where debates in this area usually go only so far as considering the extension of the franchise to those aged sixteen and over. Nevertheless, among the tasks that properly fall to political philosophers is the task of considering political proposals that may in some respects still be seen as unlikely or, at least, ahead of their time. In that spirit, I aim here to make a case in favour of this shift towards the democratic inclusion of teenagers, in the hope that the merits of

doi:10.1017/S135824612200008X
Royal Institute of Philosophy Supplement **91** 2022

the case for enacting this kind of democratic transformation will in time come to seem unanswerable.

The structure of the essay is as follows. In Section 2, I discuss the significant respects in which our current political societies fail their younger citizens. In Section 3 I present the core argument in favour of extending the vote to those aged twelve and over, respond to a number of criticisms that this view might face as regards the status, interests and capacities of teenage citizens, and I highlight the broader changes in the culture of democratic politics with which this change would be associated. Section 4 defends the proposal to lower the voting age to twelve against some (more or less radical) rival proposals. Section 5 concludes, while offering some thoughts on the particular context for this change in the light of the Covid pandemic and the climate emergency.

2. Societies That Fail Their Young Citizens

It is difficult to avoid the conclusion that Britain – like many other economically developed democratic societies – is now a society that does not serve its young people at all well. Indeed, to put things more strongly, this is now a country that has let down the next generation rather severely, and in a variety of different ways. It has become common to hear about particular geographical communities that have been 'left behind', but alongside this we have to realise that we live in societies where the younger generation are being 'kept behind', with their life-chances systematically restricted and their aspirations frustrated. It is a sign that something has gone badly wrong in the operation of our democratic societies when, despite aggregate levels of societal wealth continuing to rise, the next generation face a future of uncertainty, debt, and economic precarity, with their mental health suffering in the face of trying to adjust to a society that seems designed to operate against their interests. Furthermore, this is all happening at a time in which our collective democratic institutions continue to fail to address the unfolding climate crisis with anything like the required level of seriousness of purpose.

It is unsurprising that many young people turn away from political engagement, through a mixture of frustration, hopelessness and disaffection, and so it is also unsurprising that electoral turnout is lowest among the youngest cohorts.[1] This of course only exacerbates the

---

[1] See for example 'Age and Voting Behaviour at the 2019 General Election', British Election Study, 27 January 2021. Online at: https://www.britishelectionstudy.com/bes-findings/age-and-voting-behaviour-at-the-2019-general-election/. The British Election study data shows that the

problems of intergenerational inequality in both the economic and political domains, as older cohorts find themselves able to get the political system to respond to their social and economic interests, further tilting the playing field away from the interests of the young. Even relatively advantaged young people in the UK face some rather unappealing future prospects. In this regard, I often think of the situation faced by my own students. In many ways, they are in what should be a wonderful position at an early stage in their lives, having secured places at a good university in a prosperous society; yet their prospects are deeply uncertain, and even those who secure good jobs will (in the absence of the particular unfair advantages enjoyed by those who can expect large financial transfers from parents or grandparents) be likely to find themselves spending years when they pay forty or even fifty percent of their income as rent to landlords, alongside their repayments of large amounts of student debt, not knowing when they might be able to purchase a home, or start a family. For many even of this relatively advantaged group, their lives are beset by the phenomenon described by Jonathan Wolff and Avner de-Shalit as 'planning blight', with a sense of precarity and uncertainty making it difficult for them to move confidently forwards in their lives in the way that their parents or (even more so) their grandparents would have been able to do at a similar age.[2] It is absolutely unsurprising, therefore, that there is an epidemic of mental ill health among young people in our societies – such a response can be seen not as a disconnected pathology, but as an entirely reasonable response to objective circumstances.[3]

It is not just those in their late teens and twenties who are being so systematically ill-served by our social and economic institutions. Those in the immediately younger cohort are, if anything, being treated even worse. Real terms levels of education funding were cut significantly in the UK over the 2010s, and this came in the wake

---

level of turnout among the 18-24 age cohort was only around 50% in the 2015, 2017 and 2019 elections (albeit rising gradually across these three elections), whereas among those aged 75 and above, turnout in these elections was over 80%. It is also important to note that rates of electoral registration are much higher among older voters.

[2]   See Wolff and de-Shalit (2007, p. 69). See also Bidadanure (2018).

[3]   Mark Fisher wrote movingly and insightfully on this subject. See for example Fisher (2012) and Fisher (2014). See also the work of David Smail, which Fisher cites, e.g. Smail (2015).

of the abolition of the Education Maintenance Allowance (EMA) in 2010, which had provided some significant financial support for less-advantaged young people continuing in full-time education.[4] Although examples from countries such as Iceland have shown the enormous benefits of public funding of sporting and social activities for teenagers, no such programme of public investment in the well-being of teenagers ever makes its way onto the political agenda in most countries.[5] And, of course, teenagers know well what is ahead of them in terms of the difficulties faced by young adults in their societies, with the understandable consequence that for them too it is difficult to face the future with optimism and confidence.

In short, our younger generations find themselves in a predicament where they face intertwining and mutually reinforcing social problems. Given the reliance of their life chances on potential future capital transfers from their parents and grandparents, which in so many cases make individuals' economic prospects depend not on their own talents, ideas, energy or hard work, but simply on the economic position they inherit from predecessor generations, we have a crisis of opportunity and of social mobility.[6] These sorts of circumstances constitute a direct violation of even the most minimal requirement of social justice: whereas at one point the readers of Rawls's *A Theory of Justice* might have considered the idea of 'fair equality of opportunity' to be a remarkably modest and uncontroversial principle of justice, it now seems like a distant or even mockingly unattainable ideal.[7] Alongside this, the phenomenon of 'planning blight' mentioned above, with young people left economically dependent on their parents for longer, and facing economic precarity, a mountain of debt from university, and for those who can get their own place to live, frequently facing years with insecure housing tenure as they transfer much of their income to a landlord, means that we see something close to a crisis of social reproduction, as it becomes increasingly difficult for people to form families of their

---

[4]   See e.g. Forrest (2021); Sibieta (2021). On the Education Maintenance Allowance, see Bolton (2011); Murray (2010).

[5]   For the Icelandic Youth Fund, and the Icelandic Sport Fund, see the website of Rannis (*Rannsóknamiðstöð Íslands*), the Icelandic Centre for Research, here: https://en.rannis.is/funding/youth-sport (for sport funding) and here https://en.rannis.is/funding/youth-sport/youth-fund/ (for general funding for youth activities). See also Young (2017).

[6]   See Piketty (2014); O'Neill (2017, esp. pp. 357-58).

[7]   Rawls (1999, §12, §14). See also Rawls (2001, §§13-14); O'Neill and Shields (2017); O'Neill and Williamson (2009); O'Neill (2012).

own, and to advance through their lives in the ways that previous generations would have simply taken for granted.[8]

Taken together, these crises of social mobility and social reproduction can be seen not only as bad in themselves, but also as fundamentally undermining younger people's freedom: the current younger generation simply does not have the range of live open options for how they might want to live their lives that their parents and grandparents were able to enjoy. What we would expect all of this to lead towards is a further crisis – a crisis of social inclusion and social allegiance – whereby it becomes increasingly difficult to see why younger generations should give their affiliation and support to a socioeconomic system that constricts their sense of agency, facilitates their economic exploitation, and stymies their long-run life chances.

There are many aspects of economic and social policy that would need to change in order to transform the position of the younger generation in a more favourable direction. But it is difficult to envisage such measures being implemented in the absence of a more foundational change: that is, a change in the distribution of political voice and power within our societies. Younger people have become accustomed not only to having their interests largely ignored in the political system, but also constantly to finding themselves on the losing side in democratic decision-making. In recent years in the United Kingdom, younger cohorts did not vote for Brexit in 2016, and in 2017 and 2019 backed the more egalitarian social democratic option presented by the Labour Party, only to find themselves serially, repeatedly defeated; meanwhile, the political system again and again delivers on the preferences, and protects the interests, of retired voters. Those with less of a long-run stake in the society again and again get their way over those whose lives lie mostly still ahead of them, all the while turning the younger generation into something akin to a permanent internal minority: ripped-off, unsupported, marginalized, and frequently even exploited and demonised.

It is natural to think that a flourishing society is one where the life prospects of each succeeding generation are an improvement on the preceding generation. The French political theorist, one time Prime Minister and Nobel Peace Prize winner Léon Bourgeois, whose thought has in recent years gained renewed influence on writers such as Thomas Piketty, defended a plausible 'solidaristic' conception of intergenerational justice, according to which each generation has an obligation to improve the life situation of the next

---

[8] On the crisis of social reproduction, see Fraser (2016); see also Bidadanure, op. cit..

generation, as a way of solidaristically acknowledging and symbolic-
ally repaying the benefits they had received from previous generations.[9] In more recent decades, philosophers have defended a
related, but more modest, conception of intergenerational justice,
which requires, as Philippe Van Parijs puts it, 'each generation,
each birth cohort, to make sure the situation of the next generation
[…] is no worse than its own'.[10] Given the background environmental
crisis and the social problems outlined above, neither the solidaristic
standard of continual onward improvement nor the more modest
standard of making things no worse is being met under current circumstances.[11] We live in societies that are failing completely to
meet even modest requirements of intergenerational justice, and so
our younger generations are absolutely justified in feeling that they
are being treated in a manner that is both unjust and unacceptable.

This introductory section has presented a brief sketch of the situation in which we find ourselves, in which our societies are now
failing their younger citizens in various, mutually reinforcing ways.
Younger people face deep intergenerational injustices, in the
context of a political system that is structurally indisposed either to
take their interests sufficiently seriously so as to remedy those injustices, or to give them sufficient voice or influence so as to be able to
undertake a fundamental reorientation of that system in the direction
of more just outcomes. Writing over twenty years ago, Philippe Van
Parijs talked about the situation in advanced industrial societies that
saw a confluence of (a) deep injustices being wrought on younger generations, and (b) a political system that makes any attempt to address
these injustices almost impossible, given the excessive political power
of older generations, so that 'the political feasibility of [any] reform
that would prevent such injustices is exceedingly problematic,
given how our democracies are currently organized' (Van Parijs,
1999, pp. 295-96). Van Parijs's prediction in 1999 was that, with
the median age of voters only likely to rise in subsequent years,
getting closer to the retirement age in advanced industrial societies,
these problems were only likely to become deeper, more pronounced,
and more troubling. Unfortunately, history has proven that this pessimistic prediction was completely correct, although what Van Parijs

---

[9] See Bourgeois (1902); see also Piketty (2020) and O'Neill (2021). On
conceptions of intergenerational reciprocity see Gosseries (2009).
[10] Van Parijs (1999, p. 294). See also Rawls's discussion of the 'Just
Savings Principle' in Rawls, op. cit., on which see also Meyer (2021).
[11] On the dimensions of the environmental crisis, see Lawrence and
Laybourn-Langton (2021).

could not have known at the time he was writing was the way in which some of the most burdensome consequences of the crises of the twenty-first century – most notably the Great Financial Crisis of 2007-8 and the Covid pandemic from 2020 onwards – have been further loaded onto the shoulders of the young, making the situation now even more baleful than could have been predicted in extrapolating in a linear fashion from the trends of the late twentieth century.[12] The contours of these problems of intergenerational injustice, and the difficulty of solving them within our existing institutions have, then, been known for quite some time, but they are now manifesting with a worryingly increased severity. What then is to be done?

3. A Radical Remedy: Votes for Young Citizens

In the context of these age-based injustices, I want to suggest that the vote should be extended to young citizens from the age of 12, so that the population of teenagers who are in secondary education are fully enfranchised. The franchise has expanded continually over the history of democratic societies, and this is a clear and obvious next step in this process of broadening the basis of democratic politics. To take the case of the United Kingdom, we have only really had a genuinely broad democratic franchise since the Representation of the People Act of 1918, which abolished property qualification among male voters, and extended the vote to a subset of women aged over 30, in the process roughly trebling the size of the electorate. The franchise was only extended to all women over the age of 18 in the Equal Franchise Act of 1928 (for comparison, France did not extend the vote to women until as late as 1944, a change voted through by De Gaulle's government-in-exile in London). And those aged 18-20 in the United Kingdom only became voters as late as the 1969 Representation of the People Act.[13] In short, the limits and contours of the right to vote have been far from stable, and have undergone periodic expansions in the direction of greater democratic inclusion. There is no reason to think that a limitation

[12] For the impact of the Great Financial Crisis on the young, and its knock-on effects in creating a collective sense of political consciousness among a specific generation see Milburn (2019). On the monetary policy response to the Covid pandemic increasing existing asset values (and thereby exacerbating intergenerational inequalities), see Tooze (2021).
[13] On the history of the expanding franchise, see Foot (2005); see also Vallance (2009); Johnston (2013).

of the franchise to those 18 and over is a deep or inviolable feature of electoral politics and, indeed the 2014 Scottish Independence Referendum operated with a franchise extended to 16 year olds, as have elections to the Scottish Parliament since that time. Democratic inclusion is a work-in-progress, in the UK as in other developed democratic societies and, as I hope to be able to show in what follows, it is a process that we have very strong reasons to keep pushing forward.

An extension of the vote to those 12 and over would give voice and standing to young people in our society, and ensure that their views, values and interests were given greater attention in our democratic deliberations. By dropping the voting age from 18 down to 12, we would also be making a significant move in the right direction as regards the redistribution of political power away from older and retired voters, giving ourselves the opportunity to have a society that moves beyond the current marginalisation of the young, in favour of one that treats them more fully as fundamentally our equals. In this section, my aim is to give the (rather straightforward) basic argument in favour of democratic inclusion of those of secondary school age, to rebut some possible lines of criticism, and to embed the proposal in a broader discussion of what it would be to have a more genuinely democratic society.

(a) Taking All Citizens' Interests Seriously

Why should we include the young in our democratic institutions? The positive argument is remarkably simple and straightforward: it is that young members of our society (a) are participating citizens whose lives are lived as part of our shared social and institutional environment; (b) have fundamental interests that are deeply at stake when it comes to how they are treated by the social, political and economic institutions of our society; and (c) do not in general lack any specific capacity that would allow them to exercise their democratic rights as voters, or as citizens more generally. My position is that these three claims, taken together, constitute a jointly sufficient case for the democratic inclusion of young people.

Claim (a) and claim (c) hold that there is not a relevant difference between those in the 12-17 age range and their older fellow citizens. But with claim (b) one could put things rather more strongly; indeed, one might say that younger citizens have especially weighty and long-run interests with regard to the evolution over time of our societies as, quite simply, those with more years ahead of them are going to be more enduringly affected by current political and economic decisions, certainly much more so than much older voters, who may be coming towards the latter years of their lives. Moreover, other things being equal, we would expect that those whose interests are going to be more fully at stake, over a longer time period, would have more reason to take a long-term time horizon in their thinking, and to be able to take long run considerations more seriously than those for whom the future of their society will not be a future through which they themselves will live.[14] Indeed, one sees some striking evidence of this in the generally much higher level of awareness of, and mobilisation around, environmental issues evinced by younger people.[15]

(b) Rebutting Some Common Objections – on Status, Interests and Capacity

The straightforward positive case for democratic inclusion of young people should, on the face of it, be hard to resist. Why, then, might people nevertheless be unmoved by it, or look to resist it? One claim might be that those under the age of 18 do not really meet the first element of the description given above – i.e. that they are not participants in our shared institutions, and hence lack a relevant stake, or the relevant standing, that would be a precondition for full democratic citizenship. One could imagine narrower accounts of what it is to be a full participant in society, emphasizing economic contribution through work or contribution to the state's budget (e.g. as a 'tax payer'), or some other level of positive contribution that younger cohorts are held not to meet. Nevertheless, one can rebut this line of argument in more than one way. At a relatively superficial level one can point out that many young people, under the age of 18, do indeed contribute in these ways, whether through part-time work, or through paying taxes of various kinds. Conversely, many people aged 18 or over are not themselves in full-time employment, and may find themselves outside the scope of the income tax system, and no more involved in paying other taxes than are other, younger people. But more fundamentally, this

---

[14] For discussion of this point, see Bidadanure (2016).

[15] See for example the remarkable spread of the Youth Strike for Climate / Skolstrejk för Klimatet movement founded by Greta Thunberg in 2018. See, e.g., Taylor (2021) and Carrington (2021). See also Thunberg (2019).

economistic way of measuring social participation is both unreasonable and anachronistic – indeed, it smacks unpleasantly of the kind of thinking that stood behind nineteenth century property qualifications for the vote. People can be full participating members of society in all sorts of ways, through the contribution they make to their communities, their families, and to the intermediate institutions of which they are part; and people aged 12-18 absolutely can and do make social contributions of just these kids. Moreover, given that most people in this age group are in full-time education, they are typically daily participants in one of the most important kinds of institutions within our societies, actively involved in developing their capacities and, through that current institutional participation, building their capability to make a valuable social contribution in many other ways in the years ahead.

An unsympathetic reader might say that I'm here unduly weakening the relevant idea of participation, but in response it should be borne in mind that, over the long-run history of democratic societies, the evolution of thinking about the franchise has in essence been about shifting from unduly pinched and narrow conceptions of what it is to be a full citizen in the relevant sense, towards a more open and expansive conception. In her remarkable book on the history of the emergence of democratic constitutions, *The Gun, the Ship and the Pen: Warfare, Constitutions and the Making of the Modern World*, Linda Colley emphasises the way in which the extension of the franchise was at first, in the late eighteenth century, internally associated with the extension of military conscription (Colley, 2021). To be a full citizen was to be someone available for military service and so, indeed, the demand for democratic rights often came from within the ranks of military men. Here, then, was an idea of full participation associated with one's standing as a member of a society's fighting force, and hence we see the restriction of the franchise in early democratic constitutions to men. While historically revealing, nobody would now want to defend a conception of democratic participation connected in this way to martial capacity. One can see the expansion of the franchise in the nineteenth century as a turn away from this martial idea of citizenship to a more economic conception, but with the abolition of property qualifications for women's voting rights in the UK in 1928, this too was something that a democratic society such as the UK managed to move beyond. People can be full participating members of society in all sorts of ways, and we would not now think it justifiable to exclude someone on the basis of their economic status – indeed, we should see that as being as absurd as a removal of the vote from those who had not served or were not available to serve in the military.[16] The conflation of 'voter' and 'tax payer' in some parts of the popular political imagination should be seen for what it is – an unjustifiable and indeed rather sinister anachronism.

So much for some of the common objections to claim (a) above. I would hazard the view that, when it comes to claim (b) nobody would be so perverse as to claim that young people do not have fundamental interests that are deeply at stake when it comes to the direction of politics and policy in their societies. To deny that would be not so much merely to deny the political status of young people as to fundamentally deny their underlying moral status; that would be a view as implausible as it is offensive. The significance of the interests at stake here becomes still more pronounced when we take a more complex, intertemporal view of citizens' interests. For it is not only true that teenagers have weighty current interests, extending into the future, as regards the political and economic decisions made within their societies. Alongside this, it is also the case that current teenagers have future interests in respect of how the political system treats them now, and in terms of the ways in which their views are addressed and accommodated, not only in terms of the ways in which their future selves would be glad that policy has been made in a way that reflects the impact on those in the future, but also because their future selves will have been glad of having grown up in a political system that embeds their status as full democratic citizens from an early age, and which gives them a clearer path to becoming active and engaged members of their political society (a point to which I will return below).

What then of claim (c), the idea that people aged 12-17 do not in general lack any specific capacity that would allow them to exercise their democratic rights as voters or as citizens more generally? Here one could imagine objections that teenagers are too feckless, unfocussed or unintelligent to follow political issues and to exercise political judgement in the way that one would expect of competent voters. Such objections, though, can be countered at more than one level. While some teenagers might make inattentive democratic citizens, we all know teenagers who take an active interest in the politics of their societies, and would be likely to exercise their votes

---

[16]   For a very funny satire of a quasi-fascist society in which political rights are tied to military service, see Paul Verhoeven's 1997 film, *Starship Troopers*. The novel of the same name, on which Verhoeven's film was based, seems not to have been satirical at all, but rather to endorse this kind of militarism. See Heinlein (2015).

judiciously. If one is focussed on the existence of the requisite capacities, it seems to be the most clear violation of basic fairness to exclude a whole group just because *some* of its members might not evince the virtues needed by responsible citizens. Indeed, the readiness with which some opponents of votes for teenagers are ready to exclude *all* from the entitlement to vote on the basis of a lack of capacity among only *some* of that group itself displays a kind of unmotivated bias towards the status quo, and a readiness to hold this group to different standards than those applied to their older fellow citizens. It would be question-begging to justify the unequal treatment of teenagers on the basis of the unequal application of a standard to which other citizens are not held. Needless to say, there are many older voters who may be unreflective, feckless or even plainly deluded in their political thinking and in the ways in which they deploy their vote, but this of course does not mean that we think it justified to have some public test for sorting the 'responsible' voters from the less responsible, much less that we are thereby justified in excluding broad swathes of citizens from democratic inclusion on the basis of the failings of some of their number.

It would, moreover, be entirely against the spirit of democratic societies, and it would represent a failure to treat citizens with respect and in a spirit of equality, to think that some regime of individualised testing to assess citizens' capacities could be appropriate. That is part of why, when I stated condition (c) above, I did so not in terms of *individual* capacities, but in terms of whether the group of potential new voters *in general* lacked any specific capacity needed for the exercise of democratic rights. Young citizens of secondary school age, with seven or more years of full-time education behind them, will in general have the requisite basic capacities in terms of comprehension, numeracy and general intelligence to be able to follow political issues with sufficient attention, and to be able to exercise their vote responsibility. Some may not do so, of course, but that is no different than for any other group or cohort, and that would give us no reason to exclude this younger group in particular from democratic life, any more than it would give us a reason to exclude any other group.

In his discussion of the case for votes for children, Daniel Weinstock introduces what he calls a 'Principle of Minimal Realism', 'which states that we should not exclude categories of persons from the franchise on the basis of epistemic standards that would be appropriate only for an idealized democracy that lies at a significant remove from reality of the practice of actually existing democracies' (Weinstock, 2020, p. 757). Weinstock's principle gives a judicious and appropriate standard for avoiding one kind of faulty reasoning in this kind of territory, where people can be minded both to apply standards inconsistently to different groups, and also suddenly to switch to a rarefied register of an imagined idealized democratic system when constructing arguments for electoral exclusion, when much of the practical urgency of the need to think about expanding democratic *inclusion* is driven precisely by the highly non-ideal operation of actually existing democratic systems, and the far-from-ideal outcomes to which they typically lead. In short, and in endorsing Weinstock's principle, we should neither hold the young to standards that we do not apply to others, nor in general make use of a standard for democratic citizenship that is unrealistically utopian and disconnected from the range of behaviours displayed by real voters in real polities.

(c) Schools, Democracy, and an Enhanced Democratic Culture

When we imagine a polity that drops its voting age to 12, and thereby enfranchises those attending secondary school, we need to imagine the broader consequences that would be entailed by this act of radical democratic inclusion. Once we look at our younger fellow citizens as in some sense political equals within a democratic society, it is clear that certain other elements of our social world, and in particular of our educational system, would need to change.[17] For a start, political education would become a more pressing matter, with a need for secondary schools to do more to equip their pupils for democratic citizenship. As things stand, citizenship education is often done very poorly within our educational system, and many citizens leave school without much sense of the potential power of the political system to change the conditions of their lives, or of how they might practically come to play a significant role within that system.[18] A world in which those aged 12–17 were *already* full democratic citizens would be a world in which the need for schools to do better in terms of citizenship education would be much more vivid, and a world in which the relevance and importance of democracy could be more easily communicated to young citizens.

[17]   On what is involved in relating to one another as equals, see O'Neill (2008), and Schemmel (2021). On schools as places where people learn to relate as equals, see Laden (2013). On how things often go wrong under current conditions, see Bruch and Soss (2018).

[18]   For valuable discussions of how the education system could do much better at educating *citizens*, even under the current political system, see for example Callan (1997); Brighouse (2005) and Kitcher (2022).

Where the minimum voting age is 12, and the typical gap between elections is 5 years or less, all citizens will encounter their first general election while still in full time education, with the opportunities that this would bring for education on the facts and issues under discussion, and for collective deliberation within a supportive environment. This would obviously place a responsibility on schools to do more in terms of the political education of their students, and to do this in an open, professional and non-partisan way, but this is something that is well within the competence of an educational system, and which many teachers would relish. The suggestion, then, is that the shift in the voting age would need to go alongside an enhanced role for schools as part of what Jan-Werner Müller has called the 'critical infrastructure' of democracy: that is, the set of institutions that make a thriving and engaging democracy possible (Müller, 2021). As it stands schools tend to do too little to help to support emerging democratic citizens, which is perhaps understandable when one thinks of the way in which those aged 12-17 are separated from the realities of democracy. Abstract nostrums about democratic values and the significance of the vote could be transformed into something much more real and vital when political issues can be discussed among a group who all already possess the basic democratic rights and entitlements of full citizens, and who will be able to use their votes as they come to see as appropriate. Democratic education can be transformed for the better when democracy is seen as something in which everyone can participate, rather than something that happens only to other people.

This likely transformation of the democratic culture can also be seen from the other side of the democratic process, when one thinks of the way that it would transform the way in which politicians and political parties would relate to younger citizens. With those aged 12 and over now recast as full democratic citizens with voting rights, no local constituency election campaign would be complete without the candidates visiting local secondary schools and making their case directly to younger citizens. This would change the dynamic between politicians, parties, and those young voters, giving politicians and parties strong reasons to communicate their message clearly to this audience, and to take the ideas, values, and interests of the young seriously. The political culture would, as a whole, no longer communicate to the young that they are marginal or unimportant, but would in general be reconfigured so that young citizens found themselves treated with a great deal more respect. What would instead be communicated to the young would not be their irrelevance or marginality, but their status and standing as citizens in a genuine democratic community.

When one thinks of these broader changes in the democratic culture, some of the lines of criticism of lowering the voting age come to seem rather misdirected, or beside the point. In their influential treatment of the case *against* lowering the voting age even to 16, Tak Wing Chan and Matthew Clayton examine empirical studies that show that the young lack political judgement, knowledge and engagement – that, as Chan and Clayton put it, the young lack 'political maturity' – and that therefore extension of the franchise would be misguided (Chan and Clayton, 2006). But what they are reporting on, with regard to their empirical findings, are the understandable consequences of a system that treats the young with disrespect, and which gives the young very little reason to engage seriously with the democratic process.[19] To take the consequences of the current pattern of democratic exclusion as evidence against the case for democratic *inclusion* is completely back-to-front. We should not expect that political groups with stable and thoughtful political positions should just exist *ex nihilo* before the members of those groups are included in the political process; rather, one of the functions of democracy is to give people the opportunity to forge those stable political identities through debate and deliberation with one another, and through the individual and collective exercise of their capacities as citizens (Müller, 2021). Democratic inclusion is a precondition for the transformation of the democratic culture, and should not be held off on the basis that the current, untransformed political culture is one that, entirely reasonably, leaves many young people disengaged and disaffected.

(d) Creating Democratic Citizens – Vote Early, Vote Often!

One intriguing phenomenon demonstrated by current empirical research, though, is the degree to which democratic participation is a *habit*. Those who start off voting at an early age generally retain that pattern of participation. As Eric Plutzer puts it, most voters display *inertia* with regard to political participation – they are either habitual voters or habitual nonvoters.[20] Under our current system, the general pattern is that younger voters are likely to start off as habitual nonvoters, with the problem of democratic activation then in

---

[19] As regards the 'path-dependence' of the phenomena described by Chan and Clayton, see Weinstock (2020, p. 760). See also Peto (2018).
[20] Plutzer (2002). On voting as a *habit* see also Gerbet et al. (2003). I am grateful to Harry Hathaway for helpful guidance on the empirical dimensions of voting as a *habit*.

effect a problem of habit change over time, of shifting people from the column of habitual nonvoters to the column of habitual voters. Once the shift happens, the effect of habit makes people 'sticky' in their role as activated and engaged citizens: for example, one 2009 study estimated that voting in one election increases the probability of voting in a subsequent election by 13% (Denny and Doyle, 2009). And so the key problem in increasing turnout among younger voters is to establish a pattern of political engagement at an early opportunity.

It is not surprising that younger people in general are less likely to vote, both due to problems generated by the kind of reasonable disillusion, disengagement and demobilisation discussed above in section 1, but also due to wholly understandable practical and logistical issues related to the fact that, as things stand, people first become voters at a very tricky time in their lives. As former Labour Party leader Ed Miliband puts it, we currently expect people to start voting at a stage in their life that 'often coincides with a time of flux – moving away from home, getting a job, starting further or higher education. Given those distractions, these years can reasonably be described as 'arguably the worst possible years to have one's first vote' (Miliband, 2021, p. 167). Miliband makes that remark in the context of arguing for the voting age to be dropped down to 16, but with general elections up to 5 years apart, the relatively marginal change that Miliband supports would not fully address the problem that he identifies, as many first time voters would still find themselves in that 'time of flux' after the end of full-time school attendance.[21] With a shift to votes at 12, by contrast, we ensure that for everyone the first time they vote in a general election is when they are still in secondary education, and still able thereby to call upon the supportive infrastructure that their school can provide in helping them to navigate their new status as full, voting citizens. This change would, therefore, create a really strong opportunity for more people to get into the *habit* of voting: through bringing citizens' initial experience of exercising their democratic rights into an earlier phase of their lives, we create the conditions where it is more likely that those citizens will go on to exercise those rights over the subsequent course of their lives. To sloganize, and appropriating for less nefarious ends a phrase at times attributed to James Michael Curley of Boston or Richard J. Daley of Chicago: it is a case of *vote early, vote often.*

---

[21]   Despite the inadequacy of dropping the voting age to 16, the seemingly beneficial consequences of even this change are striking, when one looks at the case of Austria, which shifted to votes at 16 in 2007. See Zeglovits (2013); Zeglovits and Aicholzer (2014).

(e) A Preponderance of Reasons: the Overdetermined Case for Votes at 12

My hope is that the foregoing discussion makes the case that we have overwhelmingly strong reasons to accept the reduction of the voting age to 12. The case can be made both in *instrumental* terms, as regards the way in which this kind of extension of democratic inclusion can be seen as a precondition for overcoming the various pathologies of intergenerational injustice to which our societies are subject; but the case can also be made more *directly*, in terms of the appropriate way in which institutions should respond to its younger citizens, given their status, (current and future) interests, and capacities. More broadly, one can also see the proposal for dropping the voting age substantially as part of a wider case for how we can create a more vibrant and active democratic culture, and how to make the most of our existing educational institutions in helping to turn democratic inclusion from an abstraction to a reality. This is, then, a change to the rules of democracy that one can support on a number of different grounds, and which might in time hope to attract the support of those approaching these issues from a variety of different starting points.

4. The Policy of Votes at 12, and its (More or Less Radical) Alternatives

Let us assume, then, that there is a strong case for lowering the voting age. We might nevertheless ask why the right way forward would be to lower the voting age to 12 in particular, as against any other particular age. In this section I will look to justify my proposal against both the (less radical) claim that the voting age should be reduced to 16, and the rather more radical claim, as recently advanced by David Runciman, that the voting age should be dropped all the way to 6, with primary school children as well as those attending secondary school being brought within the scope of full democratic participation.

(a) Votes at 16: An Insufficient Step in the Right Direction?

The first thing to say about Votes at 16 is that, insofar as one is convinced by the case for lowering the voting age, this is probably the strategic position that one should endorse in political terms, if one's primary objective is to support a policy that has a chance of being enacted in the near run. As mentioned above, Austria already has a voting age of 16, as does one other European Union member, Malta. Sixteen is also the voting age in a number of South American democracies, including Argentina, Brazil and Ecuador. In the United Kingdom, although the voting age is 18 for most national elections, and for local elections in England, the voting age was lowered to 16 for the Scottish independence referendum of 2014, and is also in use for elections to the Scottish Parliament, the Welsh Senedd, and for Scottish and Welsh local elections. One might have the sense, then, that in advocating for Votes at 16, one would be pushing at an open door, and advocating for a distinctively realistic policy that one might well expect to see eventually adopted for United Kingdom general elections (it is notable that the Labour Party went into both the 2017 and 2019 general elections advocating a voting age of 16), and in other democratic countries.[22] Certainly, there is nothing in the argument of this essay to deny that a move from a voting age of 18 to a voting age of 16 would be a move in the right direction.

However, I think there is a strong case for why it would not be enough. In almost every instance, the arguments for shifting the voting age to 16 carry through to the more radical conclusion that the voting age should be further reduced to 12. We have already seen this above, with regard to Ed Miliband's point about trying to avoid the situation where young voters' first vote happens during the 'time of flux' immediately after leaving school, and instead can be exercised while still within the more supportive environment of their secondary school, as this is clearly an argument that takes us beyond votes at 16 and instead leads us to endorsing a considerably younger voting age. If the electoral cycle is x-years long, then the minimum voting age should be no higher than x-years before people typically leave school, suggesting that in a country with a maximum of five years between elections, and with people leaving

---

[22]   Bills have been introduced to the UK Parliament to reduce the voting age for general elections to 16, most recently Jim McMahon's Representation of the People (Young People's Enfranchisement and Education) Bill of 2017, which had support from Labour, the SNP, the Liberal Democrats, Plaid Cymru and the Green Party, but which did not become law due to a lack of government support. (See https://bills.parliament.uk/bills/2074) Perhaps most notably, Tony Benn's comprehensive Commonwealth of Britain Bill of 1991 also contained provision to drop the voting age to 16. Benn's plan for a new republican constitution for Britain never got so far as a second reading in the House of Commons. See Rush (2021).

school at 18, the minimum voting age should be no higher than 12 or 13.

In a similar manner, as regards the way in which the case for Votes at 16 can so easily be tweaked in a more radical direction, if our argument is about the significance of representation of interests, given the fact that (again to cite Miliband's argument) 'if you are a voter, politicians are more likely to take your interests into account' (Miliband, 2021, p. 165) this applies just as much to those in the 12-15 age bracket as it does to those aged 16 and above. There seems, indeed, to be no pressing relevant difference, unless it is the difference that, with younger citizens further from the time of economic independence, and with more years ahead of them when they are reliant for their future prospects on the performance of their country's educational institutions, the interests of this younger group perhaps stand in even stronger need of being taken seriously into account within the democratic process. Or to take a different line of argument explored above – the point about political *habit* and the creation of active democratic citizens – again the case takes us beyond the modest conclusion of votes at 16 towards a more radical realisation that the voting age should be dropped further.

In general, there seems no general reason to think that there are relevant and significant differences between the status, interests or capacities, with regard to the requirements of political engagement and participation, of those in the 12–15 age range and those in the 16–17 age range. Given this, it is unsurprising that in most cases, an argument for extending the franchise to those in the second group very quickly can be extended so as also to apply to those in the first group. More might be said in favour of holding the line for a voting age higher than 12 and, as I've said above, I think there is good reason to treat even the milder policy of votes at 16 as an important step in the right direction, but to my mind a more powerful and interesting challenge actually comes from the opposite direction, from those who would argue that the voting age should be reduced so as to include young children. It is to those views that I shall now turn.

(b) Why Not Go Further? Runciman, Weinstock and Votes at Six

In a much-discussed 2018 lecture on 'Democracy for Young People' and more recently in a 'Long Read' essay for *The Guardian*, 'Votes for Children! Why We Should Lower the Voting Age to Six', David Runciman has made the case for an extension of the franchise, with a new minimum voting age of six, that might make my own putatively radical suggestion seem like a rather tepid, milquetoast halfway house (Runciman, 2018; 2021). In a similar vein, Daniel Weinstock has also recently considered a wholescale extension of voting rights to children, concluding that 'we may be duty-bound to consider what may have seemed at the outset as an outrageous suggestion – namely, that children be given the same voting rights as their elders' (Weinstock, 2020, p. 771). While I am highly sympathetic to Runciman's and Weinstock's views, and would indeed be delighted if by some miracle any democratic polity were to follow their advice and implement such a radical new extension of the vote, I think there are a number of good reasons to prefer my more moderate position. Let me take some of these in turn:

(i) *The Critical Infrastructure Argument*: according to the view developed in this article, one of the related changes to our democratic institutions that would be necessitated by a much lower voting age would be the enhanced role that schools would have to play in providing an important element of the background 'critical infrastructure' of democracy. It seems plausible that secondary schools, as part of their role in preparing young people for the lives that lie ahead of them, could be especially well-suited to this kind of infrastructural and preparative role. By contrast, such a role would sit less easily with primary schools, which one can see as addressed to the work of helping children to develop their more foundational capacities. Given that we typically already embed a significant transition from one kind of educational setting to another when children move from primary to secondary education, it seems wise to align this new line of transition to full democratic citizenship along with that educational transition, in a way that allows each kind of educational setting to play a distinct kind of background role in children's development.

(ii) *The Value of Symbolic Transitions Argument:* related to the previous point is the idea that there is much that is of value with having the transition to full democratic citizenship being something of which the recipient of that change of status is fully aware, and which they can consciously integrate into their sense of their own personal development. In this way, there is a further case in favour of alignment with the change of educational setting, but from the perspective of the new voter rather than considered in terms of the role and function of the educational institution itself. By contrast, if everyone aged 6 and over could vote, then younger voters would have little sense of this being a status into which they had transitioned, as opposed to it being something in the background, taken for granted.

It seems to me that there is much to be learned here from how the transition to full community membership are handled by religious communities, something that is often achieved in a way that communicates the significance and value of that transition in a far more vivid way than is done in secular contexts. The Catholic sacrament of Confirmation – often described as the 'sacrament of maturity' – is typically conferred around the age of 12–14, or sometimes slightly younger.[23] Similarly, the Jewish ceremonies of Bar Mitzvah and Bat Mitzvah, at which boys and girls come to full community membership, are performed at the age of 12. It seems plausible that both the Catholic and Jewish traditions have got at something valuable and significant here, in treating seriously the public acknowledgement of the point at which young people move into full membership of their communities, and take on the associated status and entitlements of that new status. This is not to say that secular, democratic states need to be led by religious conceptions of maturity or status – far from it, indeed – but it is to say that there is no reason not to try to learn from the practical insights of religious traditions.

(iii) *The Argument from the Burden of Voting and the Value of Childhood:* a third consideration against the further reduction of the voting age so as to include younger children turns on a different way of understanding the interests of those younger children themselves. It seems plausible to think that, for younger children, one of the valuable aspects of their status outside full membership of the political community is that it excludes them from the burden of having to engage with political issues, and gives them more of a protected space for development. And so we might well think that it would be backwards to enfranchise younger

---

[23] Debates about younger or older ages for Catholic confirmation have interesting affinities with debates about the voting age. See, e.g., Cornwell (2016).

children on the basis of giving full consideration to their interests, when those interests would best be served by being freed from the responsibilities of full citizenship. By contrast with children of secondary school age, who are generally already taking a keen interest in the wider world and developing their views and outlook, it might seem like a rather cruel imposition to draw younger children away from their own concerns and to direct their attention towards the often rather dismal world of politics.

In the conclusion to his own discussion of these issues, Daniel Weinstock considers whether children might be after all 'entitled to not have to consider the tawdry realities that participation in political life inevitably places one in contact with'.[24] Weinstock's own position on this question is inconclusive, but he is certainly correct that there is good reason to think that these kinds of considerations about the burdens of voting and the value of a (non-political) childhood should be given at least some weight. Obviously, though, this is a consideration that should not be over-extended: one could imagine someone making a parallel argument about younger teenagers, but this can look grotesquely patronising if a competent, engaged and articulate young person aged 13 or 14, who may be passionate about issues of social and environmental justice, is told that, for their own good they should be protected from having to think about politics. And so we might here take the view that the position of votes at 12 presents a plausible middle way for trying to offer some protection of younger children from politics, without patronising those in the older age range. Those who might seem still to have a complaint here would be the engaged and knowledgeable 10 or 11 year old, who might plausibly complain that their exclusion from full political status is arbitrary and unfair; but at least under a democratic regime of votes at 12 they would not have too long to wait.

Taken together these three kinds of consideration point towards the greater plausibility of my more moderate proposal, rather than the full enfranchisement of everyone old enough to read a ballot paper.

---

[24] Weinstock, (2020, p. 771). For a related argument see also Beckman (2009).

Alongside these considerations is also, of course, the more straight-forward point that any concerns we may have about the threshold of basic capabilities and capacities required by democratic citizens, which really do not seem to generate plausible worries for young people in secondary school who have completed their primary education, would certainly get more purchase when we start to think of the case of 6 and 7 year olds, for whom the cognitive demands of citizenship might be too much. The policy of votes of 12, then, is very much in the spirit of Runciman's and Weinstock's lines of argument, while avoiding some of the less attractive features of their more radical proposals.

5. The General Case and the Special Case: Lowering the Voting Age After Covid, and in Light of the Climate Emergency

I want to end this discussion by suggesting that, implausible though it may be to imagine such a radical change in our voting system being enacted any time soon, this really ought to be an issue that is taken fully seriously, and which should be treated with a reasonable degree of urgency. The argument of this essay has been that there is a *general* case for the enfranchisement of young citizens, given their status, interests and capacities. But, writing in 2022, in light of recent events and developments, I think we can see that there is also an additional and urgent *special* case for democratic transform-ation. In this regard, it is worth thinking about the Covid pandemic, but most importantly about the climate emergency.

During the Covid pandemic, huge sacrifices were made by the younger generation, sacrificing time in education, leisure and sport-ing activities, and valuable time with friends, in order to make an enormous contribution in protecting their fellow citizens from the threat of the virus. This was typically a case of those who were at lower relative risk, and less clinically vulnerable, sacrificing their own interests and well-being to protect the older and more vulnerable. In a less pathologically unjust political society, this extra-ordinary collective act of social solidarity would have generated a level of gratitude and acknowledgement appropriate to the degree of sacri-fice involved. A society that took the young less for granted might have marked that sacrifice with a collective decision to provide extra years of educational funding to make up for time lost, or a commit-ment to write-off student loans, or a new determination to solve the housing crisis faced by young people. It should have prompted more serious thinking about wealth taxes, and the intergenerational transfer of resources. In short, it should have occasioned an overdue decision to acknowledge this extraordinary social contribution by doing at least some of what would be necessary to redistribute opportunities to the younger generation. None of this happened. Instead, the older beneficiaries of the sacrifices made by the young responded much like Michael Corleone in *The Godfather, Part II*: 'My offer to you is: nothing'. This grotesque violation of basic reciprocity, which we have just all witnessed playing out in plain sight, could hardly have provided a more vivid demonstration of the need to redistribute political power, and hence the need to transform our democratic institutions in a way that gives more voice and influence to younger citizens.

But the most pressing 'special' case for urgent reform to the democratic system is not about acknowledging what has happened with Covid, but is instead about looking forward to what is ahead of us. It is a horrifying but transparent truth that our existing political system, with its inveterate short-termism and inability to act against the near-run interests of older and wealthier parts of society, is fundamentally failing to respond at the right scale to the climate emergency. We are in a ship heading towards the rocks, with those in charge refusing to listen to the pleas of younger passengers that we are headed for disaster. Under these conditions, the very least that we should do is to find a better way to steer the ship. The dangers ahead of us are such that finding a better way to forge a political response to crisis is far from an abstract or idle matter; the need for structural change in how we organise our politics is a matter of pressing necessity.[25]

University of York
martin.oneill@york.ac.uk

[25]   For helpful discussion of the case for lowering the voting age, I am very grateful to the students in my Autumn 2021 MA module on 'Advanced Topics in Political Philosophy', and in particular to Harry Hathaway (whose own view is in favour of the abolition of the voting age altogether). I have also benefitted from discussing these issues with the participants in the World Economic Forum 'Great Narrative' meeting in November 2021. Further thanks for useful discussion, online or in reality, to Anita Allen, David Axelsen, Richard Bellamy, Juliana Bidadanure, Paul Bou-Habib, Eamonn Callan, Christina Easton, Suzanne Fortier, David Grinspoon, Malte Jauch, James Johnson, Mary Leng, Dominic Mahon, Thierry Malleret, Joe O'Neill, Tommy O'Neill, David Owen, Tom Parr, Michael Rosen, John Steele, Daniel Weinstock, and Miklós Zala. I am especially grateful to Julian Baggini for the invitation to contribute this essay.

References

Ludvig Beckman, *The Frontiers of Democracy: The Right to Vote and Its Limits*, (Palgrave Macmillan, 2009), 114–19.

Juliana Bidadanure, 'Youth Quotas, Diversity, and Long-Termism', in Iñigo González-Ricoy and Axel Gosseries, eds., *Institutions for Future Generations*, (Oxford University Press, 2016).

Juliana Bidadanure, 'Towards a Democratic Ethics of Youth Policies', in Annabelle Lever and Andrei Poama, eds., *The Routledge Handbook of Ethics and Public Policy*, (Routledge, 2018), 460–471.

Paul Bolton, 'Education Maintenance Allowance (EMA) Statistics', Research Briefing, *House of Commons Library*, (13 January 2011). Online at: https://commonslibrary.parliament.uk/research-briefings/sn05778/

Léon Bourgeois, *Solidarité*, (Armand Colin, 1902).

Harry Brighouse, *On Education*, (Routledge, 2005).

Sarah K. Bruch and Joe Soss, 'Schooling as a Formative Political Experience: Authority Relations and the Education of Citizens', *Perspectives on Politics*, 16.1 (2018), 36–57.

Eamon Callan, *Creating Citizens: Political Education and Liberal Democracy*, (Oxford University Press, 1997).

Damian Carrington, 'Young global climate strikers vow change is coming – from the streets', *The Guardian*, (24 September, 2021).

Tak Wing Chan and Matthew Clayton, 'Should the Voting Age be Lowered to Sixteen? Normative and Empirical Considerations', *Political Studies*, 54.3 (2006), 553–58.

Linda Colley, *The Gun, the Ship and the Pen: Warfare, Constitutions and the Making of the Modern World*, (Profile Books, 2021).

Megan Cornwell, 'Bishop brings forward Confirmation age to increase numbers receiving the sacrament', *The Tablet*, (5 October, 2016).

Kevin Denny and Orla Doyle, 'Does Voting History Matter? Analysing Persistence in Turnout', *American Journal of Political Science*, 53.1 (2009), 17–35.

Mark Fisher, 'Why Mental Health is a Political Issue,' *The Guardian*, (16 July, 2012).

Mark Fisher, 'Good for Nothing', *The Occupied Times*, (19 March, 2014). Online here: https://theoccupiedtimes.org/?p=12841.

Paul Foot, *The Vote: How It Was Won and How It Was Undermined*, (Viking, 2005)

Adam Forrest, 'School spending set to remain below 2010 levels – as poorest areas are "hammered" by big cuts', *The Independent*, (1 September 2021).

Nancy Fraser, 'Contradictions of Capital and Care', *New Left Review*, 100 (2016), 99–117.

Alan S. Gerber, Donald P. Green and Ron Schachar, 'Voting May Be Habit-Forming: Evidence from a Randomized Field Experiment', *American Journal of Poitical Science*, 47.3 (2003), 540–50.

Axel Gosseries, 'Three Models of Intergenerational Reciprocity', in Axel Gosseries and Lukas H. Meyer, eds., *Intergenerational Justice*, (Oxford University Press, 2009).

Robert Heinlein, *Starship Troopers*, new edition, (Hodder, 2015).

Neil Johnston, 'The History of the Parliamentary Franchise', *House of Commons Library*, Research Paper 13/14 (2003).

Philip Kitcher, *The Main Enterprise of the World: Rethinking Education*, (Oxford University Press, 2022).

Anthony Simon Laden, 'Learning to be Equal: Just Schools as Schools of Justice', in Danielle Allen and Rob Reich, eds., *Education, Justice and Democracy*, (University of Chicago Press, 2013).

Mathew Lawrence and Laurie Laybourn-Langton, *Planet on Fire: a Manifesto for the Age of Environmental Breakdown*, (Verso, 2021).

Lukas H. Meyer, 'Intergenerational Justice', in Edward N. Zalta, ed., *The Stanford Encyclopedia of Philosophy* (Summer 2021 Edition).

Keir Milburn, *Generation Left*, (Polity Press, 2019).

Ed Miliband, *Go Big: How to Fix Our World*, (Bodley Head, 2021).

Janet Murray, 'Students hit by scrapping of education maintenance allowance', *The Guardian*, (25 October, 2010).

Jan-Werner Müller, *Democracy Rules*, (Allen Lane, 2021).

Martin O'Neill, 'What Should Egalitarians Believe?', *Philosophy & Public Affairs*, 36.2 (2008), 119–56

Martin O'Neill, 'Free (and Fair) Markets without Capitalism: Political Values, Principles of Justice, and Property-Owning Democracy', in Martin O'Neill and Thad Williamson, eds., *Property-Owning Democracy: Rawls and Beyond* (Wiley-Blackwell, 2012).

Martin O'Neill, 'Philosophy and Public Policy after Piketty', *Journal of Political Philosophy*, 25 (2017), 343–75.

Martin O'Neill and Liam Shields, 'Equality of Opportunity and State Education', *The Philosophers' Magazine*, (7 June, 2017).

Martin O'Neill, 'Justice, Power, and Participatory Socialism: on Piketty's *Capital and Ideology*', *Analyse & Kritik*, 43.1 (2021), 89–124.

Martin O'Neill and Thad Williamson, 'Property-Owning Democracy and the Demands of Justice', *Living Reviews in Democracy*, 1 (2009), 1–10.

Tommy Peto, 'Why the Voting Age Should be Lowered to 16', *Politics, Philosophy and Economics*, 17.2 (2018), 277–97.

Thomas Piketty, *Capital in the Twenty-First Century*, (Harvard University Press, 2014).

Thomas Piketty, *Capital and Ideology*, (Harvard University Press, 2020).

Eric Plutzer, 'Becoming a Habitual Voter: Inertia, Resources, and Growth in Young Adulthood', *American Political Science Review*, 96.1 (2002), 41–56.

John Rawls, *A Theory of Justice*, revised edition, (Harvard University Press, 1999).

John Rawls, *Justice as Fairness: A Restatement*, (Harvard University Press, 2001).

David Runciman, 'Democracy for Young People', *Talking Politics podcast*, (5 December, 2018). Online at: https://www.talking politicspodcast.com/blog/2018/129-democracy-for-young-people

David Runciman, 'Votes for children! Why we should lower the voting age to six', *The Guardian*, (16 November, 2021).

Martyn Rush, 'Tony Benn's Plan to Democratise Britain', *Tribune*, 26 February 2021.

Christian Schemmel, *Justice and Egalitarian Relations*, (Oxford University Press, 2021).

Luke Sibieta, 'School spending in England: trends over time and future outlook', Briefing Note, *Institute for Fiscal Studies*, (2 September, 2021). Online at https://ifs.org.uk/publications/15588.

David Smail, *The Origin of Unhappiness: a New Understanding of Personal Distress*, (Routledge, 2015).

Matthew Taylor, 'Global climate strike: thousands join coordinated action around the world,' *The Guardian*, (24 September, 2021).

Greta Thunberg, *No One Is Too Small to Make a Difference*, (Penguin, 2019).

Adam Tooze, *Shutdown: How Covid Shook the World's Economy*, (Allen Lane, 2021).

Edward Vallance, *A Radical History of Britain*, (Little Brown, 2009).

Philippe Van Parijs, 'The Disenfranchisement of the Elderly, and Other Attempts to Secure Intergenerational Injustice', *Philosophy & Public Affairs*, 27. 4 (1999), 292–333.

Daniel Weinstock 'What's So Funny about Voting Rights for Children?', *Georgetown Journal of Law & Public Policy*, 18 (2020), 751–772.

Jonathan Wolff and Avner de-Shalit, *Disadvantage*, (Oxford University Press, 2007).

Emma Young, 'How Iceland Got Teens to Say No To Drugs', *The Atlantic*, (19 January, 2017).

Eva Zeglovits, 'Political Interest of Adolescents Before and After Lowering the Voting Age: the Case of Austria', *Youth Studies*, 16.8 (2013), 1084–1104.

Eva Zeglovits and Julian Aichholzer, 'Are People More Inclined to Vote at 16 than at 18? Evidence for First-Time Voting Boost Among 16- to 25-Year-Olds in Austria', *Journal of Elections, Public Opinion and Parties*, 24.3 (2014), 351–61.

Membership Rights for Animals

WILL KYMLICKA

Abstract
It is increasingly acknowledged that animals have an intrinsic moral status, in part
due to the influential work of many moral philosophers. However, surprisingly
little has been written by philosophers on whether animals are owed social membership and the rights that attach to membership in society. In this paper, I explore why
the idea of social membership matters, particularly in relation to domesticated
animals, and how it can guide legal and political reforms. Focusing on social
membership identifies neglected avenues for transformative change, and offers
new ways of challenging the deeply-embedded 'human use typologies' that currently
govern our relations to domesticated animals. It also raises fascinating philosophical
questions about the definition of 'society' and the role of an ethics of membership.
Ultimately, we will need to develop a new philosophy of interspecies society.

The facts about our treatment of animals are grim. Upwards of
10 billion land animals are raised and killed for food each year in
North America, almost all under conditions of intense confine-
ment. And the average population of wild animal species has
dropped by 50% in the past forty years, as human colonization
and despoliation of wild animal habitat continue unabated.
Moreover, the United Nations estimates that both of these
trends will continue: forty years from now, we will be confining
and killing even more animals for food, and leaving even less
space for wild animals. These facts reflect a remarkable sense of
entitlement, or what Ted Benton calls 'a quite fantastic species
narcissism' (Benton, 1988, p. 7).

What can philosophy contribute to addressing this challenge?
On the one hand, philosophy has played a vital role in catalyzing
both personal ethical reflection and a social movement. Since the
publication of Peter Singer's *Animal Liberation* (1975), Mary
Midgley's *Beast and Man* (1978), and Tom Regan's *The Case
for Animal Rights* (1983), moral philosophers have been at the
forefront of both academic and public debates about our
obligations to animals. Indeed, social scientists have argued that
the influence of moral philosophers as catalysts of the animal
rights movement is perhaps an unparalleled example of academic

doi:10.1017/S1358246122000078   © The Royal Institute of Philosophy and the contributors 2022
Royal Institute of Philosophy Supplement **91** 2022   213

philosophy shaping a social movement (Jasper and Nelkin, 1992, p. 90).

On the other hand, when it comes to specific public policy proposals or legal reforms, philosophers have been less prominent. This may reflect a striking divide between moral philosophy and political philosophy on the animal question. While moral philosophy has been a trailblazer in raising questions about our treatment of animals, political philosophy – the branch of philosophy most naturally inclined to think about law and public policy – has been a laggard. Virtually all of the work done in contemporary political philosophy – whether on democracy, justice, citizenship, sovereignty, freedom, power – makes no reference to animals, and implicitly assumes that we can theorize these issues without taking animals into account. A good indicator of this is textbooks: Sue Donaldson and I surveyed thirty recent textbooks in political philosophy, and we discovered not one that encourages readers to think critically about human entitlement to use animals (Kymlicka and Donaldson, 2016). The vast majority make no reference to animals at all, and the few that do mention animals do so in a way that simply presupposes this entitlement. For example, David Miller's *Political Philosophy: A Very Short Introduction* mentions fish, but only in the context of deciding how to fairly allocate rights to fish in international waters: our right to kill fish is taken for granted, and the only question is how to fairly distribute this right (Miller, 2003). Another textbook (Farelly, 2004) mentions cows, but only in the context of how to regulate slaughter in a multicultural society. Here again, the right to eat cows is taken for granted: the only issue is how fairly to resolve disputes about appropriate slaughter methods. In short, all thirty textbooks implicitly or explicitly assume that animals are resources to be used for human benefit, leaving untouched readers' sense of species entitlement. Whereas moral philosophy has been a catalyst of the animal rights debate, political philosophy has, in Regan's words, been 'caught napping' (Regan, 1990, p. xi).

We need to move the animal question beyond the confines of moral philosophy and into broader terrains of social and political philosophy. In this paper, I will focus on one possible route forward. I will begin by describing the existing state of animal policies and their underlying ideology of 'humane use' – what Nozick called 'utilitarianism for animals, Kantianism for persons' – and how this permits the moral catastrophe we find ourselves in. I then explore two influential critiques of this status quo: the first defends utilitarianism for both humans and animals; the second defends Kantianism for both humans and animals. I will suggest that, whatever their philosophical merits, neither is well-positioned to generate usable policy proposals. I then consider an alternate approach which focuses on what I will call membership rights: rights tied to membership in particular social roles, relationships and practices, such as 'family member' or 'worker'. These social categories play a crucial role in organizing our everyday understanding of what we owe each other, and I will argue that including animals in these legal categories could radically disrupt the prevailing ideology of humane use.

1. Diagnosing the Problem: the ideology of humane use

Current public policy is premised on the assumption that humans have the right to use animals for our benefit, but that we should avoid 'cruelty' or 'unnecessary suffering' in this use. This proviso against unnecessary suffering is sometimes described as a commitment to 'animal protection,' but the basic logic of such laws inherently subordinates animal protection to human use. We protect animals only if and insofar as this protection is consistent with our use of them. For example, it is consistent with our interest in eating meat to require that cows be insensate when killed, but it is not consistent with our interest in eating wild fish to require that fish be insensate when killed. There is no way to kill most wild fish without inflicting intense pain, and to insist on a principle that fish be insensate when killed would require us to give up using fish as food. Since we assert the right to use fish in this way, we abandon the principle of 'humane' slaughter. The fish's interest in a painless death counts for nothing since it is incompatible with our using fish for food.

Ani Satz (2009) calls this the 'interest-convergence' principle: we recognize the interests of animals only if and insofar as it is consistent with our prior claim to use them in a particular way.[1] It operates through what Jessica Eisen (2010) refers to as 'human-use typologies': we categorize animals based on how we intend to use them, and then we define standards of protection that do not interfere with that use. This is quite explicit in animal law and policy. To take one example, Switzerland's Federal Animal Welfare Act (2005) says that animals have 'intrinsic value' and so must be treated with

---

[1] The 'interest-convergence' principle was originally developed by critical race theorists in the US to explain the inadequacies of racial equality law (Bell, 1980), but as Satz notes, it fits perfectly the logic of animal law.

respect, and that this requires that anyone who handles animals must ensure their wellbeing insofar as their 'designated use' (*Verwendungszweck*) permits. We see versions of this in every Western country: we protect animals' interests insofar as is this is compatible with their 'designated use'. For this reason, it is misleading to talk about 'animal protection' policies: the fundamental purpose of these policies is not to protect animals, but on the contrary to assert the right to use animals. We have animal use laws, not animal protection laws. At its core, animal law authorizes the harming of animals.

Robert Nozick famously characterized the philosophical foundations of these policies as 'utilitarianism for animals, Kantianism for persons' (Nozick, 1974, p. 39). In relation to humans, we endorse 'Kantianism'[2] – that is, we recognize that humans have rights which set limits on the extent to which we can be sacrificed for the good of others. Killing one human to harvest organs to save five other humans would fail to treat us as ends in ourselves: it would instrumentalize us, when we should instead be seen as bearers of inviolable respect and dignity. All Western democracies – and international human rights law – accept this basic premise of 'Kantianism for humans', reflected in the prohibition on experimentation on humans.

By contrast, in the case of animals, we endorse utilitarianism – that is, we accept that their interests should be counted when engaging in utilitarian calculations about the greater good, but there is no limit on the extent to which those interests can be sacrificed for the good of others. Killing one baboon to save five humans is permissible, and perhaps even morally required. As McMahan puts it, animals are 'freely violable in the service of the greater good', whereas human persons are 'fully inviolable' (McMahan, 2002, p. 265). All Western democracies accept this basic premise of 'utilitarianism for animals', reflected in the humane use provisions of animal law.

This then is the current state of animal policy: an ideology of humane use, tied to human use typologies, grounded in inviolable Kantianism for humans, violable utilitarianism for animals. Virtually everyone who has studied animal law agrees that this framework is a moral failure, permitting and legitimizing the wholesale instrumentalization of animals, sacrificing even the most basic interests of animals to the most trivial interests of humans.

---

[2] Kantianism in this context does not refer to the entire structure of Kant's philosophical thought, but to the specific idea that respecting someone as an end in themselves requires setting limits on the extent to which they can be sacrificed for the good of others.

2. Philosophical critiques

As I noted earlier, moral philosophers have played a pivotal role in challenging the ideology of humane use and its philosophical underpinnings, and these philosophical critiques have inspired both individual change and social movements. These critiques have come from a wide range of positions, including feminist care theory, Wittgensteinian ethics, Aristotelian virtue ethics, pragmatist ethics, Christian and other religious ethics, and Indigenous ethics. In this section, however, I will focus on two lines of critique. If we want to challenge 'utilitarianism for animals, Kantianism for humans', then two options readily come to mind: we might defend utilitarianism for both humans and animals or we might defend Kantianism for both humans and animals. These are the positions defended by Singer and Regan respectively, and they continue to shape much of the debate. I will suggest, however, that neither is easily translatable into policy reform.

The Utilitarian critique: Singer has argued that it is speciesist to give more weight to the interests of humans than to the comparable interests of animals: all interests should be counted equally in determining the greater good. He thus objects to the status quo of 'utilitarianism for animals, Kantianism for humans'. But as a utilitarian, the part of the status quo he objects to is not 'utilitarianism for animals'. On the contrary, he fully supports utilitarianism for animals (so long as the interests of animals are in fact duly counted). What he objects to, philosophically, is Kantianism for humans. Whether someone has 'rights' is itself a question to be determined by assessing what promotes the greater good: there are no such things as inviolable natural rights that pre-empt the pursuit of the greater good. What he proposes, therefore, is not to extend inviolability to animals, but rather to insist that humans too should be seen as violable in the service of the greater good. He argues for a more even-handed calculus when deciding who is violable to serve the greater good.

For example, in a famous 2006 BBC documentary, Singer said that if infecting 100 monkeys with Parkinson's and then killing them was necessary to develop a therapy that could cure 40,000 humans, then it was 'justified'.[3] Some commentators were surprised by Singer's endorsing of lethal animal experimentation, and suggested that it must reflect some change of mind in 'the father of animal rights',

---

[3] Jonathan Wishart, dir., *Monkeys, Rats and Me*, aired November 27, 2006, on BBC2. For discussion, see Walsh (2006); Jaschik (2006); Giraud (2019).

and some retreat from his stance against speciesism (Walsh, 2006). In fact, as he clarified afterwards in interviews, he has never denied that animal experimentation is justified if it promotes the greater good, and he explains that this is entirely consistent with his critique of speciesism, since he would apply the same test to experimenting on 'human beings at a similar mental level'.[4] What is wrong is not experimenting on monkeys to promote the greater good, but the fact that humans have exempted themselves from the utilitarian calculus and accorded themselves inviolable protection from utilitarian violability. His recommendation, in short, is utilitarianism for both humans and animals.

This is a non-starter as a basis for policy reform. There is no public support whatsoever for the idea that we should start experimenting on humans. The vast majority of citizens believe deeply in 'Kantianism for humans'. They believe – as do I – that respecting others as ends in themselves requires setting limits on the extent to which they can be sacrificed for the good of others. Indeed, the legal institutionalization of such rights is widely viewed as one of the great moral achievements of the twentieth century.

So there is no prospect of replacing 'utilitarianism for animals, Kantianism for humans' with 'utilitarianism for both animals and humans'. And, predictably, in the debate triggered by Singer's 2006 interview, no one took seriously the idea that we might start experimenting on 'human beings at a similar mental level' in pursuit of new Parkinson's therapies. Kantianism for humans is simply too entrenched to be worth discussing. The entire debate focused on his justification for animal experimentation: that is, he was widely seen as recommending 'utilitarianism for animals'. His endorsement of utilitarianism for humans dropped out of the policy debate.

And so the net effect of his intervention was to reinforce the prevailing ideology of humane use: he was seen as endorsing the idea that experimenting on animals to benefit humans is justifiable. To be sure, as Singer and others have demonstrated, Western societies badly misapply the principle of utilitarianism for animals, consistently undercounting animals' interests, and thereby overestimating the cases where sacrificing animals would in fact advance the greater good. A more rigorous application of utilitarianism for animals would show that the benefits to humans of many of our research practices (or agricultural practices) do not in fact outweigh the harms to animals. However, a more consistent application of 'utilitarianism for animals' would still leave untouched the basic

---

[4]   Singer quoted in Jaschik (2006).

premise of Kantianism for humans, utilitarianism for animals. Singer himself may believe in 'utilitarianism for humans, utilitarianism for animals', but in a context where human rights are deeply entrenched, the former is immediately dismissed in policy contexts. And this leaves us right back where we started. In a context where Kantianism for humans is beyond question, endorsing utilitarianism for animals is not a challenge to the philosophical foundations of the status quo but a reinforcement of them.

The Deontological critique: If utilitarianism for both humans and animals is a non-starter, an obvious alternative is to defend Kantianism for both humans and animals. This is the crux of Regan's deontological rights-based position: animals too should be seen as having inviolable rights not to be sacrificed for the good of others. Animals have their own lives to lead, and we have no right to sacrifice them for our benefit. They are not a caste group that exists to serve us.

On this view, the central policy task is to ensure that animals are accorded the legal status of a rights-bearing subject. In our legal system, that status is 'personhood'. Since Roman times, Western legal systems divide the world into 'persons' (those who are right-bearing subjects), and 'property' (that which is the good of another). And so the central policy goal of deontologists is to secure legal personhood for animals.

From a philosophical perspective, I find the arguments for animal personhood to be compelling. In co-authored work with Sue Donaldson, I have argued that personhood − or some functional equivalent like 'selfhood' − is essential to interspecies justice, and hence a crucial long-term goal.[5] However, as a policy proposal for the foreseeable future, it is unrealistic, at least with respect to the animals who are most intensely used in our society, such as farmed animals. It is difficult to know what percentage of the general public would support the idea of personhood for pigs and chickens, but if we take the number of ethical vegans as a quick proxy, the number is perhaps 3% in most Western countries. The idea is not

---

[5]   Donaldson and Kymlicka (2011, chap. 2). There may be good reasons to replace the language of 'personhood' with 'selfhood' or 'subjecthood', given the historically racist, ableist and speciesist connotations of 'person-hood' (Deckha, 2021). But whatever the term, sentient animals can and should be accorded the legal status of rights-bearing subjects. The goal is to move animals from being a legal 'something' to being a legal 'somebody', whether 'being a somebody' is best captured in the language of personhood, selfhood (as we propose) or beingness (as Deckha proposes).

supported by any major political party, and is not even discussed in mainstream political and public debate.

This helps explain why existing legal campaigns in defense of animal personhood have focused on a handful of wild animals who are peripheral to the 'animal-industrial complex',[6] such as primates, elephants, whales, and dolphins. This is true, for example, of the Great Apes Project and the Nonhuman Rights Project (NhRP).[7] This is a deliberate part of the legal strategy: pursuing personhood for primates, whales and elephants is politically feasible in large part because their use is not central to contemporary Western economies or ways of life. We can grant them basic rights with only minimal change in everyday practices.

Recall that the interest-convergence principle rests on some idea of the 'designated use' of animals – on human use typologies - and then accords weight to animal welfare if and insofar as it is consistent with this designated use. Pursuing personhood for apes, elephants and whales is politically feasible precisely because the average citizen has no clear idea of the 'designated use' of such animals. On the contrary, most citizens think that the appropriate life for such animals is to live freely in their own habitat. Of course there are some apes, elephants and whales in labs, zoos and aquariums – and these are the focus of legal campaigns – but these species are not primarily defined by their human use, and many citizens are quite prepared to accept that they have no designated human use, and so should be exempt from the interest-convergence logic.

The deeper challenge is to gain rights for those animals who are central to the animal-industrial complex, and who have been defined socially and legally by their designated use. These are the animals who are most trapped by the current interest-convergence logic, and for whom legal reform is urgent. In particular, we need to reform the status of domesticated animals: the animals brought into human societies to serve us, and whose designated use is a central part of our ways of life.[8] It is a striking fact that NhRP and

---

[6] The term 'animal industrial complex' originates in Noske (1989). See also Twine (2012).

[7] It is also true of two recent Argentine cases where advocates sought personhood for primates: a 2015 case involving Sandra the orangutan, and a 2016 case involving Cecilia the chimpanzee, discussed in Stucki (2016).

[8] By domesticated animals, I refer to those animals who have been selectively bred over generations to be able to live and work alongside us, which includes companion animals (e.g., dogs and cats), farmed animals (e.g., cows, sheep, pigs, chickens, salmon), and some lab animals (e.g., domesticated mice, zebrafish).

other campaigns for personhood have been unable to imagine a strategy for achieving personhood for domesticated animals.

3. An Alternative Approach

So we seem to be caught in a bind. The status quo of 'Kantianism for humans, utilitarianism for animals' is a moral failure, but the two obvious alternatives – namely, Kantianism for both humans and animals, or Utilitarianism for both humans and animals – are non-starters for policy purposes. Is there a third option?

I am particularly interested in what we might call 'transformative' policy reform – reform that not only reduces or mitigates a particular harm, but also challenges the underlying premises used to justify those harms in the first place.[9] And in my view, that requires above all repudiating the idea of designated use. The reason why recent legal moves to recognize animal 'sentience', 'intrinsic value', 'dignity' and 'respect' are hollow is that they are subordinated to an animal's designated use. A minimum condition of transformative reform, therefore, is that we 'Break Free from Human-Use Typologies' (to quote the title of Eisen's article).

I am also particularly interested in transformative reforms in relation to domesticated animals (hereafter DAs), whose very existence has been defined by human use. Unlike wild animals, DAs are bred by humans to serve us. Many people find it difficult to imagine a life for DAs that is not defined by human use: serving us is who they are, what they do, and what they are for.

Given the extent to which DAs have been defined by human use typologies, we need a strong effort of imagination to break free from these typologies and to visualize alternative futures. If we want to identify options for transformative legal change, we need a clearer idea of our ultimate goal. What would a just interspecies society look like, and what kinds of relationships between humans and DAs would it involve? Once we have this ideal in view, we can then work backwards and identify openings for viable reform.

So what would an ideally just interspecies society look like? We know part of the answer: justice requires that we stop harming, exploiting and killing animals. We must recognize that they are individuals with their own lives to lead, not resources for us. But this is only part of the story: it tells us how we *must not* treat animals, but

[9] On the idea of transformative change in relation to animals, see Donaldson and Kymlicka (2022).

it does not yet tell us how we *should* relate to them. What kinds of relationships, activities, and interactions should we have with them?

It seems likely that we would and should have different types of relations with different groups of animals. Think about wolves and dogs. Since dogs are domesticated wolves, they are very similar in their basic biology, with similar forms of sentience. Yet we would surely have different relations with them. In respect to wolves, our obligation would largely be to leave them alone, to live freely on their own habitat. But having bred dogs to be part of our society and to be interdependent with us, we have obligations to care for them and to provide the conditions for their flourishing in community with us.

How can we make sense of this distinction between dogs and wolves? Domestication has made DAs members of a shared society with humans, and as such, they have membership rights, in addition to the basic personhood rights owed to all sentient animals. Recognition of social membership is an essential component of justice for DAs: having taken them out of the wild, and bred them to live and work alongside us, we must accept that they are now members of a shared society, a society that belongs to them as much as to us. Through domestication, they have acquired a birthright in this shared society.

Recognition of social membership would have far-reaching implications. The idea of social membership is central to our social and political life: contemporary liberal-democracies operate on the basis of an 'ethics of membership'. T.H. Marshall famously argued that the rise of the post-war welfare state, and its associated ideas of social solidarity and democratic citizenship, was predicated on 'a direct sense of community membership based on loyalty to a civilisation that is a common possession' (Marshall, 1950, p. 96). The starting premise is that we form a 'society', and that the function of the democratic welfare state is to ensure that all members of society feel equally at home in the community, that everyone can equally partake in its social and cultural life and enjoy its civilization, that everyone can feel that they belong to the community and that the community belongs to them.[10] Marshall was centrally concerned with how the welfare state enables the working class to claim common possession of society, but if we accept that DAs are also members of society, the same logic applies. If DAs are members of

---

[10] In other work (Kymlicka, 2022), I explore in more depth how an ethic of membership underpins both liberal-democratic politics and social-democratic welfare states.

society, then they too are entitled to shape the social norms that govern our shared life, to have their interests included when determining the public good, to benefit from public goods, public services and public spaces, and to a fair distribution of the benefits and burdens of social cooperation. Concretely, this would include a range of rights, including, for example, a right to a system of publicly-funded health care for DAs, and a right that emergency services be trained and equipped to rescue DAs in case of fires or floods, and a right to accessible public spaces.[11]

This suggests that justice for DAs operates at two levels. First, there is a set of basic rights owed to all sentient animals – wild or domesticated – such as the right not to be killed, experimented on or enslaved. Let's call these the universal rights of personhood, many of which are negative rights. Second, we have a set of rights that vary with the relationship that animals have to human society, which in the case of DAs involves membership rights to flourish within a shared society. (For wilderness animals, by contrast, these relational rights might include rights to habitat and to autonomy, to protect them from encroachment by human society).[12] Let's call these 'group-differentiated' or 'relational' rights, since they vary with an animal's relationship to human society. These tend to be positive rights, to particular relationships or resources.

On this two-level view, justice requires both universal basic rights of personhood and relational rights, such as membership rights for DAs (or territorial rights for wilderness animals). To achieve justice for DAs, we need to promote both an ethic of personhood (DAs cannot be endlessly sacrificed for the good of others) and an ethic of membership (DAs have a birthright in society, which belongs to them as much as to us).

While the first level of personhood rights has been much discussed in animal rights theory, less attention has been paid to the second level of membership rights. This partly reflects the dominance of moral over political philosophy in animal rights theory: the idea of

---

[11]   This is just a cursory sketch of the membership model for DAs. See Donaldson and Kymlicka (2011, chap 5) for a more detailed discussion of its normative rationale and political implications.

[12]   In *Zoopolis*, we discuss a third group who are non-domesticated but live amongst us rather than on their own habitat (e.g., urban wildlife). We suggest that justice for these 'liminal animals' also requires both universal rights of personhood and group-differentiated relational rights: in their case, rights to residency and accommodation (Donaldson and Kymlicka, 2011, chap. 7).

social membership is central to political theories of citizenship and social justice, but less central to moral philosophy (in either its utilitarian or deontological versions). However, the inattention to DAs' membership rights also reflects a perception that talk about membership rights seems utopian. After all, as we've seen, personhood rights are largely negative rights not to be harmed, whereas membership rights are often positive rights. If it's unrealistic to expect public support for negative rights of personhood, how can we hope to get support for positive membership rights?

This two-level view of personhood rights and membership rights is indeed unabashedly idealistic, miles away from the status quo. However, I would argue that having this ideal in mind helps us to identify some real-world possibilities for transformative reform. While the path to personhood for DAs is blocked for the near future, there are forces in society pushing for recognition of their membership rights. Moreover, these efforts have had some success. While still fragile and small-scale, there are emerging spaces where DAs are indeed breaking free from human-use typologies and joining an ethic of membership. These developments have largely gone under the radar of animal rights theorists, but I will argue they are potentially transformative, and that philosophy has an important role to play in advancing them. In the next section, I will consider two such efforts.

4. Membership Rights: Domesticated Animals as Family Members and Workers

According to the ideal I've just articulated, one fundamental task is to ensure that DAs are recognized as members of society, and that our relations with them are governed by an ethics of membership. What would this mean, legally? Where might we look for glimpses of the legal recognition of social membership?

One place to start is with the very term 'domesticated'. The word domesticated refers to the 'domus' – the household. We refer to DAs as domesticated because they have been brought into the domus to live and work alongside us in our homes and workplaces.[13] The home and the workplace are the sites where DAs and humans first formed a society together, and so it makes sense to start here. As I will

---

[13]   The advent of factory farming in the West has removed most farmed animals from anything we would recognize as a domus or domestic setting, so that some commentators talk about a 'post-domestication' era (e.g., Bulliet, 2005).

discuss later on, justice requires that DAs be seen, not just as members of (private) families or workplaces, but also as having claims on society more generally, including public spaces and public institutions. Society is a broader category than family and work. Nonetheless, family and work are good places to start our investigation of membership rights.

Historically, DAs have been defined, for legal purposes, not as members of families and of workplaces, but as the property of families and workplaces. Consider family law. According to the law, pets living in a family home are the property of a family member, not themselves a member of the family. It is therefore entirely permissible for the owner to sell the dog, kill the dog, or in cases of family breakup, to demand custody of the dog as a property right. If the dog is owned by the husband, for example – if he is the one who purchased the dog – then he can claim custody of his property in case of divorce, even if it is clearly in the best interests of the dog to stay with the spouse or children or with other family pets to whom the dog has become attached. Family law gives rights to family members (including the right to maintain family ties wherever possible), but companion animals are not recognized as family members (and hence have no right to maintain family relations). Whereas an ethic of membership would say that the family belongs to both its human and animal members – that the family is a 'common possession' of its members – the law gives animals no membership rights in the family.

Similarly, according to the law, animals who work for an organization are the property of those organizations, not members of them. For example, dogs in the US Army have until recently been defined as property, and as such, have often been left behind when the military pulled out of foreign countries. Similarly, police dogs have often been killed when they are no longer able to perform their jobs. Labour law gives rights to workers in the workplace, but does not recognize animals as workers. Whereas an ethic of membership would say that the workplace belongs to both human and animal workers as a common possession, labour law gives animals no membership rights in the workplace.

This is a long-standing feature of animal law, and follows naturally from the ideology of humane use. In both the family and work contexts, we count the animals' interests only when it is compatible with our use of them. However, what is striking for our purposes is that this legal status quo is increasingly out of touch with public attitudes, and we can see glimpses of a move towards a membership-based model. I will start with the family, and then turn to work.[14]

---

[14] My summary here draws on the fuller discussion of these reforms in Kymlicka (2017).

Animals as Family Members: Surveys show that the vast majority of North Americans with companion animals consider them as 'one of the family', to be treated according to an ethic of membership, and they increasingly expect the legal system to respect and honour this membership relationship.[15] The result is a growing gulf between the self-understandings of average citizens and the law, and growing calls for legal reforms to acknowledge animals as family members.

Consider the issue of custody in the event of divorce. In the case of children, the established rule is that custody should be based on 'the best interests of the child', including a commitment to maintaining family ties wherever possible (e.g., courts try to avoid splitting up children). In the case of companion animals, however, since they are merely property, custody is based on whoever has the best ownership claim. Custody can be determined, for example, on the basis of who originally paid for the animal, without any attention to who has cared for the animal or whom the animal prefers, and without any commitment to preserving family ties (e.g., no effort is made to avoid splitting up companion animals and those they are attached to).

Many citizens are appalled that the legal system treats companion animals this way. And in response, many scholars have advocated legal reforms that recognize companion animals as 'members of the family' for the purposes of custody decisions (including 'petimony' in cases where the person best equipped to care for the companion animal is poorer), adapting legal rules developed for custody of human members of the family (Rook, 2014).

A similar dynamic is at work in relation to liability for harms caused by animal companions, such as dog bites. In some jurisdictions, owners of companion animals are subject to strict liability for any harm their dogs cause. The result is to equate possessing a dog with possessing dangerous property, such as storing dynamite in one's backyard. Anyone who stores dynamite is subject to strict liability for any explosion, and it is no defense to say that one took

---

[15] A 2011 Harris Poll showed that over 90 per cent of Americans with companion animals considered them to be members of the family (Harris, 2011). Nor is this just a ritualized phrase. Studies using standard psychological measures of attachment (e.g., proximity seeking, safe haven, secure base, and separation distress) show that people's closeness to their companion dogs is equal to their closeness to their mothers, siblings, and best friends (Amiot and Bastian, 2015). This is particularly true of children, who often report that the family member they feel closest to and trust is a companion animal (Melson, 2001).

reasonable precautions to avoid such an explosion. This is a sound legal principle if one wants to discourage people from having dangerous property. But the same principle is now being applied in many jurisdictions to animal companions: anyone who keeps a dog in their backyard is subject to strict liability for any dog bites, no matter how conscientious and careful they are. The (intended) result is to either discourage people from having animal companions or to keep them continually confined or chained, since they are categorized legally as a threat to others.

This equation of animal companions with dangerous property is out of step with social perceptions. For many people, companion animals are valued members of the family, and so should be subject to the same liability rules as, say, harms done by young children. In the case of young children, parents have a duty to exercise reasonable supervision and control, so as to reduce the potential risk that children might harm others, but children are seen as presumptively sociable members of the family and of society who have a right to be part of social life. We could reduce the risk that children will harm others if we kept children locked up all the time, but children are not dangerous property to be confined. They are members of society with a right to engage in social life, subject to parental duties of reasonable supervision. And so here too we see proposals to replace strict liability for dog bites (animals as dangerous property) with a model based on parental duties of supervision (animals as sociable family members) (Epstein, 2006).

In these contexts, and others (such as legal reforms allowing the creation of trusts for pets whose human guardians predecease them),[16] there is a push to redefine companion animals not as the property of the family, but as members of the family, with membership-based claims (to the preservation of family bonds in the case of divorce; to engage in social life in the case of liability; to be eligible for family benefits in the case of wills). All of these reforms involve rejecting the older use-based principles of animal law and replacing

[16]   Foster (2011). Other reforms that embody a family membership ethic include the recognition in the law of a duty of veterinarians to report suspected abuse of companion animals based on the precedent of health care providers having a duty to report child abuse; legal challenges to bans on animal companions in public housing, which effectively prevent poor people from keeping their more-than-human family together; and legal amendments changing 'ownership' language to 'guardianship'. All of these reforms take principles from family law and apply them to companion animals.

them with principles taken from family law for governing the relationships amongst family members. In my view, this trend will only grow in strength. The social reality is that companion animals are indeed members of the family, and whenever the law is so far out of touch with social realities, it needs to adapt.

Do these changes represent a genuinely new type of animal law reform that replaces the older logic of interest-convergence grounded in human use typologies with a new ethics of membership? Perhaps not. A skeptic might argue that these reforms are less about recognizing the membership-based rights of the animals, and more about advancing the interests of the humans in having secure use of the animal. We have a long history of using animals for companionship, and these legal reforms can be seen as operating to provide greater legal security to humans who use animals for companionship. In that sense, we can see them as strengthening the rights of the owners of companion animals, not as recognizing the rights of animals themselves. Humans assert a right to use animals for companionship, and these reforms simply specify how that right to use animals will be legally protected.

That is undoubtedly part of the story. However, it is not the only, or primary, dynamic at work. When people mobilize to secure these legal reforms, they are not saying 'please respect my right to use animals for companionship,' they are saying 'please recognize that companion animals are members of my family.' Just as they do not think of their companionable relationships with children or spouses as use-based relationships, so too they do not think of their relationships with dogs or cats as use-based relationships. They are, rather, relations of co-membership in a shared social unit – in this case, the family. People are not saying that 'we' (humans) have a right to use 'them' (companion animals), but rather are saying that companion animals are members of the 'we,' and are demanding legal recognition of this interspecies we-ness, this interspecies familial relationship. Recognition of family membership is precisely a membership relationship, and it carries with it membership claims, rather than claims to 'humane use.' Animals have always provided companionship but recognizing them as co-members of the family is new, and entails claims to shared membership of the home.

Animals as co-workers: Many DAs were originally brought into human society to labour, and humans and animals today continue to work alongside each other in a striking array of workplaces, from farms and labs to hospitals and seniors homes to military installations and airports (Coulter, 2016). As we've seen, legally speaking, these animals are not considered workers, but as the property of the workplace. However, as in the case of the family, this is increasingly contested. In some of these workplaces (though by no means all), the human workers have come to think of animals as their co-workers, with similar working hours and working conditions, undergoing similar training, facing similar risks, enjoying shared accomplishments. And once animals are seen as co-members of a shared workplace, there is a natural tendency to ask whether animals should have the membership rights of co-workers. These rights might include rights to safe working conditions, to maximum working hours, to union representation, to a retirement, to workers' compensation if injured, to a living wage, and rights against forced labour.[17]

This idea is nonsensical within the old use-based paradigm. However, an increasing number of human workers refuse to accept this framework for thinking about the status of their animal co-workers. One example concerns dogs in the US Army. As noted earlier, until recently these animals were seen as property – literally listed as 'equipment' – and as such, were often left behind (or killed) when the military pulled out of foreign countries. However, in response to pressure from their human co-workers, the Army now defines military dogs as 'personnel', and as such they have rights to repatriation and to rehoming upon retirement (Cruse, 2014). Similar developments have occurred in relation to police dogs – for example, the Nottinghamshire police force in Britain provides retired police dogs with a pension. And there are glimpses of a similar trend regarding emotional support animals. In all of these cases, it is the human workers who are mobilizing for recognition of DAs as colleagues and co-workers – as members of a shared interspecies workplace – rather than as property or equipment belonging to a human workplace.

Can we view these reforms as examples of transformative policy change that replaces the older logic of interest-convergence with a new ethics of membership? A more sceptical interpretation is certainly possible. Humans have a long history of seeing animals simply as 'beasts of burden' who exist to work for us, and these reforms could be seen as reaffirming our right to the 'humane use' of animals for their labour. But that does not seem to fully capture these developments. When soldiers in the US Army mobilized to secure these legal reforms, they did not say 'please respect my right to use animals for work,' they said 'please recognize that animals are my co-workers.' Just as they do not think of their collegial

---

[17]   For discussion of such labour rights, see Cochrane (2016), Blattner (2019); Shaw (2018).

relationships with other human soldiers as use-based relationships, so too they do not think of their collegial relationships with military dogs as use-based relationships. They are, rather, relations of co-membership in a shared social unit – in this case, the workplace. People are not saying that 'we' (humans) have a right to use 'them' (animals), but rather that animals are members of the 'we,' and are demanding legal recognition of this interspecies we-ness, this inter-species working relationship. Recognition of collegiality is precisely a membership relationship, and it carries with it membership claims, rather than claims to 'humane use'. Animals have always la-boured for us, but recognizing them as co-workers is new, and entails claims to shared membership of the workplace.

So we have two examples of potentially transformative member-ship claims, as family members and co-workers. It is worth noting that philosophers have been largely invisible in these debates regard-ing family and worker status. These issues have not been central to mainstream animal ethics, and not have not been prioritized by the animal advocacy movements inspired by philosophers. Rather, these membership developments have largely occurred as a result of pressure from members of the general public who have demanded that the state recognize the ties they have developed with their com-panions and co-workers. Some philosophers are now playing catch-up with these developments, trying to make theoretical sense of them. But in general, philosophy has been 'caught napping' with respect to membership claims. Philosophers did not identify this as a potential sphere for transformative legal reform, and have not actively engaged with public debates on these reforms. I think this is regrettable, since these reforms raise a number of puzzles and dilemmas that cry out for philosophical analysis.

5. Advancing an Ethic of Membership

If the analysis so far is correct, we are at a crossroads with respect to membership rights for DAs. We can see glimpses of transformative legal reforms that embody an ethic of membership, but also a risk that these reforms will collapse back into ideologies of humane use. The fact that these reforms are ambiguous in this way – wavering between an ethics of membership and an ethics of humane use – is significant, and raises important issues that require philosophical attention.

One way to unpack the ambiguities of a membership approach is to compare it with another, perhaps more familiar, strategy for achieving animal liberation: namely, 'let them be'. This is the slogan Regan and other theorists have used to summarize their vision of animal liberation: we liberate animals by leaving them alone (Regan, 1983, p. 357). Palmer calls this the 'laissez-faire intuition', and discusses how central it has been to many theories of animal rights (Palmer, 2010). If the ideology of humane use has involved incorporating animals into our society, culture and economy to serve us, animal liberation involves de-incorporation: disengaging animals from human society, culture, and economy, and leaving them free to live on their own.

This 'laissez-faire intuition' is indeed an appropriate route to animal liberation for many wild animals. In many cases, we should leave them (and their habitat) alone.[18] However, this is not a viable strategy for most DAs. Having been taken out of the wild, and bred to live and work amongst humans, many DAs would not survive if we just 'let them be'. In any event, as I argued earlier, DAs have a birthright in the society that they have helped to build. DAs may choose to leave human society, through some process of gradual rewilding, but we have no right to expel them from society.[19]

The membership strategy is therefore a very different route to liberation from laissez-faire. Rather than severing DAs' relationship to society, it refounds that relationship by giving DAs a fuller stake in society. On the membership model, society is a 'common possession' of its members, and so society belongs to DAs as much as to humans.

This idea raises distinctive risks as a strategy for animal liberation. To be a member of society brings with it various rights – including the family and workplace rights discussed in the previous section – but also various expectations and responsibilities. A shared society is only possible if everyone is able and willing to comply with some basic rules of sociability: sharing space, taking turns, avoiding violence and intimidation. Minimally, therefore, to be a member of society involves expectations of civility and sociability. Membership may also involve expectations of contributing to the common good, of doing one's share for the production and reproduction of the shared social world.

---

[18] Even here, however, it is inaccurate to describe this as 'laissez-faire'. For wild animals to live autonomously, they will require legally guaranteed territorial rights, as well as legal and political standing to address a range of international issues (climate change, pollution, migration corridors etc) and to make claims for rectificatory justice. See Donaldson and Kymlicka (2011, chap. 6).

[19] On how we might institutionalize a right to exit for DAs, see Kymlicka and Donaldson (2014).

And all of this requires some degree of socialization. All members of society – human or DA – need to learn to exercise self-restraint and to regulate their natural instincts so as to comply with social norms and social roles. For DAs to enjoy the family and workplace rights discussed in the previous section, they must first be socialized into the expectations of family and work life, to be able to live and work peaceably alongside others.

The membership approach, therefore, seems to involve some of the same problematic practices as humane use. Whether we adopt a membership model or a humane use model, in either case we seem to be involved in 'molding', 'disciplining', 'normalizing' or 'policing' DAs to secure their compliance with social norms and their contribution to public goods.[20] So how exactly is membership liberating?

This is a serious challenge, and is one reason why many animal rights advocates have embraced the laissez-faire model of animal liberation. A laissez-faire approach denies that we have any right to socialize animals, or that we have any right to impose expectations of compliance or contribution upon them. In that sense, a laissez-faire strategy of animal liberation seems safer and cleaner: it avoids the dilemmas that arise when take seriously the idea of living together in a shared social world, with all the restraints and accommodations that are required to live together socially.

However, as I noted earlier, the laissez-faire strategy is simply not feasible or legitimate for most DAs. So in my view, we have no option but to confront these dilemmas head on. We need to think more deeply about what precisely defines an ethic of membership, and how we can prevent it degenerating into an ethic of humane use.

I suggested earlier that the crux of a membership ethic is the idea of society as a common possession, in which society belongs to all its members. The ideology of humane use rejects this: DAs are seen as belonging in society, but society does not belong to them: it belongs only to humans. Humans are the possessors of society, and as such have the right to determine its social norms and social roles. By contrast, the ethic of membership has a symmetrical view of belonging: DAs not only belong in society, but society belongs to them as a common possession of all members. And this in turn means that, on a membership model, DAs have a right to co-determine its social norms and roles. A full-throated ethic of membership rests on these two ideas: common possession of society and co-authorship of its social norms and roles.

---

[20]   For the argument that the membership strategy involves policing and disciplining DAs, and hence is not really a form of liberation, see Nurse and Ryland (2013).

These are the ideas that underpinned Marshall's conception of the democratic welfare state, and in my view, they should equally define an ethic of membership for DAs.[21]

This is a demanding vision, and as soon as we make it explicit, it becomes clear that existing reforms to family and work fall short of it in at least two key respects. First, they are highly selective in terms of which membership rights are accorded, falling short of rights of common possession and co-authorship of society. These reforms have invoked membership to address specific problems – e.g., custody disputes in the case of companion animals; retirement in the case of working animals – but have not embraced a fuller vision of social membership. Second, they are highly selective in terms of which DAs are recognized as members. In short, they extend a limited conception of membership to a limited number of DAs.

However, justice is not built overnight, and so a crucial question is whether these reforms are just one-off tweaks to the status quo, or are they likely to spur further membership claims. Will they have spill-over effects, provoking membership claims for a wider set of DAs, over wider areas of social life?

And here, I think, there are reasons for cautious optimism. Let me start with family reforms. As I just said, these reforms are limited in two key respects as compared to a full ethics of membership. First, these reforms have focused on acknowledging animals' membership within private families, whereas a full ethic of membership requires that DAs be recognized as members of the broader society and polity as well. To be fully recognized as a member of society would not just involve being treated as a member within private familial settings, but also being treated as a member of the public, with rights to public goods, public services, public spaces and public voice. So the first challenge is whether the recognition of private family membership can be a springboard to recognition of a wider public and political membership.

The second challenge is that legal reforms to recognize family membership have only applied to companion animals, and not farmed animals or lab animals. People rarely view sheep, cows, pigs, mice or rats as members of the family (although some do, of course), and so extending membership rights based on perceptions

---

[21]   This arguably distinguishes the social-democratic image of membership from certain Confucian ideas of role ethics which offer a more hierarchical account of society. See, for example, the discussion of 'just hierarchy' between humans and domesticated animals in Bell and Pei (2020, chapter 4).

of familial bonds is less likely to help them. So the second challenge is whether we can extend this recognition beyond dogs and cats to farmed animals and lab animals.

These are both big challenges. There is growing evidence that companion animals are being treated in the law as family members, but we need to extend this membership from the private to the public, and from companion animals to all DAs. I am optimistic about the first challenge. We can already see evidence that the recognition of private family membership is having implications for broader social membership. Consider the legal changes adopted after Hurricane Katrina requiring emergency services to be trained and equipped to rescue companion animals. Or consider the growing movement demanding that cities provide dog parks, and access to public services and spaces. Or consider proposals for public health insurance for companion animals. All of these involve claims to public goods and services in the name of companion animals as family members.

This should not be surprising, since once we acknowledge that companion animals are members of the family, people will want to take their families with them into the broader society. They will want to vacation with their more-than-human family, or to bring their more-than-human family into commercial spaces or onto public transportation, or to ensure the health and safety of their more-than-human family. All of these involve claims on public services and public spaces. More-than-human private families will, sooner or later, demand a more-than-human conception of the public and of social membership.

And this in turn might generate claims to political representation. If companion animals are members of the public, and not just the family, their good should be included when determining the public good, and this requires that their interests be represented. There already are some examples around the world of appointing 'advocates' or 'ombudspersons' for animals within policy-making processes. In some cases, their mandate is simply to ensure effective implementation of existing laws regulating humane use, but more ambitious versions argue that DAs are owed political participation and representation because of their social membership, as members of the public in whose name the state governs.[22]

So there are grounds for optimism that the scope of membership norms will expand from private family membership to broader public/political membership, at least for companion animals. The second challenge, however, is more daunting: it is difficult to see

---

[22] For various models of the political representation and participation of DAs, see Smith (2012); Garner (2017); Hooley (2018); Donaldson (2020).

how this model of family membership can be extended to most farmed or lab animals, who are not perceived as members of the family. This perception might change over time, due to the rise of sanctuaries for formerly farmed animals, especially urban and suburban micro-sanctuaries, which allow more and more people to experience first-hand the possibilities of living alongside such animals.[23] Humans are certainly capable of having companionable relations with most DAs if given the chance, and bylaws prohibiting 'farm' animals in urban settings are increasingly being challenged in order to make room for such relationships. As more and more people come to know of friends and neighbours who have formerly farmed animals as family members, perhaps the very distinction between companion animals and farmed animals will gradually break down.

Indeed, some opponents of extending family membership to companion animals criticize it precisely on the grounds that 'with many communities increasingly permitting farm animals as pets, drawing a line even broadly at companion animals can be exceedingly difficult' (Goldberg, 2013, p. 48). Far from being a 'difficulty' with the reform, I view this as one of its most potentially transformative features. The political significance of extending family membership to companion animals is much greater if it goes hand-in-hand with efforts to dissolve the line between companion animals and farmed animals – for example, by challenging bylaws that prohibit farmed animals in the city, and by establishing urban and suburban micro-sanctuaries for formerly farmed animals.

In short, while existing reforms to recognize family membership represent a highly limited vision of an ethics of membership, we have good reasons to think they can be a springboard to fuller social membership, certainly for companion animals, and also perhaps – more speculatively – for other DAs, if accompanied by efforts to dissolve the hard division between companion animals and farmed/lab animals.[24]

Let me turn now to the case of workplace reforms. As with family reforms, we see the same double challenge: existing reforms to recognize animals as workers offer only a narrow set of membership rights

---

[23] On the growing presence of formerly farmed animals in (sub)urban settings, see Ranalli (2008); Van Kleek (2014). On the role of farmed animal sanctuaries in challenging the ideology of humane use and prefiguring membership relations, see Donaldson and Kymlicka (2015); Blattner et al (2020).

[24] This distinction is also being challenged by calls to establish rehoming and adoption programs for animals used in research labs.

to a narrow set of DAs. To date at least, the key right gained by those animals who have been legally recognized as workers is the right to a decent retirement. The general public seems uncomfortable with the idea that animals who have worked loyally for us should be killed or abandoned when they are no longer able to work, particularly if this work involved risk or sacrifice, as with military and police dogs. Recognizing animals as workers has largely been motivated by the desire to secure a decent retirement for such working animals.

This is very far from the full membership idea that would entail common possession and co-authorship of workplaces and work life for DAs. However, I suspect that recognizing animals as workers will over time generate a wider set of membership claims. Commentators have called this the 'labour recognition transformation thesis'.[25] Both as a matter of formal law and as a matter of public ethos, the category of 'worker' carries moral weight. It entails not only rights regarding the workplace (such as maximum working hours and safe working conditions), but also rights in relation to the broader economy and society (such as a right to share in the benefits of society's overall scheme of cooperation). Drawing on international labour law, Blattner argues that recognizing animals as workers would entail both a prohibition on forced labour and effective representation in workplace management (Blattner, 2019), perhaps through some form of microboard'.[26] Once we recognize animals as workers, they should be seen as having the right to shape the design of jobs and the workplaces – in short, the right to co-author the future of work in our shared society.

This is speculative: there is a vast distance between current reforms aimed at preventing the killing of animals when they stop working and Blattner's vision of animals as co-authors of workplaces and economies. It is too early to tell whether the 'labour recognition transformation thesis' will bridge this gap. However, it's worth noting that many social justice struggles have grounded their claims for recognition and respect on work. Historically, when excluded or stigmatized groups have claimed social membership, it is often through work (Shklar, 1991). Participating in labour provides a

---

[25] The term was coined by Eisen (2019), summarizing the views of various contributors to Blattner, Kymlicka and Coulter (2019). See also Niesen (2021).

[26] The microboard structure was developed to assist the self-determination of people with severe cognitive disability, composed of people who are known to and trusted by the individual. Donaldson (2020) extends this model to the case of DAs in the workplace.

basis on which subaltern groups can establish their claim to be participants in and contributors to schemes of social cooperation. Of course, people fight to escape or abolish degrading and stigmatizing forms of work, but there is ample evidence that participating in socially-recognized and socially-valued work is an important source of meaning and identity for humans, and an important basis for claims to social membership, and there is no reason to assume that the same is not true of DAs (Donaldson and Kymlicka, 2019).

So we have grounds for optimism that recognizing animals as workers can trigger broader claims to social/political membership. However, that leaves us with the second problem: existing reforms only extend this social recognition to a small category of working animals. In principle, compared to the family membership route, the workplace membership path seems more inclusive, since it does not require intimate companionship or family ties. Social recognition comes through relations of collegiality, as co-workers in a shared workplace, not intimate family relations. As a result, this trend could in principle apply to a wider range of DAs engaged in a wider range of labour in diverse workplaces, outside the private home.

In practice, however, only a narrow range of work, done by a narrow range of animals, has so far achieved social recognition. It is above all military and police work that has generated social recognition, primarily for horses and dogs. As a result, the trend to recognize animals as workers, to date at least, has failed to challenge the cleavage between companion animals, whom we socially recognize, and farmed/lab animals, whom we ignore and exploit. Even though social recognition for military and police dogs is tied to work, not family bonds, it seems that the animals we are most inclined to recognize as 'co-workers' are the same types of animals that are viewed as 'members of the family'.

However, I do not see any conceptual obstacle to a gradual extension of the social recognition of animals as co-workers to farmed animals. If sniffer dogs at the airport can be seen as co-workers, why not Bill and Lou, the oxen who worked alongside students plowing fields at Green Mountain College farm?[27] Or the sheep who graze environmentally-sensitive grasslands at the San Francisco airport, or the goats on Faroe Island who take Google Earth cameras into otherwise inaccessible places, or

---

[27] On the infamous case of Bill and Lou – where the College decided to kill and eat the oxen as soon they were unable to continue work despite offers to give them sanctuary – see Kymlicka and Donaldson (2014).

the pigeons who carry pollution sensors to monitor air quality in the skies above London? And why not the animals who perform what Les Beldo calls 'metabolic labour', producing manure, or wool, or eggs (Beldo, 2017)? Indeed, there is growing interest amongst both academics and advocates in the transformative possibilities of labour as a route to recognition and membership for a wide range of DAs.[28]

To be sure, this is an uphill battle. For one thing, social recognition of others as co-workers is easier when we interact with them on an everyday basis, in a setting of trust, cooperation, and sociability, where we greet others at the start of the workday, socialize, and then embark on working together. It is more difficult when large numbers of animals are confined in pens or cages, with little or no human interaction or interspecies cooperation. The sociological conditions that make it possible to see others as co-workers in a shared workplace are simply not present in most modern farms or labs.

Moreover, even if we could make this cognitive leap to reimagine farmed animals as our co-workers, those with vested interests in the animal industrial complex will surely mobilize against any recognition of farmed animals as co-workers, since it would threaten the basis of their commercial exploitation of animals. The recognition of military/police dogs as co-workers has been uncontroversial because it is peripheral to the basic structure of the animal industrial complex, but as soon as ideas of workplace-based membership rights start to challenge inherited agricultural practices, and the lifestyles they make possible, the backlash would be quick. So it is an uphill battle to hope that ideas of animals as co-workers can significantly affect, in the near future, the abject status of farmed or lab animals (Eisen, 2019).

In short, in relation to both family and work, we see a similar story. Existing legal reforms have introduced a narrow set of membership rights for a select handful of animals, but in both cases, there is evidence of a multiplier effect, as small initial reforms have triggered further debates and claims for stronger membership rights amongst a wider range of DAs.

Whether this trajectory will ultimately lead to a genuine ethics of membership is far from clear. And even if we could make real progress on the membership front, we would still face unfinished business regarding the other crucial track of interspecies justice – namely, personhood rights. As I've emphasized, justice ultimately

---

[28] For an overview of recent academic analysis and advocacy on animal labour, see Lercier (2021).

requires both membership rights and personhood rights. Membership without personhood is a radically precarious and unjust status. To take just one example, under Ontario law, if companion animals who are lost are not claimed within three days, shelters are allowed and indeed may be required to sell them to research labs to be experimented on. When membership status fails, as in the case of lost dogs, they have no personhood rights to fall back upon, and so are subject to pure instrumentalization. Recognition of personhood makes clear that animals, like humans, have intrinsic moral status, prior to and independent of specific roles or relationships.

Our long-term aim, therefore, should be to achieve both universal rights of personhood and relational rights of membership. I have focused on membership in this paper because it has been relatively neglected within the literature, and because it may be a more politically feasible path for the foreseeable future, but we clearly need both. Membership cannot take the place of personhood (or vice versa): they are both irreducible elements of justice. What is less clear is how the two tracks interact. Someone might think that personhood must come first, that we can only recognize DAs as family members and workers if we first recognize them as persons. One might think, for example, that society will only recognize dogs as 'personnel' if it first recognizes them as 'persons.' But as we've seen this is not true. And indeed my hunch is that the reverse is often the case: we will come to recognize DAs as persons because we have first come to see them as family members and co-workers. Hannah Arendt famously argued that the first step towards the denial of universal human rights was to strip people of their social membership: once we lose the ability to see humans as social members, we lose the ability to see them as individual persons. So too in the reverse: enabling people to see DAs as social members may facilitate and expedite the recognition of personhood.

6. Conclusion

In this paper, I have defended an under-explored route to legal reform for domesticated animals - namely, through inclusion into the everyday categories of social membership, such as family members and co-workers. Rather than restate that argument, however, I want to conclude by returning to the role of philosophy in these debates. As I noted earlier, philosophers have largely been 'caught napping' with respect to these developments. There has been a recent flurry of work by philosophers to try to catch up with these developments,[29] but we might hope that philosophers could in fact lead the way, as they did in the 1970s and 1980s with the original debates about speciesism and moral status. Why did philosophers miss these developments, and what sort of philosophy do we need to make sense of these issues, and to help inform their evolution?

I've already suggested that part of the explanation is the relative imbalance of moral and political philosophy on the animal question: we desperately need to get political philosophy on board. But I want to make a more specific suggestion. If the distinguishing feature of DAs is that they have been brought into our society to live and work alongside us, then what we need, above all, is a *social* philosophy, in the literal sense. We need a theory of 'society'.

I mentioned earlier that most theories of democracy and social justice implicitly start from the premise that we form a 'society', and defend the ideal that this society should be a common possession of its members. However, political philosophers have a variety of ways of making sense of this idea of 'society'. Rawls famously says that we should think of society as a 'scheme of cooperation for mutual advantage', and argues that theories of distributive justice concern the benefits and burdens of this 'scheme of cooperation' (Rawls, 1971, p. 4). Other theorists offer subtly different formulations, emphasizing shared norms and rules. A. John Simmons, for example, argues that the distinctive focus of political philosophy, as compared to other fields of normative theory, is neither intimate personal friendships nor cosmic relationships, but rather 'society', understood as a 'stable, intergenerational group of persons characterized by peaceful, cooperative, rule-governed conduct with a wide range of activities' (Simmons, 2008, pp. 7-8). Similarly, John Christman argues that political philosophy focuses on 'people as they live within rule-governed social institutions' (Christman, 2002, p. 3). Thomas Christiano suggests that society in this sense creates a 'common world', which he defines as one 'in which the fulfillment of all or nearly all of the fundamental interests of each person are connected with the fulfillment of all or nearly all of the fundamental interests of every other person' (Christiano, 2008, p. 80), and he argues that democracy is about the governing of such a common world.

It would be interesting to parse the subtle differences amongst these definitions. But for our purposes, what is striking is that all of

---

[29] See Sandøe et al (2015); Overall (2017) on companion animals; Blattner et al (2019) on animal labour.

these philosophers take for granted that 'society' is a human-exclusive phenomenon. This is demonstrably false. DAs are clearly part of society on any of these definitions: they participate in schemes of cooperation, comply with rule-governed institutions, and have interdependent interests. To theorize justice for DAs, we therefore need to think about society in interspecies terms. And this in turn raises a host of subsidiary questions about the kind of cooperation that humans and DAs engage in; the nature of the norms and rules that define an interspecies community; the kinds of 'publics' and 'commons' that bring members together (public goods, public spaces and public things); and the kind of social solidarity that binds members of society together and leads members to accept the burdens of justice. In my view, this is an exciting frontier of animal ethics that philosophers are just beginning to explore. If we are to move forward in a more transformative direction, towards a fuller ethic of social membership, we need a more developed philosophy of interspecies society.[30]

Queen's University
kymlicka@queensu.ca

References

Catherine Amiot & Brock Bastian, 'Toward a Psychology of Human–Animal Relations' 141 (2015) *Psychological Bulletin* 6.

Les Beldo, 'Metabolic labor: Broiler chickens and the exploitation of vitality', *Environmental Humanities* 9 (2017) 108-128.

Daniel Bell and Wang Pei, *Just hierarchy*, (Princeton University Press, 2020).

Derrick Bell Jr, 'Brown v. Board of Education and the Interest-Convergence Dilemma', 93 (1980) *Harvard Law Rev* 518.

Charlotte Blattner, 'A Right to Freely Choose One's Work'. In Charlotte Blattner, Kendra Coulter, and Will Kymlicka, eds. *Animal Labour: A New Frontier of Interspecies Justice?* (Oxford University Press, 2019).

Charlotte Blattner, Sue Donaldson, and Ryan Wilcox, 'Animal Agency in Community.' *Politics and Animals* 6 (2020) 1-22.

Charlotte Blattner, Kendra Coulter, and Will Kymlicka, eds. *Animal Labour: A New Frontier of Interspecies Justice?* (Oxford University Press, 2019).

[30] This paper draws on ideas developed in collaborative work with Sue Donaldson, and I'm grateful for her comments on an earlier version.

Ted Benton, 'Humanism = Speciesism? Marx on Humans and Animals'. *Radical Philosophy* 50 (1988) 4-18.

Richard Bulliet, *Hunters, herders, and hamburgers: the past and future of human-animal relationships*, (Columbia University Press, 2005).

Thomas Christiano, *The Constitution of Equality*, (Oxford University Press, 2008).

John Christman, *Social and Political Philosophy: A Contemporary Introduction*, (Routledge, 2002).

Alasdair Cochrane, 'Labour rights for animals'. In R. Garner and S. O'Sullivan, eds., *The Political Turn in Animal Ethics*, (Rowman and Littlefield, 2016) 15-32.

Kendra Coulter, *Animals, work, and the promise of interspecies solidarity*, (Palgrave, 2016).

Sarah Cruse, 'Military working dogs: classification and treatment in the US Armed Forces', *Animal Law* 21 (2014) 249.

Maneesha Deckha, *Animals as Legal Beings*, (University of Toronto Press, 2021).

Sue Donaldson, 'Animal Agora: Animal Citizens and the Democratic Challenge', *Social Theory and Practice* 46 (2020) 709-735.

Sue Donaldson and Will Kymlicka, *Zoopolis: A Political Theory of Animal Rights* (Oxford University Press, 2011).

Sue Donaldson and Will Kymlicka, 'Farmed Animal Sanctuaries: The Heart of the Movement?', *Politics and Animals* 1 (2015) 50-74.

Sue Donaldson and Will Kymlicka, 'Animal Labour in a Post-Work Society?'. In Charlotte Blattner, Kendra Coulter, and Will Kymlicka, eds. *Animal Labour: A New Frontier of Interspecies Justice?* (Oxford University Press, 2019) 207-228.

Sue Donaldson and Will Kymlicka, 'Transformative Animal Protection' in Kristin Voigt, Valéry Giroux, and Angie Pepper (eds) *The Ethics of Animal Shelters* (Oxford University Press, 2022).

Jessica Eisen, 'Liberating Animal Law: Breaking Free from Human-Use Typologies', *Animal Law* 17 (2010) 59-76.

Jessica Eisen, 'Down on the Farm: Status, Exploitation, and Agricultural Exceptionalism'. In C. Blattner, K. Coulter, & W. Kymlicka (Eds.), *Animal Labour: A New Frontier of Interspecies Justice* (Oxford University Press, 2019) 139-59.

Lynn Epstein, 'There are no Bad dogs, only bad owners: Replacing Strict Liability with a Negligence Standard in Dog Bite Cases', *Animal Law* 13 (2006) 129-45.

Frances Foster, 'Should Pets Inherit?', *Florida Law Review* 63 (2011).

Robert Garner, 'Animals and democratic theory' *Contemporary Political Theory* 16 (2017) 459-77.

Phil Goldberg, 'Courts and Legislatures Have Kept the Proper Leash on Pet Injury Lawsuits', *Stanford. Journal of Animal Law & Policy* 6 (2013) 30.

Harris Poll, 'Pets Really Are Members of the Family', (10 June 2011), *The Harris Poll*, <http://www.theharrispoll.com/health-and-life/pets_really_are_Members_of_the_Family.html>).

Dan Hooley, 'Animals and Political Standing', *Palgrave Handbook of Philosophy and Public Policy*, (Palgrave, 2018) 291-301.

Scott Jaschik, 'Did Peter Singer Back Animal Research?', *Inside Higher Ed*, (December 4, 2006) https://www.insidehighered.com/news/2006/12/04/did-peter-singer-back-animal-research

John Jasper and Dorothy Nelkin, *The Animal Rights Crusade* (Free Press, 1992).

Gail Melson, *Why the Wild things are: Animals in the Lives of Children*, (Harvard University Press, 2001).

Will Kymlicka, 'Social membership: Animal law beyond the property/personhood impasse', *Dalhousie Law Journal* 40 (2017) 123.

Will Kymlicka, 'Nationhood, Multiculturalism and the Ethics of Membership', in Liav Orgad and Ruud Koopmans (eds) *Majorities, Minorities, and the Future of Nationhood* (Cambridge University Press, 2022).

Will Kymlicka and Sue Donaldson, 'Animals and the Frontiers of Citizenship', *Oxford Journal of Legal Studies* 34 (2014) 200-219.

Will Kymlicka and Sue Donaldson, 'Locating animals in political philosophy', *Philosophy Compass* 11 (2016) 692-701.

Marine Lercier, *Animal Labour: A Social Justice Issue for the 21st Century* (Global Research Network, Canterbury, 2021).

Jeff McMahan, *The Ethics of Killing* (Oxford University Press, 2002).

Mary Midgley, *Beast and Man* (Cornell University Press, 1978).

David Miller, *Political Philosophy: A very short introduction*, (Oxford University Press, 2003).

Peter Niesen, 'Animal agriculture and the 'labour turn'', *Politics and Animals* (2021).

Barbara Noske, *Human and Other Animals* (Pluto Press, 1989).

Robert Nozick, *Anarchy, State and Utopia* (Basic Books, 1974).

Angus Nurse and Diane Ryland, 'A question of citizenship', *Journal of Animal Ethics* 3 (2013) 201-207.

Christine Overall, *Pets and people: The ethics of our relationships with companion animals.* (Oxford University Press, 2017).

Clare Palmer, *Animal ethics in context*, (Columbia University Press, 2010).

Ralph Ranalli, 'The New Faces Settling into Suburbia: Owners Cite Practical, Spiritual Rewards of Farm Animals as Pets', *Boston Globe*, (June 29, 2008), http://archive.boston.com/news/local/articles/2008/06/29/the_new_faces_settling_into_suburbia/

Tom Regan, *The Case for Animal Rights*, (University of California Press, 1983).

Tom Regan, 'Foreword', *Political Theory and Animal Rights*. Ed. Andrew Linzey and Paul Clarke. (Pluto Press, 1990).

Deborah Rook, 'Who Gets Charlie? The Emergence of Pet Custody Disputes in Family Law: Adapting Theoretical Tools from Child Law', *Int J Law Policy Family* 28 (2014).

Peter Sandøe, Sandra Corr, and Clare Palmer, *Companion animal ethics*, (Wiley, 2015).

Ani Satz, 'Animals as Vulnerable Subjects: Beyond Interest-Convergence, Hierarchy, and Property', *Animal Law* 16 (2009) 1–50.

Rosemary Shaw, 'A Case for recognizing the rights of Animals as Workers', *Journal of Animal Ethics* 8 (2018) 182-98.

Judith Shklar, *American Citizenship: The Quest for Inclusion* (Harvard University Press, 1991).

A. John. Simmons, *Political Philosophy*, (Oxford University Press, 2008).

Peter Singer, *Animal Liberation*, (Harper, 1975).

Kim Smith, *Governing Animals: Animal Welfare and the Liberal State* (Oxford University Press, 2012).

Saskia Stucki, 'Toward Hominid and Other Humanoid Rights: Are We Witnessing a Legal Revolution?', *Verfassungsblog* (2016), http://verfassungsblog.de/toward-hominid-and-other-humanoid-rights-are-we-witnessing-a-legal-revolution/

Richard Twine, 'Revealing the Animal-Industrial Complex', *Journal for Critical Animal Studies* 10 (2012) 12-39.

Justin Van Kleek, 'The Sanctuary in Your Backyard: A New Model for Rescuing Farmed Animals,' *Our Hen House*, (June 24, 2014), http://www.ourhenhouse.org/2014/06/the-sanctuary-in-your-backyard-a-new-model-for-rescuingfarmed-animals/

Gareth Walsh, 'Father of Animal Activism Backs Monkey Testing', *The Sunday Times*, (November 26, 2006). https://www.thetimes.co.uk/article/father-of-animal-activism-backs-monkey-testing

Individual Freedom in the Post-Corona Era

HEISOOK KIM

Abstract
In this essay, I examine the concept of individual freedom that varies depending on cultures through different attitudes toward the administrative policy of wearing masks. Many Westerners criticized the enforcement of the policy in East Asia as the oppression of individual freedom. I argue that the criticism is based on a narrow understanding of the problem and that individual freedom becomes obscure even in the West as we are entering the society of surveillance capitalism due to technological revolution. Confucian cultures give us a context in reference to which we reflect on individual freedom in the post-pandemic situation.

A column published in the French business daily *Les Echos* in April 6 under the title 'COVID-19 and tracking: let's not sacrifice our individual liberties' opined that South Korea's administrative policy of tracing the movements of confirmed cases and making tracing information available to the public was perhaps one of the worst cases in terms of the respect for individual freedom. The author, lawyer Virginie Pradel, opposed discussions in France that were in favor of adopting a similar contact tracing system as Korea's. The Korean Embassy in France immediately complained to *Les Echos*, and Jun Hae-oung, the director of the Korean Cultural Center in Paris, submitted a rebuttal to the daily under his name on April 14. He said, 'The South Korean government and its citizens are very committed to the fight against the virus', adding that 'all measures taken are based on laws' and 'approved by Korean citizens'.

In the age of COVID-19, we are witnessing the conflict between the right to pursue individual freedom and the moral obligation to ensure the safety of the community and our neighbors from the spread of the virus. This conflict often arises in instituting policies concerning wearing masks, building contact tracing systems and limiting various cultural activities including religious gatherings. The efficacy of wearing masks to avoid the virus is now widely accepted across the East and the West. Not long ago, however, some considered the refusal to wear face masks as an act of protecting

doi:10.1017/S1358246121000412

individual freedom, and some politicians, such as the former US President Donald Trump, exploited the 'anti-mask' movement as a political symbol to create solidarity among their supporters.

A societal controversy of this kind draws my attention to philosophical questions arising from the debate on the state control over individual citizens and the protection of individual freedom in an emergent case like Covid-19. In the early stage of this crisis, China appeared to undergo a great deal of turmoil due to the exponential growth in confirmed cases, but the full deployment of its considerable state authority under the centralized socialist system allowed it to avoid catastrophic damage at a relatively early point in time. As the success of pandemic response hinges on the efficiency of centralized disease control systems and the voluntary compliance of citizens, East Asian countries including Taiwan and Korea have experienced relatively low numbers of cases, as compared to the U.S. and European countries. In response to this, Western societies have begun to voice the criticism that the deployment of national surveillance systems, mandatory mask use, and movement restrictions infringes on the freedom of individuals and that East Asian countries have traditionally neglected individual freedom.

1. Can individual freedom be measured?

'Individual freedom' involves a number of connotations and complex philosophical issues that cannot be settled down by providing a specific set of behaviors and criteria. It is like other abstract values of love, justice and righteousness. From a superficial perspective, as Virginie Pradel pointed out, a government would indeed be violating individual freedom and the right to privacy if it imposes penalties on the refusal to wear a mask, prohibits entry into buildings without wearing a mask. It may be even more serious a problem if the government utilizes location tracking software on smartphones to identify the movements of infected persons and makes such information public. How can the conflict of interest between the pursuit of individual freedom and public control be navigated in situations like the pandemic that affects the entire world as well as individual countries? How does the notion that restrictions on individual freedom are unavoidable to ensure the public interest and the safety of society accord with the ideology of liberalism? A number of Americans including the former US President Trump and Europeans regarded the mandatory use of facial masks as an invasion of individual freedom, and Virginie Pradel presumed that the location tracking of confirmed cases infringed on individual freedom and undermined the core values of liberal democracy.

With regard to conflicts between authority and individual liberty, English philosopher and liberal John Stuart Mill asserted in his book *On Liberty* that individual freedom should in no case be violated unless it harms others: 'That the only purpose for which power can be rightfully exercised over any member of a civilized community, against his will, is to prevent harm to others. His own good, either physical or moral, is not a sufficient warrant. He cannot rightfully be compelled to do or forbear because it will be better for him to do so,... In the part which merely concerns himself, his independence is, of right, absolute. Over himself, over his own body and mind, the individual is sovereign' (Mill, 1860, p. 22).

Based on Mill's standards, the enforcement of mask wearing for infected persons does not infringe on individual freedom since their refusal to do so is likely to spread the coronavirus to others. Likewise, it is difficult to view the mask use mandate as a violation of individual freedom, because even those who are not confirmed to have been infected may pass on the virus through asymptomatic spread. What about releasing information on the movements of infected persons to the public through location tracking? If the disclosure of such information can minimize the risk of infection for others, the restriction of the individual's right to privacy would be justifiable. Then, why are the descendants of Mill in the West enraged by policy measures taken by East Asian countries? And why do citizens of the said East Asian countries quietly comply with such measures?

In Korea, although there was only one intellectual, as far as I know, named Han Sang-Jin who expressed concern over the increasing state control over the public during the pandemic, the issue did not become a controversy under the public spotlight from the perspective of the infringement of individual freedom, and a majority of the Korean public did not associate the matter of disease control with that of individual freedom. Rather, social criticism was directed toward those who hid or lied about their movements, which demonstrates the fundamental difference of attitude between the East Asia and the West concerning the relationship between the individual and the society. Considering another interesting news that China has developed a mobile application that can pinpoint individuals with bad credit within a 500 meter radius of a user, it is clear that the norms adopted by each society to pursue social safety can greatly vary and a criterion of individual freedom accordingly. In order to understand such norms, it is crucial to first understand the cultural backgrounds and contexts in which they are produced and consumed.

2. Individual Freedom in the Western Tradition

Individual freedom is closely linked to the existence of an individual. The existence of an individual is essential as freedom must be possessed and enjoyed by an agent or a subject. Democracy is a political system based on the existence of diverse individuals as citizens who are free and equal. Mill and other liberals believed that the worth of a society or a nation was based on the sum total of happiness or satisfaction individuals that comprised it might have. A prerequisite for individual freedom in a society to be secured is the existence of an individual as a whole being or as an absolute unit. The notion that an individual is the most basic element of a society is widely accepted in Western societies, as is the idea that we all exist as separate individuals with our own rights, desires, and values. The concept of an individual or individuality, however, is not as simple as it seems at first glance.

Throughout the history of Western philosophy, the definition of an individual or individuality has been a difficult and longstanding metaphysical question. Human beings do not simply exist in abstraction; rather, a human being exists as a woman or a man who is old or young, long haired or short haired, and fat or skinny. In reality, an individual is a being of myriad qualities and empirical properties. But, no matter how many properties and characteristics may be used to identify an individual, it is almost impossible to identify and to pin down with all those descriptions a particular individual who exists here and now. For there could be, in principle, many others who might fall under those general descriptions.

For centuries, Western philosophers have struggled to identify the conditions under which an individual 'a' can be identified as 'a'. The emphasis on individuality and the search for its conditions are deeply related with certain aspects of the Western Christian culture. One of the core elements that comprise the Christian worldview is the salvation of soul after death. In order to attain ultimate salvation, an individual must establish a positive relationship with God and cherish Christian values by leading a moral and religious life. And what is saved after death is 'my' soul, not the soul of my family or my friend. The soul must remain absolutely individual and cannot be shared with other beings. It must be simple (not divided), and unique. My soul belongs to me only. Good deeds of mine can only save me, but not others.

Responsibilities, duties and rights are completely vested in an individual who carries out actions. What is at stake is my conscience and my own moral decision to act. Morality and religious belief are something that I myself take responsibility on as person. Even my parents and family members have little to say about moral decisions I make and about the matter concerning the soul. The relationship between the soul of an individual and God is absolutely covenantal, that is, formally binding only between the two. Even though the authority and the social binding force of Christianity have waned, the idea that an individual human being stands as a solitary existence facing God *vis a vis* is deeply ingrained in laws and other social practices in Western societies as an ideal.

If an individual is accepted as an absolute unit, freedom can be referred to as the original state of an individual. The following paragraph by John Dewey helps us understand the concept of individual freedom as accepted in Western culture.

> Cicero had maintained that every man had its principles innate within him....The Roman law itself was most often used in the interest of absolutism, but the idea of a natural law, and so of a natural right more fundamental than any human dictate, proved a powerful instrument in the struggle for personal rights and equality. 'All men naturally were born free,' wrote Milton. 'To understand political power right,' wrote Locke, 'and derive it from its original, we must consider what state all men are naturally in, and that is a state of perfect freedom...' These doctrines found eloquent portrayal in Rousseau, and appear in the Declaration of Independence of 1776. (Dewey, 1978, p. 143)

Underlying the strong resistance against the coercion of a person's will in any way is this conception of individual freedom or individuality. The infringement of the right to privacy under the pretext of a government's pursuit of public interest is also to be rejected in the name of individual freedom.

In the initial stage of the COVID-19 pandemic, Westerners expressed their disapproval of government measures or social forces to adopt practices that individuals may dislike, such as wearing masks, and showed anger at tracking infected people. These phenomena are related with the aforementioned conception of individual freedom running deeply in Western cultures. The conception can be put in a phrase, 'I belong to no one but myself'. But we are now facing threats to such conception in the postmodern and post-coronavirus era. Even in the Western world, individual freedom seems to become an epitaph written on the gravestone of modernity no longer fitting in the world built on digital technology, virtual space, and platform business. I will address this issue in the last part.

.

3. Individual Freedom in East Asian Cultures

The cultural traditions of Korea, Taiwan and other East Asian countries were strongly influenced by such religious traditions as Confucianism, Buddhism and Taoism. Among them, Confucian values have come to dominate everyday rituals, social norms, modes of political power and governing practices in many Asian countries. This is partly because Confucianism is closely related to the specific moral norms that are complied with in everyday lives and bureaucratic rules of governance, while Buddhism and Taoism to metaphysical questions transcending this-worldliness.

In the Confucian tradition, an individual never exists as an absolute unit. Individuals always exist in the network of relations carrying out their roles, and fulfill moral responsibility and duty imposed upon them within familial relationships. Moral rules are regarded to reflect the order of heaven, the universe and the nature. Within the family, there are specific roles, moral norms and duties that must be followed by the father, the mother, sons, daughters and daughters-in-laws. Because of the longstanding cultural focus on filial piety, even an individual's body is considered to be bestowed by their parents, thus my body being not truly my own. Happiness of one's life depends on how well one performs the role allotted by the community and the value system one belongs to. The phenomenon that an individual in the East Asian culture pays much more attention to moral obligation and responsibility than to individual rights originates from the Confucian tradition centering on tightly knit human relations.

In Korean culture, the existence of an individual is established as a function of networks, not as an abstract unit independent of various social contexts. There have been various kinds of socially working networks developed throughout the history. These include not only networks like families and clans, but many pseudo-familial networks such as networks of hometown acquaintances, school friends, and religious groups. Countless social communities in Korea very often work like a family network. Many Korean CEOs are still fond of using the word 'our family members' when they refer to their employees. When people get close in Korea, they use terms to each other expressing familial relations like grandmother, aunt, brother and sister. Individual freedom in this type of society is thought to be obtained when individuals fulfill given roles within their networks by living up to their names and completing moral responsibilities that define the roles. Individuals are very likely to have inhibitions being conscious of other people's judgments because the roles are given from outside of their own selves. An individual does not belong to its own self but to a greater social self like families, clans, or a group with larger public identity, i.e. the nation. Individual freedom is supposed to be achieved only when the networks that form individuals function as intended. As an individual cannot be separated from the community and the network, individual freedom can only be achieved, or at least is thought to be achieved, when the network serves its own purpose. Individual freedom as developed in the West becomes more or less superfluous, if not spurious, or remains as an empty ideal in the Confucian culture.

The problem of individual freedom may be dealt with differently according to the way in which an individual is defined. If individuals are recognized as independent beings and separate units that possess unique values of their own, individual freedom can be achieved (or felt to be achieved) at the level where individuality is maximally procured. In Western culture, individual freedom is deeply related with other important concepts such as individual autonomy, inalienable rights of a person, and free will. On the other hand, the concept of individual freedom entered the East Asian cultures from the late 19th century when the Western democracy and the modern legal systems began to take root as an essential part of modernization.

In Confucian culture, the prime state of existence for an individual is to perform a given role in familial or social networks and fulfill the moral responsibilities set in accordance with the roles one plays. Individual freedom is not to be separated from the wellbeing and harmony of a close-knit community such as family or clan. The successful fulfillment of proper roles is considered to be the most valuable thing a human being born into a concrete network of relations may feel. My freedom is achieved by sharing happiness with family members and with those who bear family-like relations with me. If my family members are not happy, then I feel unfree as well as unhappy, being bound to them in many aspects; social, political, economical, cultural, religious, psychological, and so on. Individual desires that disregard family or social relations are deemed to be selfish, and in most cases, the private (私) is considered to have lower value than the public (公). The optimal state of individual existence is to be in harmony with others in the community by following moral laws which are universally valid as the mandate of heaven.

Naturally, an emphasis on the importance of existence and the will of individuals can also be found in the Confucian tradition. For example, *The Analects* includes a passage as 'The commander of three armies may be taken away, but the will of even a common

man may not be taken away from him' (Chan, 1963, p. 36). In
Mencius, we may also find a passage saying, 'Therefore all things of
the same kind are similar to one another…. The sage and I are the
same in kind' (Chan, 1963, p. 55).

These claims on the equality in the aspect of rational ability and
human dignity, however, did not make clues to the protection of
individual rights. Why? How did the notion of natural endowment
in human beings give rise to, on the one hand, the concept of
natural rights in the West, and that of natural duties, on the other,
in the East? An individual as a being situated in the network of
human relations must take responsibility for ensuring the effective
working of the network. There has been a strong belief in Korea
that an individual and the network are bound together by
a common lot. Very often, reward and punishment were given on a
group basis, rather than an individual basis. The guilt-by-association
system has worked until quite recently.

When a person holds fast to one's own rights and runs counter to
the general will of a community, that person is often regarded as
selfish enough to cause the malfunctioning or even the destruction
of a community. While the Chinese character '公' carries the
meaning of public, open, official, fair, and universal, its counterpart
'私' has the negative connotation of being selfish, rather than its literal
meaning of being private. Within this culture, individual freedom is
thought to be achieved when the network operates in utmost
harmony. The existential meaning of being an individual is manifested in being with others: I am part of you, and you are part of
me. Any role-playing cannot be completed without different many
other role players. The sense of fulfillment in life comes from the recognition that we all are participating in the same play. It is not like the
recognition of the equality of you and me.

An intriguing point that may have ethical significance is that there
is a moment in which individuality reveals itself in the Confucian
tradition, namely when a subject stands against the established
order of a king or a government by placing one's own name on the
public appeals. In cases of political resistance in the past Joseon
Dynasty, an individual revealed its individuality even more starkly
and the spirit of defiance toward authority in which an individual
staked its own life was sometimes accepted as one of cardinal
virtues of Confucian intellectuals. In some ways, it can be said that
individual freedom is negatively acquired through a struggle for recognition against the ruling power by risking one's own life.
Throughout East Asian history, it was not uncommon practice to
mount an open rebellion by leaving behind a public testament or

committing suicide by self-immolation in public to resist unjust authority or to defend moral values such as chastity, loyalty, and faith. Such cases represent extreme ways for an individual to pursue moral responsibility and freedom.

In the traditional Confucian culture, as I mentioned, social prizes or punishments were imposed on a collective basis. In particular, the tradition of attributing punishments to the group to which one belonged played a crucial role in reinforcing collectivist behaviors among people. Family or clan was not merely a community based on consanguinity but also a political community bound by a common fate. Churches in modern Korean society where Confucian values are waning seemingly function in a way that clans in traditional society did. In many cases, Koreans tend to project emotions that they might have for their families onto the groups to which they belong. They frequently form a sense of unity with others or an outside group to which they feel close. In this type of society, individual freedom is not an absolute or an objective value manifested by a certain measure but somewhat a vague or a subjective value created from numerous relationships. As such, it is the value that is flexible enough to be readjusted depending on situations.

In this context, East Asians tend to show greater leniency in comparison to Westerners towards the social policy decisions enforced upon individuals under social emergencies. Instead of regarding the compulsory mask use or the disclosure of the information about infected persons as the suppression of individual freedom, they regard such actions as the price they should pay to protect 'our' society under the specific situation of the COVID-19 pandemic. The so called 'compliance' shown by individuals in East Asia toward state-instituted policies can also be understood in terms of the aforementioned relativistic weighing of an individual's freedom and rights. At this point, a question may arise. When does an individual in the East Asian culture where individuality seems obscure see individual freedom as being infringed upon or damaged? This issue is inextricably linked with oppression, discrimination, and injustice, which are inflicted upon groups to which individuals belong. When their groups or communities suffer from oppression or damage in any form, individual members belonging to them tend to feel as though their own rights have been violated and their own liberty damaged. This aspect of East Asian culture provides an explanation for collectivist and conformist behaviors among East Asians.

Today, the surveillance capitalism that is unfolding within the development of digital technology poses diverse challenges to individual freedom in both the East and the West alike. In a society where individuals are relegated to the level of consumers, the desire of an individual is inevitably linked to the desire of other consumers. Individual freedom is nowadays reduced to the freedom to purchase goods that other consumers like to purchase. Countless commercial advertisements and social networking services make it difficult for an individual to have desires on its own independently from what other people desire. Ironically, individual freedom in a digitalized capitalist society where an individual enjoys more freedom than ever before in human history appears to be in danger. I examine the issue in more detail in the following section.

4. Individual Freedom in the Post Pandemic Era

The COVID-19 pandemic accelerated the advancement of online communication across the globe. Traditional communication methods are rapidly changing due to the development of digital technology, which affects all the aspect of human life including politics, religion, art, and education. The post-pandemic world will never be the same as what we have been used to. The development of 'fintech' (financial technology) implies that capitalism will also be subject to many changes in the future. Companies such as Amazon or Google are shifting into corporate entities whose identities are difficult to define, while the propagation of platform labor is creating an another kind social problem. All the online activities conducted by individuals, including online transactions or Google searches, leave digital traces that are stored, analyzed and processed as data for intended purposes, mostly likely for the purpose of creating profit.

Like it or not, and intended or not, we all exist today as chunks of big data. We are almost transparently encapsulated by unknown strangers who handle our data for their own purposes. Those strangers could be individuals or institutions or business firms. Human beings are trapped in a massive network of surveillance and the companies that operate the invisible surveillance systems are accumulating enormous wealth. The era of surveillance capitalism is expected to expand to the degree no one ever can imagine. As the Internet of Things becomes more common making everything that exists in the world 'smart', it appears as though human beings come to satisfy their desires more effectively living in a better world abundant with a variety of goods. Individual freedom seems to blossom with the increases of individual choice and autonomy. In an era of unprecedented convenience and plenty, there seems to be no limit to what one can desire. Are people living in a surveillance capitalist society freer than ever in human history?

The source of power that would dominate the post-pandemic world is digital technology. But a horrible thing is that there are no headquarters of technological domination. Technological developments and the utilization of data are not governed by a certain centralized sector of society, neither by a heroic leader. Technological onslaught on human civilization is ubiquitous, pervasive, and smeared all over our lives. Many dichotomous distinctions we were used to are now becoming blurry. There is no clear distinction between the exploiter and the exploited within a society. Whereas I can play a role of consumer on one platform, I can also become a producer by establishing another platform. I can buy books at an online bookstore, then sell them online as used books. I may even construct a platform to sell used books on specific subjects alongside other sellers. Increasingly, it is difficult to guess where digital technology will eventually take us. At the time when all are abstracted to mere data, how should individual freedom be understood? On Amazon, every choice that I make is analyzed to guide my future choices and also other consumers' choices. AI will guide me to other items I might like. The information about other people's choices often stimulates my desire to better off than others. Does this give us a stress or a happy moment to exercise free will to buy goods?

Nowadays, it is very difficult to regard individual freedom as something that has an absolute value. Concepts of my own rights, my own possessions, and my own desires are turning more and more equivocal. Upon choosing a book on Amazon, Amazon immediately tells you what other books were purchased by other users who chose the same book as mine and leads you to make further purchasing decisions. This appears to be a similar mechanism to the practice of releasing the movement routes of persons infected with COVID-19 in Korea and Taiwan, though in this case, infected persons are simply referred to by serial numbers. The only difference between the two aforementioned examples is that the information on books purchased by other users recommends me to make a purchasing decision, whereas the information about confirmed cases of COVID-19 suggests that I should avoid taking the same routes. Although Virginie Pradel regarded the disclosure of the movement routes of infected persons as 'surveillance that disregards freedom', this kind of practice is already taking place on numerous platforms under surveillance capitalism in which we willingly choose from the options recommended to us in the name of free will under an overwhelming deluge of information. My desires and freedom exist as a function of enormous digital networks, or rather as the result of the working of such enormous networks. What is especially intriguing is that this resembles the way in which the freedom of individuals is defined in East Asian culture in the previous sections. It is important to take note that the situation that Western intellectuals might describe as 'barbaric' will become much more commonplace in the future society of surveillance capitalism. I am afraid that the gloomy aspect of surveillance capitalism will be intensified in the post-pandemic world. In the traditional Confucian Korean culture, people have placed great value on the act of resistance against injustice to defend humanity and moral spirit. In general, Confucian culture places strong emphasis on the protection of moral principles based on humanistic values to which one holds steadfastly to foster moral sincerity towards the community of pseudo-familial relationship. The reason I reflect on the aspect of Confucian culture that emphasizes the community values more than individual freedom is that individual freedom in the contemporary West becomes an issue more obscure than ever. Individual freedom is put in danger not only in the East but also in the West. Nowadays it becomes nearly impossible for people all over the globe to live without Google or the like amidst the digital revolution. If we take individual freedom as an absolute value, we have to face a gloomy future. In order to avoid falling into a nihilistic or pessimistic vision of what we are in the age of technological development, we must begin to approach individual freedom from a different perspective. In view of the contingent nature of human life and the fragility of human existence, we must embrace the concepts of individuality and individual freedom as values that are constantly being readjusted and revalorized within the network to which we belong. Individual freedom in Confucian culture would do well to make reference to the reality of situation that we face globally in the post-pandemic era of surveillance capitalism. I would like to conclude the essay with one question: Is individual freedom as a final end of our life valuable in itself or a means to accomplish greater values beyond?

Ewha Womans University
hkim@ewha.ac.kr

References

The Analects, tr. Wing-Tshit Chan, *A Source Book in Chinese Philosophy* (Princeton: Princeton University Press, 1963).

Mencius, tr. Wing-Tshit Chan, *A Source Book in Chinese Philosophy* (Princeton: Princeton University Press, 1963).

John Dewey. *Ethics. The Middle Works of John Dewey, 1899-1924 vol.* 5 (ed.) Jo Ann Bovdston. (Carbondale and Edwardsvill: Southern Illinois University Press, 1978).

John Stuart Mill. *On Liberty* (2 ed.). (London: John W. Parker & Son, 1860).

In Defense of A Mandatory Public Service Requirement

DEBRA SATZ

Abstract

This paper defends mandatory national service as a response to democratic decay. Because democracy cannot be maintained by laws and incentives alone, citizens must care about the quality and attitudes of their society's members. In an age of increasing segregation and conflict on the basis of class and race, national service can bring citizens from different walks of life together to interact cooperatively on social problems. It offers a form of 'forced solidarity'. The final sections of the paper consider objections to this proposal.

1. The obligations of democratic citizenship

Democratic citizenship is an achievement. Modern citizenship offers the most powerful way we have of integrating the demands of justice with membership in a community. Most crucially, it links a commitment to free and equal individuals – who have differing ways of life, religions, and identities but the same fundamental status as members – with the idea of society as a fair system of cooperation. It thereby sharply breaks – at least in its aspirations and assumptions – with older ways of organizing societies, on the basis of social caste, privilege, dictatorship, or minority rule.

This achievement is under a great deal of stress right now. Public confidence in democracy is at the lowest point on record in the United States, the major democracies of Western Europe, sub-Saharan Africa, and Latin America. In some countries, including the United States, this metric has now reached an important threshold: the number of people who are dissatisfied with democracy is greater than the number of people who are satisfied with it. A report from the University of Cambridge's Centre for the Future of Democracy found that the decline was especially pronounced in countries which were supposed to be democratically stable: high income democracies in Europe and North America (Foa et al., 2020). It may (or may not) be an exaggeration to claim, as many have done, that there is a 'crisis of democracy' but it is certainly true that the rise of populist movements, extremists, political polarization, and rising inequality indicates a serious problem.

doi:10.1017/S1358246121000370   © The Royal Institute of Philosophy and the contributors 2022

Debra Satz

This paper explores one response to this democratic challenge, that of mandatory national service. To set the stage, I begin by briefly recapping the history of democratic citizenship. This history reveals that the architecture weaving citizenship into the lives of society's members has become thin and fragile.

The British sociologist TH Marshall in his classic work *Citizenship and Social Class* (1964) describes the path to modern citizenship in terms of three stages, each stage correlated with an expansion of rights: from the 17th-mid 18th century, we see consolidation of the *civil rights* needed to engage in a range of social activities, including the rights to religious freedom and to engage in trade and to own property; from the late 18th to early 20th, citizenship evolved to include *political rights* such as the right to vote and to stand for an election; finally post-world war II democracies featured the creation of *social and economic rights* to give citizens a right 'to share in the social heritage and to live the life of a civilized being according to the standards prevailing in the society'. *Modern democratic citizenship is meant to include all three sets of rights: civil rights, political rights, and economic rights.* Where any of these rights are violated or ascribed unequally, some people are excluded from full membership in society. Marshall was particularly concerned to integrate the working classes whose lack of education and economic resources had excluded them from the 'common culture' which should have been a 'common possession and heritage' (1964, pp. 78, 101-102).

The arc of creating these new rights owes much to generations of activists, labor unions, and social movements. (Of course, these rights are imperfectly realized in today's societies.) As the rights of citizenship expanded, it might be expected that the obligations associated with citizenship also expanded. That is because rights are correlated with obligations: it makes little sense to say that I have a right to something if there is no duty on anyone to provide for and enforce that right. Rights without corresponding obligations, while not nothing, run the risk of being 'mere words'. (This is sometimes a charge levelled at human rights.) Marshall himself saw this reciprocal relationship between rights and responsibilities, writing, 'If citizenship is invoked in the defense of rights, the corresponding duties of citizenship cannot be ignored' (1964, p. 123).

Yet the duties of citizenship have steadily eroded over time even as citizen's rights have grown; today, for the most part, our obligations as citizens are understood as aspirations and not requirements.[1] For

---

[1]   It might be said, too, that many of the benefits of citizenship have bled over to those living within a territory regardless of whether they are citizens or not.

example, it is often said that a good citizen is someone who votes, pays their taxes, obeys the laws and otherwise participates in collective self-government. But a sizeable proportion of citizens in democracies never or rarely vote and play little role in collective decision-making at any level.

What about the obligation to pay taxes? Taxation, like obeying the law, is not so much a feature of citizenship but of residency. For example, in the United States, all persons physically living and working within its boundaries are required to pay taxes and obey the law. (There is one exception where citizenship makes a difference to that obligation: citizens working outside the US are required to pay US taxes, while non-citizens are not – but the US is the only country in the world except for Eritrea that taxes permanent expatriates and this practice remains quite controversial.)

For much of American history, serving in the military was seen as a core obligation of citizenship (although initially only for men.) In 1973 that changed when the draft was abolished and an all-volunteer force was established. Britain abolished its own system of conscription after some fits and starts, in 1960. Many well-known factors led to ending the draft in the US, including an unpopular war in Vietnam. Far less well known is the fact that the libertarian economist Milton Friedman played a significant role in the ending of military conscription.[2] Friedman and his followers successfully argued to President Richard Nixon that the draft was the equivalent of indentured servitude; Friedman denied – adamantly – that such service was an obligation stemming from membership and his argument carried the day. The result is that in the US – and in most developed country democracies – military service has become voluntary, yielding a smaller and more focused group of enlistees, enticed at least in part by market considerations. Fewer than 1% of the US population today serves in the military.

In fact, the only obligation that American citizens currently have *as citizens* is the obligation to serve on a jury. Political Scientist Robert Putnam recently has noted that the ratio of the use of the term 'responsibility' in American publications has declined with respect to the use of the term 'rights' over the last fifty years (2020, p. 193). Considerations of what we owe to each other have taken a back seat to how much we can each get for ourselves. The upshot is that, in the twenty-first century, the obligations of citizenship have become, for the most part, an empty set. My aim in this paper is to

---

[2]   Friedman's role in this is described in the first chapter of Binyamin Applebaum's (2019) excellent book.

argue that the fact that this set is empty poses a serious problem for democracy, especially in an age of growing population heterogeneity and inequality; to propose a policy to address that problem – mandatory public service for all citizens; and to anticipate and respond to some (but not all) important objections.

2. Citizenship: Not by Laws Alone

The problem with the empty set of obligations is that citizenship cannot be maintained by laws and incentives alone. The existence, health and stability of democratic citizenship depends in some way on the *quality and attitudes* of a society's members. This dependence arises because norms and dispositions shape what use people can make of their rights and opportunities. Democracy cannot flourish if some are indifferent to the rights and opportunities of their fellows; if they see politics as simply a vehicle to advance their own private interests; if a society's members do not trust one another; or are hostile to other's claims of equal standing. Democracy cannot flourish if individuals and groups do not approach disagreement in the spirit of a willingness to attempt to justify their own views to each other, and to be prepared to listen and engage with the views of others. Democracy cannot flourish where might makes right.

While it is has sometimes been thought that good incentives (including the threat of punishment) can make self-interested individuals into good citizens – in the words of the 17th century philosopher Bernard Mandeville, 'private vices, public benefits' – we now know that in many cases, self-interested motivations are not sufficient to produce publicly oriented behaviors, even in the face of strong incentives. Market incentives, undersupply civic values and, in some cases, undermine them.

Consider the following example. In Haifa, six day care centers imposed a fine on parents who were late in picking up their children at the end of the day. Parents surprised the day cares in how they responded to the fine – they doubled the amount of time that they were late! Even, when, after 12 weeks, the fines were revoked, the parent's enhanced tardiness persisted. Putting a price on lateness likely undermined the parent's sense of an ethical obligation to avoid inconveniencing the teachers; instead they now treated the extra time as a commodity to be bought (Gneezy, 2000). This finding, that market incentives can crowd out pro-social attitudes – such as concern for others – has been repeated in a great many studies. (Indeed, there are replicated studies that show that merely studying

economics decreases student's ability to solve collective action problems.) I have little doubt that if the fine had been sufficiently high –
one thousand dollars a minute – the parents would have responded
differently. But it's not always easy to find the right prices, and furthermore, it is not a good idea to put a price on everything (Satz, 2010).

What about legal incentives like the threat of punishment for
breaking the law – can't that generate the pro-social behaviors
needed for democratic citizenship? Not alone. One problem is that
pro-social motivation won't be well sustained in cases where many
people are flouting the rules and getting away with it: no one wants
to be a sucker. Another problem is that it's often costly to ascertain
whether citizens are following the rules or not – and as society
becomes more complex the costs go up, making the monitoring of
compliance difficult. So trust becomes especially important. A final
and perhaps key problem is that it is especially hard to sustain pro-
social motivation in a society that is cleaved along racial, ethnic or
class lines, where people's unequal circumstances and limited knowledge about one another undermine the existence of a democratic 'we'.
Under such circumstances it's too easy to see another's fate as outside
my responsibility. Even if I comply with the letter of the law, that
doesn't mean I will stand up for your rights under the law.

Market incentives and the threat of punishment are not sufficient
for pro-social motivations and behaviors in many circumstances.
And democratic societies require a special kind of pro-social motivation – the motivation to endorse and to comply with democratic
processes, even in cases where one might be better off by subverting
the rules or going around them. Members of society need to see each
other as passengers on the same ship, sharing a common fate. And it's
especially hard to build a cooperative and solidaristic ethos when, to
continue with my metaphor, rich members of society, can easily sail
away on their yachts.

The tendency of elites to lose touch with the rest of society has been
widely observed. One could see the underlying pathology on display
in the wake of the Occupy movement, when a spate of articles began
to appear, written by members of the top 1 percent, explaining that
they weren't all that rich, given the price of private schools, real
estate, yoga classes, vacations and so on. Writing against the existence
of private (e.g., 'public') schools in England, the social democrat RH
Tawney observed,

> It is at once an educational monstrosity and a grave national mis-
> fortune. It is educationally vicious, since to mix with companions
> from homes of different types is an important part of the

education of the young. It is socially disastrous, for it does more than any other cause, except capitalism itself, to perpetuate the division of the nation into classes of which one is almost unintelligible to the other. (Tawney, 1952, p. 158)

Arguably, a democratic society requires certain experiences where everyone is on an equal footing and everyone is treated the same: standing in line to vote, or to get a driver's license, for instance. Some theorists have called these situations points of 'forced solidarity'. Among other things, they serve as a check on the tendency for the ultra-rich to drift off into their own little world, and to insulate themselves from the travails of the ordinary person. They put us – at least for a time – in the same boat. In today's America, few of these points of forced solidarity remain.

The unmooring of elites from the majority of other citizens has two negative effects on society. First, since elites currently have disproportionate power in shaping national policy (Gilens, 2012), policies are proposed with little understanding of the effects of those policies on others. It is also easy to endorse policies that can have harmful effects on others but that one's privilege can make one immune to. Second, the ability of the wealthy to exit from the effects of a policy, can weaken the bargaining power and voice of those who remain. (This is a familiar observation about the interactions of what Albert Hirschman referred to as 'exit' and 'voice').

It is too easy for groups in society to lack basic understandings of each other. Polarized and fragmented along economic, racial and ideological lines, democratic societies seem incapable of addressing their most urgent social problems.

3. National Service: A new common experience

It is here, first and foremost, that I believe an argument for a universal service requirement arises. There are few bridging institutions – at least in the United States – that bring individuals together across their differences in contexts where they can relate to one another as equals. Schools and neighborhoods are deeply segregated by race and class. White nationalism is on the rise. Rural communities do not interact with urban ones; workplaces are hierarchically organized and the lives of managers and CEOs more isolated and different than ever from those of their employees. People congregate in on-line bubbles with the like-minded; there are separate lines at airports; private and public schools; in the US there are even public roads with faster traffic that are available for a fee. The rules of the game have been tilted to favor elites. The idea that we are all in this together has a hollow ring.

A carefully constructed national service program can respond to these problems. It can bring citizens together, across their differences, by mixing service groups across race, class and geographic divisions. Decades ago, the social psychologist Gordon Allport, showed that racial and other prejudices flourish in ignorance, but that close interracial contact can reduce stereotyping and hostility – if the contact is of a type that leads people to do things together (Allport, 1954). Allport also posited that the effects of such contact are greatly enhanced if 'sanctioned by institutional supports'. Allport's contact hypothesis is one of the most widely tested claims in social psychology. Meta-analyses of hundreds of studies show strong support for the hypothesis as applied to numerous group divisions.

My proposal is to establish a mandatory year of national service for all US citizens between the ages of 18 and 25, with an exemption only for those doing military service or those with underlying conditions that make it impossible for them to serve. This program would involve participants in the creation of public goods – whether maintenance of public lands; work on infrastructure projects; work in education; work with the elderly, or other kinds of public projects. Rigorous studies have shown that America's voluntary service corps – from the Depression's Civilian Conservation Corps to the Great Society's Peace Corps and VISTA provided young people with the time and space to gain experience and acquire useful work skills and directions. These are important private benefits to individuals. (They do have a public benefit as well in contributing to the economy.) The voluntary service programs that today operate in this space, such as AmeriCorps, do good work and have stunningly high approval ratings[3] from their alumni: Ninety-four percent say they gained a better understanding of differing communities; eighty percent say the program helped their careers. But the argument I am offering is not based in the private goods to individuals that service offers, but the democratic good it produces.

A number of proposals have been offered for national service in the last several years but few of them advocate *mandatory* service. In fact, there is a timidity about most such proposals given the proponents' diagnosis of the problem. While there are reasons for this caution, which I will discuss below, allowing exit is problematic from the perspective defended here. Volunteer programs cannot deliver their

---

[3] https://www.americorps.gov/

desired cultural effects if select groups (e.g., the wealthy and privileged) can easily opt out and if service opportunities are unequally distributed. It is by helping to dismantle racial, socio-economic and geographical barriers between people, and by creating common experiences, that national service creates it's most important public good – enhancing the relationships and mutual understanding among the participants themselves.

An integrated military draft once played a similar role. And even before the military was racially integrated, it did mix people up by social class. Consider President John F Kennedy's PT boat in World War 2; Kennedy was the son of one of the richest men in America. But on his boat – in the same boat – were the sons of a farmer, a plumber, an artist, and an auto mechanic.

There is no doubt that a national service program would have costs. It would involve oversight and planning. Participants should also be paid a modest income, and possibly receive benefits not unlike the GI bill – a law that provides educational and training benefits for military veterans. At the same time, there are economic benefits: there is a great deal of valuable work that is not currently being done, and that could be done through public service. The New Deal yielded the Civilian Conservation Corps, which mobilized, with the leadership of a young George Marshall, 3 million unemployed Americans who planted some 3 billion trees between 1933 and 1942. An analysis commissioned by the National Park Service[4] found if the government were to try and reduce the backlog of maintenance on public lands using conservation corps (made up of 18- to 25-year-olds considering land management as a career) rather than contractors of National Park Service crews, it would save more than 80% per project.

4. Objections

A. Liberty

There is an apparent tension between this proposal and liberal values which seek to shield individuals from undue interference by the state. This is the reason why most proposals for public service are voluntary. Milton Friedman's argument that compulsory military service is a form of labor bondage resonates with many. Is the premise of

---

[4]   https://www.govinfo.gov/content/pkg/CHRG-113shrg82796/
html/CHRG-113shrg82796.htm

individuals as free and equal – the basis of modern citizenship – really compatible with compulsory service?

This is an important concern, that relates to how we see our relationship with government and with one another. But I think we should reject Friedman's too quick analogy between a service obligation and servitude.[5] A service obligation is delimited in time and it is also delimited in scope. Serving my country doesn't mean, for example, that I can't speak up against it. Nor is this a one-sided arrangement: citizens reap many benefits from living in society, benefits that would not be possible without society e.g., rule of law). Additionally, not all politically imposed obligations are unjust. For example, if an obligation is imposed for the sake of justice (e.g., like paying taxes), then it's hard to see how it constitutes an unfair form of compulsion such as a situation of servitude.

Moreover, I have tried to frame my argument for national service in a particular way that is consistent with respecting individuals as free and equal. In the first place, my argument does not rest on paternalistic or moralistic grounds. I am not arguing for national service because I think it's good for individuals to engage in service – although I do. I am not arguing that it makes them morally better people – although it may.

Nor am I claiming that there is a direct link between national service and justice. Instead, I have tried to show that democracy is an ongoing project which requires certain attitudes and dispositions among its members if it is to be stable over time. That is, I am arguing – on the hypothesis that the lack of a *robust common experience tackling problems together* is undermining democracy – that we all have an obligation to do our part in upholding the conditions that make our democracy workable and stable.

B. *This proposal treats the symptoms, not the causes*

Another objection is that this proposal treats a symptom rather than the underlying disease. Corresponding to the decline in the support for democracy is the growth of inequality over the last five decades. Racial and class barriers, and lack of faith in the political system are fueled by inequality, along with the fact that the bottom quintiles of society have seen little benefit from the last fifty years of economic

---

[5]   In 1918, the Supreme Court held in Arver v United States that the Thirteenth Amendment is compatible with the existence of a military draft.

growth. Why not simply use the tax system to generate more equality of condition?

There are three reasons for a focus on national service. The first two are pragmatic. To begin with, you are unlikely to get substantial changes to the tax system, or to exclusionary zoning regulations which keep poor people out of many neighborhoods, without greater solidarity among members of society. (This doesn't mean, of course, that we shouldn't press for such changes.) In addition, the most successful innovations in American society – from public schools, benefits to Civil war veterans, social security and the GI Bill of Rights in 1944 – were all based on the idea of social support in response to service. One of the largest barriers to extending economic and social rights to all of our citizens is the perception that those on the bottom are free riders.

The third reason to focus on national service is deeper and goes back to the limits of relying on economic and legal incentives alone to shore up democracy. Without some degree of 'trust and solidarity' democratic societies are difficult to maintain. And trust and solidarity depend on certain social conditions – that reciprocity is not being violated, that free riders are held to account, that relevant information is shared – which are difficult to maintain in large and diverse societies. Writing over four centuries ago, Thomas Hobbes thought only an absolute sovereign with the power of life and death over us could forge unity between individuals with differing values and interests. While Hobbes was wrong about this, it remains true that uniting diverse individuals with differing ways of life and values into a social union in which they are regarded as each other's equals is an achievement. Doing so depends not only on institutions but also on dispositions and attitudes.

5. Conclusion

One's attitude towards compulsory national service is connected to the question of what we owe to one another. This is not a question whose answer can be empirically ascertained. I have tried to bring some evidence to bear on this question, arguing that democracy itself requires certain shared experiences and conditions and a commitment to democracy entails a commitment to the conditions needed to sustain it over time. But in the end, the question of our obligations is a question of moral and political philosophy. For those who see society simply as an instrument for the optimal pursuit of individual interests, the argument for compulsory national service will be unpersuasive. But for those who see society as a framework for individuals – considered as free and equal but differing in many interests and values – to come together and rule themselves, a year of compulsory national service will count as a small price of admission.

References

Gordon Allport, *The Nature of Prejudice* (New York: Knoph, 1954).

Binyamin Applebaum, *The Economist's Hour: False Prophets, Free Markets and the Fracture of Society* (New York: Little Brown & Company, 2019).

R.S. Foa, A. Klassen, M. Slade, A. Rand, & R. Collins, 'The global satisfaction with democracy report', (Bennett Institute for Public Policy, University of Cambridge, 2020).

Martin Gilens, *Affluence and Influence: Economic Inequality and Political Power in America* (Princeton: Princeton UP, 2012).

Uri Gneezy and Aldo Rustichini, 'A Fine is a Price,' *Journal of Legal Studies* 29 (2000), 1-17.

T.H. Marshall, *Class, Citizenship and Social Development* (Chicago and London: University of Chicago Press, 1964).

Robert Putnam and Shaylyn Romney Garrett, *The Upswing: How America Came Together a Century Ago and How We Can Do It Again* (New York: Simon & Schuster, 2020).

Debra Satz, *Why Some Things Should Not be For Sale: The Moral Limits of Markets* (Oxford: Oxford University Press, 2010).

R.H. Tawney, *Equality* (London: Unwin Books, 1952).

The Wisdom of Mentor

JESSE NORMAN

Abstract

Thomas Hobbes posited a social contract which legitimates sovereign authority. But what grounds, or could ground, such a contract? Through reflection on Oakeshott, and on Aristotle's *Nichomachean Ethics*, the paper argues for a so far unrecognised mode of human association: philic association. It briefly considers a possible expression of philic association in the history of English law, before making the case for programmes of mentoring as a policy both reflective and supportive of this mode. It ends by suggesting that the existence of such a mode shows why Hobbes's social contract theory, however ingenious and influential it has proven to be, is neither sufficient nor necessary for its stated purpose.

I have been asked to discuss a specific policy, but within a wider philosophical context. So this paper is aimed mainly at a general audience, with an interest but no specialist background in the subject, and I will take a rather roundabout and ruminative approach.[1]

The flow of both the paper and the original lecture moves from philosophy to history to policy, and since I do not think there are any general logical relationships between these modes of thought, I would caution the reader against thinking of either paper or lecture as offering an overall argument. Even so, I hope it is of interest.[2]

1. Society as an association

I want to start with a traditional tension in political philosophy and classical political theory, between the coercive power of the state and the freedom of the citizen. That tension raises a question of legitimacy: by what right does a sovereign govern?

---

[1]   This paper is considerably shorter than the lecture as given; zealots are encouraged to view the original online.

[2]   I am of course speaking purely from an academic perspective, not as a Minister or Member of Parliament.

doi:10.1017/S1358246122000017   © The Royal Institute of Philosophy and the contributors 2022

The most famous answer to that question was, of course, advanced by Thomas Hobbes in the 17th century, in *Leviathan*. Hobbes's answer is that the sovereign governs in virtue of a social contract. Casting it in its most schematic form, his thinking imagines a starting point: that individuals originally lived in a state of nature in which they were both isolated and defenceless, and moved by the instinct for self-preservation. Looking around, they see others like themselves, and this creates a natural but potentially disastrous competitive tension between them, towards what Hobbes calls a 'war of all against all'. As a result, their lives are dominated by the fear of violent death; lives famously described by Hobbes as 'solitary, poor, nasty, brutish and short'.

In his telling of the story, such people decide to come together and to agree with each other to give up some of their personal autonomy, and repose that power in a sovereign or magistrate. In return for this grant of authority and power, the sovereign assumes the obligation to maintain internal order and protect the people from external attack.

So, that is the foundational idea: society as a contractual association. Note the ingenuity of the approach. Hobbes lays down a small number of premises at the start – humans as individuals in a pre-social state of nature, the desire for self-preservation, the competitive context – and from it deduces a basis for the existence of human society and legitimate state action. It is an astonishing *coup de main*, almost a conjuring trick. We do not know anything, indeed we do not need to know anything about these people in order to get the idea going of a social contract, and from that, of a sovereign endowed with just authority.

So that is the core idea. Needless to say, it has attracted a vast amount of attention and commentary over the centuries, and a huge number of arguments for and against. But I want to focus briefly on just one objection, which I believe has its roots in the thought of David Hume. It goes something like this: it is all very well to talk about people making a contract with each other, but in virtue of what practice are they supposed to be able to make this contract? If they are not able to make promises and strike agreements already, there is no basis for such a contract. But if they are able to make promises already, if they have a convention of promising amongst themselves, then first of all they are not isolated and pre-social, contrary to the original hypothesis, and secondly it is unclear why there is any need to postulate a social contract as such at all. This Humean objection sets a potentially devastating dilemma to social contract theories of this form.

2. Civil and enterprise association

I turn now to a different way of thinking about political association, to be found in the work of Michael Oakeshott. Oakeshott was described at his death as 'the greatest philosopher in the English speaking tradition since Mill, or even Burke'. Yet he is almost unknown amongst the wider public today. Over the course of a very long life, he published a slim but profound body of work: two monographs, *Experience and its Modes* and *On Human Conduct*; and two sets of essays, called *Rationalism in Politics*, and *On History*. Of those, the only one that has really had any wider attention is *Rationalism in Politics*.

I want to dwell a little on Oakeshott because we can use him to set up the argument I want to make. Recall that a main current of political philosophy thinks of human society as an association of individuals. Within this broad view, Oakeshott identifies two different ideas, of what he calls civil and enterprise association. Broadly, civil association is the idea of an association considered under the heading of practice, while enterprise association is the idea of an association considered under the heading of purpose.

In a civil association, people are associating just in virtue of the knowledge and acknowledgement of a single law-like set of non-instrumental rules by which they abide. That is, they recognise an idea of law, they share that idea of law, and it becomes integral to the identity of their association. In an enterprise association, by contrast, people come together to achieve a particular collective purpose, and they are in that sense confederates in a common cause.

We can think of these as ideal types, but they can also be combined. In effect, Oakeshott is inviting us to attend to two potential aspects of a society. One is what we might call its rule-of-law aspect, the procedural aspects embodied in its constitution, its civil regulations, its administrative law and such like. The other is its aspect as a collective endeavour. These aspects are compossible, and they can vary over time. In wartime, for example, a society may feel itself under some pressure to abridge its purely civil rules in order to take collective actions dominated by a single purpose of repulsing and defeating the enemy. But you can see Oakeshott's distinction at work in other ways. Both in history and today, some societies find themselves taking on the goal of ensuring religious purity, or ethnic homogeneity, or military preparedness against an enemy, for example.

A crucial point is that the implicit view and status of the individual vary with the character of the association. In a civil association, people are seen as endowed with the presumptive rights of formal equality associated with the rule of law. In an enterprise association, dominated as it is by the idea of collective purpose, individuals are valued as contributors to the society's overall project or goal. Finally, to some extent there is a mapping from the civil/enterprise association distinction to a further distinction we see in politics today: between campaigning and governing. When you are campaigning, you are working to advance a particular goal, such as a policy goal or an electoral victory, and all your efforts are devoted to securing that. When you are governing, however, you do not have a specific goal as such. Rather, you are trying – as Oakeshott puts it, in a memorable metaphor – to keep the ship of state on an even keel. The enterprise is simply to keep afloat.

Now we can ask: is Oakeshott right about this? Note that there are several ways to misunderstand him. One is that this is just a formalism, without any genuine relevance to real-world politics. Another is that this is really a reworking of a conception of the minimal state associated with someone like the philosopher Robert Nozick in his book *Anarchy, State and Utopia*.

You will see at once that these objections cannot both be correct, since one asserts that the distinction is an empty formalism and the other asserts that it is a substantive characterisation of the minimal state. But I would argue that neither is correct, and that this is actually a deep and rather telling distinction, which can be read compositionally, as I have noted, or developmentally. Oakeshott does not offer the idea of civil association as a characterisation of a minimal state, and few if any could rationally believe that a minimal state could be established, even in principle, on the basis of its purely civil aspects. But the distinction is certainly not an empty formalism, since it usefully allows us to analyse and explain a range of specific cases. We can say, for example, that the project of setting up the London Olympics, a huge collective endeavour, was an enterprise aspect of British government, or that the Velvet Revolution in Eastern Europe started to move several those countries from a kind of totalizing communist view of society as an enterprise to one of it as a civil association, at different speeds, beginning in 1989.

So I would suggest this is an important and useful distinction. But there is a worry, which mirrors the worry I touched on with Hobbes's original rather game-theoretic analysis of the social contract. This is that while not being purely formalistic, Oakeshott's distinction under-specifies the character of association itself. It allows us to understand an association in terms of two or more people getting together to do something, conceived as an enterprise. It allows us to see an association as an institution that sustains itself over time, where a core aspect is simply the continuation of itself and its traditions and practices, in its civic aspect. But still, it feels as if something is being left out.

3. Aristotle on friendship

To see what that might be, I want to take another step back; and to look at a famous discussion in Aristotle's *Nicomachean Ethics* of what he calls *philia*, a word often translated as 'friendship'.

Philia is a central topic to the *Ethics*, where it takes up two books of a ten-book work, so one might ask the question, why does Aristotle think it is so important? One initial thing to note is that Aristotle appears to be aiming at several different targets at the same time, because *philia*, as he thinks of it, ranges much more widely than friendship. Thus, for him it includes your friends, of course, but it also includes your family, the relationship between parents and children, the relationship between lovers, your commercial relationships with your butcher or your music tutor, and the fellowship that exists between soldiers. It includes the relationship between members of the same religious society or grouping or tribe, the relationship between a king and his subjects, and the relationships within and between cities. All of those come under the category of *philia* for Aristotle.

In line with this, I want to think of *philia* as inclusively as possible. If we were to try to give it a philosophical characterization, there are a few things to note. The first point is that this appears to be a symmetrical relationship but not a transitive one. Let's use the phrase '*philos*' to mean 'has a relationship of *philia* with'. Then *philia* is symmetric because if A *philos* B then B *philos* A. They are, in the Greek word, *philoi*. But *philia* is not transitive because A *philos* B and B *philos* C do not together imply that A *philos* C. So I can have a link of this kind to you and you can have a link of the same kind to Jane, but that does not mean that I have that same kind of link to Jane. Even so, because it is symmetrical, *philia* involves what we would call a mutual relationship.

Secondly, *philia* appears to vary for Aristotle with social or psychological distance, while also carrying with it a default presumption of goodwill. So when you are a *philos* of someone you start off from a position or status of goodwill in relation to them, even though you may not in fact have any actual emotional relationship with them.

Thirdly, this is not a gendered relationship. Although Aristotle has some very unprogressive things to say about women elsewhere in his writings, he seems quite prepared to allow that women can be in relationships of *philia*.

Fourthly, *philoi* can be unequal in their places in society. Here Aristotle seems to be driving towards a distinction between what we might call substantive and presumptive equality and inequality. So it seems that a king and his subject may be substantively unequal in their wealth and rank, but when they encounter each other, at least in an informal context, they may address each other as presumptively equal; that is, they can be interested in each other's views as intelligent, thoughtful beings, irrespective of the regal or kingly aspects of the relationship.

What unites *philoi*? For Aristotle, it is the idea of *homonoia*: literally translated, something that is the same in their minds. It seems this can include having a shared history or interest, or a mutual regard for some third thing or person. This is not the same thing as what we might call sociability, the human capacity to form ties, but it is closely related. Nor is it the same as unanimity, a term derived from Latin meaning 'being of one mind'. The significance of this is that for Aristotle *philia* is what holds states together, and he says that lawgivers almost care more for it than for justice. It is the social amity that they aim at most of all, and it expels faction, which is their worst enemy.

If this is right, then it points to what I would suggest is a missing mode in Oakeshott. As we have seen, Oakeshott's ideas of enterprise and civil association are intended to be entirely general categories or modes of association. They can apply to whole societies, or more narrowly to smaller organisations and institutions, such as expeditions, or sports clubs or leisure groups.

But though these institutions may have an orientation towards practice or purpose, that is not all of what they are about. Take a dining club, or a book club. These exist, of course, ostensibly in order to eat food or to read books together. But what they are really about is human companionship and engagement, and a club that failed to attend to this aspect of its existence would very soon cease to exist at all.

We can see this phenomenon at work elsewhere. Take the example of a communal table in a pub or restaurant. Someone who eats at a communal table does not know who else will be there; they simply go for the unexpected pleasures of the company of others. Or take a football kickabout in the park on a Sunday afternoon; you are not necessarily expecting to play with anyone you have ever played with before. It is just for fun and friendship. More formally, if you look at the literature on different games, such as ultimatum games, you can see that even in one-off contexts people bring enormous amounts of expectation, goodwill and trust to their dealings with others.

4. Philic association and the growth of trusts

What I think this highlights is a further mode of association, which we might call *philic* association after Aristotle. Again, we can think of it as one ingredient or aspect of a given association, alongside its nomic or telic, that is civic or enterprise, aspects. And again, we can also think of it developmentally. Thus, one way of analysing the historical movement from agrarian to commercial societies is that in each case the philic aspect is progressively redefined as it moves from the more local to the more diffuse, from personal trust to wider norms of trust, from direct association to the associations of associations long identified by thinkers such as Burke and Tocqueville as characteristic of open civil society.

I think this starts to explain what Aristotle has more broadly in mind, and why he takes *philia* so seriously. A society whose philic aspect is flourishing is one that cherishes freedom of thought and speech and as-sociation, and the institutions, practices and habits that sustain them. It is also a tacit response to the earlier Humean objection, for relationships of *philia* are mutual ties of precisely the kind that can give rise to institutions of promising. The suggestion is that, however brilliant Hobbes's social contract theory may be as a heuristic or debating device or spur to formal game-theoretic treatments of social interaction, it postulates a world that is neither, plausibly, our own, nor logically ne-cessary to explain the legitimate basis of sovereign authority.

Finally, I want to suggest that it is an astonishing fact about British history that it has given legal expression to all three of the modes we have been discussing: the idea of civil association through the English common law, and the wider constitutional tradition into which it feeds; the idea of enterprise association through the emergence of the corporation and of contract law; and perhaps yet more interest-ingly, the idea of philic association through the emergence of trusts governed not by the common law but by the law of equity.

For it was the law of equity that became the legal basis for the growth of unincorporated associations in the UK. It is in the nature of a trust that it allows an unincorporated association to hold property, and the result was an explosion of associations over the last 300 years. These included coffee houses, societies and clubs of every kind in the 18th century, mutuals and working men's clubs in the 19th century, unions and co-ops in the 20th century. There really is no parallel to this anywhere else in Europe, because of the use of Roman law there, to which the idea of a trust is foreign. It gives a peculiarly British national expression to the idea of philic association.

5. The wisdom of Mentor

Now at last we can turn to policy.

Over the last 30 or 40 years, there has been a great concern, given canonical expression by Robert Putnam in his book *Bowling Alone*, that US society and western societies more generally are becoming increasingly fragmented and atomized. Today, worries might focus on growing inequalities, the effects of technology and especially social media, political and religious division, the pressures on home life, the changing economics of elites and manual workers, culture wars, fear and stress, all latterly shaped by our collective experience of having to deal with this dreadful pandemic.

Within this, there is growing concern about the effects of loneliness. It is important to say that whether loneliness has in fact increased in recent years is not quite as clear as one might think. I wish there were more academic research into this vital issue, and into the effects of loneliness on people's mental and physical health, and the sense of desperation. But note that loneliness is not the same thing as solitude. Solitude is a state that people choose. Loneliness, however, is an unchosen state of being cut off from others. It is a state, we might say, in which *philia* cannot apply.

And now finally, we come to what I have called the wisdom of Mentor: the social value of mentoring. Mentor himself, as you may know, was the man appointed by Odysseus to be guardian to his young son Telemachus in the *Odyssey*. The name of Mentor was then picked up at the end of the 17th century by François Fénélon in a book, *The Adventures of Telemachus*, which became both a best seller in France for its homily to the simple life, a constitutional monarchy and international amity, and a scandal for its covert attack on Louis the 14th. The book's great reveal is that Mentor is the goddess Minerva in disguise, which underlines the association of mentoring with wisdom.

So how should we think of mentoring, and why is it important? In today's world there is always a risk that a one-to-one personal relationship will only be cast in terms of grooming and the potential for abuse, and it is vital that appropriate safeguards are built into any structured system of mentoring.

But with these important protections in place, the huge potential for mentoring to do good is evident. A well-managed mentoring relationship is a two-way one between people of different age and experience. It allows for the transfer of specific knowledge or skills, and the pleasure of teaching or guiding someone in the earlier stages of their life. It is the stuff of meetings and conversation and personal contact, of shared projects and new friendships. But perhaps most importantly, it allows for the sharing of tacit knowledge, the unarticulated rules of the game, the sense of how to get on, be that in one's work of play or just in life generally, with all the extra confidence these things bring.

Mentoring has proven benefits for both parties, and many of them are benefits that can be realised at any age. Just to take one example local to me in Hereford, Funkey Maths (www.funkeymaths.com) is a mentoring maths programme set up by a brilliant constituent of mine, with my support. Their work shows the extraordinary effect that mentoring can have: older primary school children learn a body of basic mathematics through play, and then become mentors to the younger children. This mentoring relationship taps into something that seems to be deep in the human sensibility. Its effect here is that the older pupils are enormously incentivised to teach the younger ones. The older pupils make sure they know their stuff, and the younger ones learn from them. It is incredibly effective, and it costs virtually nothing.

How could we build up a really effective mentoring capability across the UK? It should not require any great political genius. There are plenty of energetic and pro-social people at any age, and an enormous pool of time-rich people over the age of 50. These latter have a vast amount of experience and vast access to networks and other forms of social capital. There are, too, national public service programmes at the moment such as National Citizen Service, which could be put to service and be tied to mentoring activities. And there are innumerable online apps and learning and counselling platforms that could be drawn into this picture and of course, we could have public examples of people in great places in public life, who wish to lead in mentoring and who can both elicit and drive a shift in our public norms.

I have myself been the beneficiary of several of the most marvellously inspired mentors through my own life, and have been able to play that same role to others on one or two occasions. In every case it has been an enormously personally fulfilling experience. And lest

Jesse Norman

you think this is mere personal anecdote, let me encourage you to ask others, and test the power of mentoring in your own case. You will not regret it.

House of Commons
jesse.norman.mp@parliament.uk

Index of Names